BRIDE'S®
WEDDING
PLANNER

BRIDE'S

WEDDING PLANNER

By the Editors of BRIDE'S *Magazine*

Fawcett Columbine · New York

A Fawcett Columbine Book
Published by Ballantine Books

Copyright © 1977, 1980, 1990, 1997 by The Condé Nast Publications, Inc.

All rights reserved under International and Pan-American Copyright Conventions. Published in the United States by Ballantine Books, a division of Random House, Inc., New York, and simultaneously in Canada by Random House of Canada Limited, Toronto. This is a revised edition of a work originally published in 1977 and updated in 1980 and 1990.

http://www.randomhouse.com

ISBN: 0-449-91129-2

Cover Photograph: Sasaki Hiromasa
Cover Dress: Galina by Judd Waddell
Cover Headpiece: Headpieces by Toni
Back Cover: Photographs: Andrew Eccles
          Left dress: Lazaro
          Right dress: Candice Soloman
Illustrations by Sharon Watts

Manufactured in the United States of America

Revised Edition: January 1997

10   9   8

Acknowledgments

BRIDE'S Magazine gratefully acknowledges the inspiration and guidance of its Editor-in-Chief Millie Martini Bratten, and Cynthia M. Edmunds, Associate Editor. We would also like to thank writer Donna Christiano, for her diligent effort to update this book for the 21st century. Thanks also to Sally Kilbridge, Managing Editor, Nancy Mattia, Features Editor, and Tracy L. Guth Associate Features Editor for their help with the production of the book and Susan Randol, Senior Editor at Ballantine, and her assistant Kristen Busch.

For their insights into each of their areas of expertise, thanks to staff members, Rachel Leonard, Denise O'Donoghue, Elizabeth Rundlett, Kim Macaione, Donna Ferrari, and Debra Chozick.

And for her contribution to the aesthetic appearance of the book, BRIDE'S thanks Art Director Phyllis Richmond Cox.

Contents

Congratulations!

You're engaged—and looking forward to a beautiful wedding. During the next several months, there'll be parties to attend, gifts to accept, and an amazing number of decisions to make.

Every bride starts with a vision of what she wants her wedding to be, but not many have any idea how to turn that dream into reality. Suddenly, everything's a question: What does a wedding cost? Who will pay for it? How do I find the perfect dress, wedding site, honeymoon destination?

No matter what kind of wedding you're planning—a romantic garden party in your parents' backyard or a black-tie dinner at the most lavish hotel in town—getting organized is the secret to a celebration that you and your guests will love.

If you're like most brides, you're working, in school, or both. You're overextended, time is at a premium, and you wonder if planning a formal wedding is even doable.

The unequivocal answer is yes—if you enlist help. That's where *BRIDE'S Wedding Planner*, newly revised and updated, comes in. The editors of *BRIDE'S Magazine* will walk you through every aspect of the wedding whirl—from announcing your engagement to choosing your dress to booking your honeymoon and settling into your new home. We've included creative ways to personalize your ceremony, contemporary ideas for wedding showers and prewedding parties, and clever suggestions for favors. We'll tell you how to buy a diamond engagement ring, choose and word invitations, and hire a caterer, florist, and band. Worried about where to seat divorced parents? How to choose bridesmaids without hurting feelings? How to share wedding expenses? You'll find options and resources that will answer these questions, plus worksheets and checklists to make sure everything stays organized, everybody stays informed.

We've put all our experience and expertise to work in making your wedding and honeymoon as trouble-free as possible. We've anticipated questions, solved problems, and quashed dilemmas before they even arise. Our goal is for you and your groom, your family and friends to enjoy a joyous celebration of love and commitment, one that will provide memories you'll cherish for a lifetime.

Millie Martini Bratten
Editor-in-Chief
BRIDE'S Magazine

Chapter 1:

GETTING STARTED

You met. Fell in love. He asked. You said yes. Or maybe it was the other way around. Whatever, it's time to start planning your wedding.

START SPREADING THE NEWS: HOW TO ANNOUNCE YOUR ENGAGEMENT

Going public with the news makes your engagement feel *really* official. Tell family first, followed by friends and coworkers. Here are more tips on getting the word out:

• **Big news should be delivered in person.** You and your fiancé should arrange a visit with your respective families to inform them of your engagement. If you live out of town and a visit is impossible, call them with the news and arrange for a visit sometime in the near future.

• **If either of you has children,** tell them about your engagement as soon as possible. Be prepared for questions concerning living arrangements, stepsiblings, house rules, disciplinary issues, and wedding plans. Be as specific as you can.

• **If you think your family might have reservations** about your upcoming marriage, speak to them alone (your fiancé should do the same if he senses opposition among his family). If your parents don't know your fiancé well, schedule a visit, or have a mutual friend speak to your parents on his behalf. If one or both of you is divorced, your parents may be concerned that this

marriage might end like the first one. Explain why you think it won't (i.e., "Back then, I was more concerned about my friends than my marriage. I've learned so much more about relationships since then"). If you'll be becoming a stepparent, have your family get to know the children so everyone will feel more comfortable.

• **If your parents are divorced,** visit one parent first, then the other.

• **If your fiancé would like to speak privately with your father** to formally ask for your hand in marriage, he can arrange a meeting. As an alternative, your fiancé can also approach both parents together, or just your mother, stepfather, or whoever took an active role in raising you.

• **Inform supervisors and coworkers.** Besides wanting to share in your happiness, they'll also want to know about the days off you'll need for wedding planning, the wedding itself, and your honeymoon. Assure them you'll keep wedding business separate from work.

• **Tell your friends and relatives.** Good news should be shared. Let anyone important to you know about the impending nuptials. If you've decided on attendants (see chapter 3), ask them to be a part of your wedding party when you tell them about your engagement. Or speak to them about it at a later date—just be sure to give them plenty of time to arrange their schedules.

- **If either of you is divorced, tell your ex-spouse.** This is particularly important if you have young children. If you're not on friendly terms, write a note.

SAVE THE DAY: SETTING YOUR WEDDING DATE

The first step to wedding planning: choosing a wedding date. While weather, work, and/or school constraints will nix a lot of days, the calendar can still seem overwhelming. Here are points to consider as you zero in:

- **Availability.** Many churches, synagogues, and reception sites are booked a year or two in advance (peak marrying months are May through October; you may have more flexibility with sites if you arrange your wedding for an off-peak month and are willing to consider alternate times).

- **Decide how much time you'll need** to pull together the wedding of your dreams. The average length of engagement for *BRIDE'S* readers is 12.1 months. You may need more or less time depending on your finances, how much time you have to devote to wedding planning, how elaborate the celebration will be.

- **Think about seasons and dates that have special meaning for you and your groom.** Perhaps it's the anniversary of your first date, your parents' anniversary, even Valentine's Day. Or maybe you'd like to schedule your wed-

ding for a time of year you're especially fond of—the spring, fall, or Christmastime, for example.

- **Consider logistics.** Getting married on Memorial Day weekend may sound great, but does your town's annual parade wind through town, grinding traffic to a halt? An August afternoon may sound terrific, too, but make sure your ceremony and reception sites offer wilt protection in the form of air-conditioning. Remember that certain religious holidays—Easter Sunday, for example, or Yom Kippur—can be off-limits.

- **Check the schedules of key family members and close friends.** Will vacation plans or impossible-to-reschedule events like graduations conflict?

- **Determine the best times to take off from work, school, or military service.** You don't want to be on your honeymoon during the annual can't-miss trade convention, for example.

- **If there are issues that need to be ironed out**—finances, combining or moving households, the decision to have or not have children—give yourself plenty of time to work on them.

READ ALL ABOUT IT: NEWSPAPER ANNOUNCEMENTS

Word of mouth can carry news only so far. After you've told close friends and family put the news of your engagement in writing—announce it in your newspaper, alumni magazine, and company newsletter.

Where to Start

Different publications have different requirements when it comes to publishing an announcement. For the specifics, call the individual publications (don't forget the newspapers of the town where you and your fiancé live and work, as well as where each set of parents lives). Ask the lifestyle editor if there's a standardized form you can fill out (if not, type the announcement, double-spaced, on a sheet of standard-size paper—8½" by 11"). Also inquire about fees and deadlines. Ask if engagement photos are published and if there are any restrictions regarding size and the use of color-prints.

What to Say

What should you include in your announcement? Career information about you and your groom—where you work, what you do, etc.—as well as the occupations of both sets of parents. Also mention the names of the schools you've attended. If you're keeping your name, add a line such as "The bride will keep her name" (friends, family, and business associates will know how they should address you in the future). The month of your wedding may be mentioned—but don't offer the date. Would-be thieves perusing the announcements will then know when your home will be unoccupied.

How to Word It

An engagement announcement is traditionally worded as follows: *Mr. and Mrs. Kenneth Larson announce the engagement of their daughter, Anne Elizabeth, to John Tyler, the son of Mr. and Mrs. Robert Tyler of Chicago. A December wedding is planned.* (Include the name of the city if it's different from the place where the paper is published.)

But in some cases, traditional wording isn't appropriate. Here are circumstances that call for special wording:

• **When the bride's parents are divorced** The parent who raised you does the announcing;

however, your other parent gets mentioned as well. For example: *Mrs. Angela Smith of Los Angeles announces the engagement of her daughter, Julia Marie, to Edward Dunleavy, son of Mr. and Mrs. Thomas Dunleavy of Sacramento. Miss Smith is also the daughter of Michael Smith of Detroit.* If divorced parents have remained friendly, they can jointly announce the engagement (e.g., *Mr. Michael Smith of Detroit and Mrs. Angela Smith of Los Angeles announce the engagement . . .*).

• **When the bride's mother has remarried** Use your mother's new surname in the announcement. For example: *Mr. and Mrs. Jeffrey Osborne announce the engagement of Mrs. Osborne's daughter, Stephanie Lee Moore, to Joshua Edmunds, son of Mr. and Mrs. Richard Edmunds of Miami. Miss Moore is also the daughter of James Moore of Baltimore.*

• **When one of the bride's parents is deceased** Both the living and the deceased parent are mentioned. For example: *The engagement of Miss Carolyn March, daughter of Mrs. David March and the late Mr. March, to Mr. Kevin O'Brien, son of Mr. and Mrs. Patrick O'Brien of Boston, is announced by the bride's mother.*

• **When both of the bride's parents are deceased** Let an honored family member or friend do the announcing. One suggestion: *Mr. Timothy Martin of Charleston announces the engagement of his sister, Cynthia Jane, to Mr. Anthony Nickels, son of Mr. and Mrs. Gerald Nickels of Houston. Miss Martin is the daughter of the late Mr. and Mrs. Samuel Martin.*

• **When the groom's parents are divorced or deceased** Follow the same general format, substituting the appropriate wording when mentioning his family.

• **When the bride and groom are hosting the wedding** You have two options: Let your parents have the honor of announcing your engagement, or announce it yourselves. For the latter, consider the following wording: *Laura Louise Grant, senior vice president for XYZ corporation, is to be married in July to Alexander Bennett, chief executive officer of ABC company in Duluth. Ms.*

Grant is the daughter of Mr. and Mrs. William G. Grant of Phoenix. Mr. Bennett is the son of Mr. Martin Bennett of Tucson and Diana H. Bennett of Buffalo.

• **When it's a second marriage** Keep the wording traditional; use your current, legal sur-name, even if it differs from that of your parents. For instance: *Mr. and Mrs. Benjamin Warner announce the engagement of their daughter, Jennifer Warner Hamilton, to George T. Keats, son of Mr. and Mrs. Donald Keats.*

NEWSPAPER ENGAGEMENT WORKSHEET

To appear: _____   _____
                 (date)   *(bride's parents' names)*

                                                _____
                                                (street address)

                                                _____
                                             (city, state, zip code)

                                                _____
                           (telephone number, with area code)

Mr. and Mrs. _____ of _____ announce the
               (bride's parents' names)   *(their city, if out of town)*

engagement of their daughter, _____ , to _____ ,
                     (bride's first and middle names)   *(groom's first and last names)*

the son of Mr. and Mrs. _____ of _____ .
                    (groom's parents' names)   *(groom's parents' city)*

The bride, a graduate of _____ , is _____ .
                                (career/place of employment/title)

Her father is _____ .
                               (career/place of employment/title)

Her mother is _____ .
                               (career/place of employment/title)

The groom, a graduate of _____ , is _____ .
                                                                        (career/place of employment/title)

His father is _____ .
                                                                        (career/place of employment/title)

His mother is _____ .
                                                                        (career/place of employment/title)

A _____ wedding is planned.
      (month/season)

Other information _____ .

THE STONE AGE: SELECTING A DIAMOND

The diamond is an age-old symbol of love and commitment. The hardness of the stone—the hardest substance on earth, in fact—has come to symbolize enduring, unbreakable love. Ancient Romans thought diamonds were splinters from falling stars; the Greeks believed they were the tears of gods. Bestowing a diamond ring on one's intended is a time-honored tradition, dating back to 1477 when Archduke Maximilian of Austria slipped one on the finger of Mary of Burgundy. Today, about 70 percent of all engaged women don a diamond ring on their third finger, left hand—a finger that ancient Egyptians thought held a vein leading directly to the heart.

If you and your fiancé are choosing your engagement ring together, shop carefully. All that glitters is not necessarily gold—or even diamonds. Here, savvy shopping pointers from the Diamond Information Center in New York City. Follow these tips when shopping for diamond wedding bands:

1. Determine your budget. Don't go stone broke—literally. Most jewelers recommend spending about two months' salary for a diamond engagement ring. Another option to consider: an heirloom ring (i.e., your mother's ring, his grandmother's ring).

2. Understand the Four Cs. Two diamonds of equal size and appearance may not necessarily be of equal value. The factors that go into determining a diamond's quality are called the four Cs—cut, color, clarity, and carat.

Cut: Dubbed the most important of the four Cs because a quality cut is what gives a diamond its brilliance. The diamond is cut, with each facet proportional in exact geometric relation to one another, then polished.

Color: The optimum color is no color. A color-free stone is best able to reflect and refract light, adding fire to the diamond. Jewelers grade a diamond's color with a letter scale, beginning with a high score of D, which is colorless.

Clarity: A flawless diamond is rare; most have some degree of what jewelers call inclusions, or "nature's fingerprints." These inclusions may be visible only through powerful magnification. A perfect diamond without flaws, is rated F1; an imperfect diamond is 13.

Carat: This refers to the weight of the diamond. There are 100 points in a carat; a diamond weight of ¹/₂ carat is 50 points.

3. Decide on a style. Try on different rings to see what you like. Diamonds come in various shapes, with some of the most popular being round, oval, marquis, pear, heart, and emerald. You may prefer to buy a stone separately (or use an heirloom one), then have a setting designed (your jeweler can help you). When buying a ring, also consider the size of your hand in relation to the ring—you might prefer a narrow band with a single stone, for instance, if you have small hands. You might also want to try on wedding bands with your engagement ring to get a sense of how the two rings will look together.

4. Shop at a reputable jeweler. Ask friends and family for recommendations of jewelers they trust.

Ring Materials

The most common choices for stone settings are gold, white gold, silver, and platinum. Many brides select gemstones along with diamonds for engagement rings. Consider offsetting the cool brilliance of your diamond with the richness of sapphire, ruby, or emerald baguettes, for instance.

Caring for Your Diamond

Keep the fire of your diamond burning bright. Here are care tips from the Diamond Information Center in New York City.

Care

• When you're not wearing it, keep the ring in a fabric-lined jewelry case or box. If placing it with other diamonds, wrap each piece in tissue paper, as one diamond can scratch another.

• To prevent scratching and chipping, don't wear your diamond while performing rough work.

• Take your ring off when washing your hands with soap, applying hand lotion, or spritzing on hairspray. All can build up on the diamond.

• Because it can pit the stone and discolor the mounting, never let your ring come in contact with chlorine bleach.

• Have your jeweler check the ring once a year for loose stones; the mounting should be checked, too, to make sure it's secure.

Cleaning

1. The detergent bath. Place the ring in a small bowl of sudsy water using a mild liquid detergent for a few minutes. While in the suds, gently brush the ring with a small, soft brush (like a toothbrush). Rinse under warm running water. Pat dry with a soft, lint-free cloth. This bath is good for light, regular cleaning.

2. The cold-water soak. Soak the ring for thirty minutes in a solution of half household ammonia, half cold water. Lift out and gently tap around the front and back of the mounting with a small, soft brush. Swish in the solution a second time. Drain on tissue paper. Use this soak for heavier dirt buildup.

3. The quick-dip method. Use any of the brand-name liquid jewelry cleaners and follow the label's instructions.

4. The ultrasonic cleaner. Many are available today; follow the manufacturer's instructions.

5. When you're at the jeweler for your ring's once-a-year checkup, also ask to have the ring professionally cleaned. To protect your investment, wait while it's being done—if you leave the ring, you give an unscrupulous jeweler the opportunity to remove your quality stone and replace it with an inferior one.

Cover Up: Insurance for Your Ring

You may feel the same way about your ring as you do your groom—till death do you part—but things can happen, namely loss, damage, and theft. In fact, in 1995 close to $1 billion worth of jewelry was stolen in this country; a measly 4.3 percent of it was recovered.

It pays to be prepared; protect your investment with adequate insurance. According to the Insurance Information Institute, standard homeowner's policies only provide about $2,000 of limited coverage for jewelry, so you may need additional protection. Contact your insurance agent about getting either an endorsement or a personal possessions floater policy. An endorsement is an addition to your homeowner's/renter's policy providing additional insurance for specific items. A floater is property insurance for items that move from location to location, such as jewelry, covering losses wherever they occur. Before you can have your ring insured, you'll need to get it appraised by a reputable jeweler or appraiser (your insurance agent can recommend one). Take a picture of your ring and place it with your appraisal certificate in a safe place. Then talk to your agent about insurance options.

ALL IN THE FAMILY: HOW TO GET YOUR BETTER HALVES INVOLVED

Wedding planning is filled with highs and lows—no bride wants to go it alone. Enlist the help of your families—both families. Here are some guidelines:

• **Get your parents acquainted.** Traditionally, the groom's mother makes the first move with a phone call or note to the bride's mother, offering congratulations and an invitation to get together. To help break the ice, you and your groom should attend. If your parents don't live nearby, suggest that his parents arrange a meeting with yours sometime before the wedding, even if they have to travel to the wedding site a day or two early.

• **Start determining wedding priorities.** The first topic of discussion: your wedding style. The second: finances. One may dictate the other. Get your families' opinions and go over options. Does one family feel they have to invite every blood relative? Do they think it's just not a wedding unless there's a seated dinner and a ten-piece orchestra? All's fair in love, war, and wedding planning; expect some tense moments. While your preferences should take precedence, it's not likely that they always will, especially if both families are footing part of the bill. In the interest of family harmony, compromises will have to be made. Bring all your negotiation skills to the table.

• **Discuss money matters.** Tradition has it that the bride's family pays for the bulk of the wedding, but that's not always the case these days. If you and your fiancé are financially secure, you might want to pay for the wedding yourselves—it will give you more leverage in planning the wedding *you* want. Or the groom's family may offer to contribute. (His parents can broach the subject during a meeting with both sets of parents, or your fiancé can extend the offer to your parents privately. Your parents may accept or decline politely.) If you're counting on your parents to foot at least part of the wedding bill but they've made no formal offer, tread gently. It could be that they're still deciding what they can afford and will bring it up soon. If you can't wait, figure out with your fiancé how much the wedding will cost, then approach your parents. Say something like "Bob and I estimate that the wedding will cost X. We were wondering if you had plans to contribute toward it." Or, perhaps ask them to pay for specifics: "Bob and I are paying for flowers, his parents are taking care of the music, would you be able to contribute for the photographer?" Based on their response, you may have to plan a simpler celebration—a smaller guest list, a brunch instead of a seated dinner, etc.

• **Keep his family informed of wedding plans.** Let his family know how many guests they may invite to the reception and when you will need the names and addresses (with correct spellings and zip codes). Traditionally, the bride's mother chooses the dress she will be wearing to the wedding first, then discusses her decision with the groom's mother, who buys a dress similar in length and complementary in color (although not the *same* color). If the groom's mother already has a dress she hopes to wear, the bride's mother might select a dress to complement it. Or, your two moms can shop together. Besides giving them a great chance to get to know each other, they'll be able to see how they'll look standing next to each other in photographs, thereby avoiding a Bobbsey Twin effect.

• **Consider ways to include his family in the wedding.** If you know and like his siblings, ask them to be part of the wedding party. You might also want to list the groom's parents on the invitations, and ask them to participate in ceremony readings and the wedding procession.

A MONTH-BY-MONTH TO-DO LIST: YOURS AND HIS

You'll need six months to a year to arrange a large wedding in an urban area at a popular site during a peak wedding month. On the other hand, it's possible to plan a wedding in a much shorter time span than the one given below (although you may not get your first choice of reception site, dress, musicians, etc.).

Bride's Twelve-Month Calendar

Twelve Months Before

• Get organized. A wedding planner will help.

• Talk to your fiancé and families about the style of the wedding you want, plus the budget.

• Select a wedding date with your fiancé.

• Choose your attendants—they'll need the time to arrange their schedules.

• Book a ceremony and reception site—expect to put down a deposit to hold the date.

• Book your wedding professionals—a consultant, caterer, florist, photographer, videographer, musicians.

Nine Months Before

• Visit with your officiant. If you're having a religious ceremony, you may need to fulfill prewedding counseling requirements. If it's a civil ceremony, your officiant may still want to meet with you to discuss your ceremony.

• Shop for and order your wedding gown and bridal accessories, such as underpinnings, shoes, veil.

• Start working on your guest list with your fiancé. Include input from both families.

• Register for gifts. If you'll be having engagement parties, you might want to do this even sooner.

• Discuss where you might like to honeymoon.

Six Months Before

• Meet with the wedding professionals you've hired to go over details. You'll want to discuss the menu with your caterer, must-take pictures with your photographer, music selections with your bandleader or DJ, etc.

- Book limousines.
- Order your wedding invitations and announcements. Send the announcements to people who were not invited to the wedding, but with whom you want to share the news.
- Make concrete plans with your fiancé about the honeymoon, and speak to a travel agent.
- Shop for and order your bridesmaids' dresses.

Three Months Before
- Finalize the guest list.
- Begin shopping for your wedding lingerie and honeymoon clothes.
- Shop for and order the wedding rings.
- Make an appointment with a hairdresser to discuss wedding-day styles.
- Check state requirements for blood testing (call your local health department).
- Reserve a block of hotel rooms for out-of-town guests.
- Call the bridal shop and verify the delivery dates of all dresses and accessories.
- Have the first fitting; select your headpiece.

Six to Eight Weeks Before
- Address and mail the invitations.
- Buy a wedding gift for your fiancé and attendants' gifts for your bridesmaids.
- Go for your last dress fitting.
- Have the photographer take your portrait.
- Submit your announcement to newspapers.
- Put together the details of the bridesmaids' luncheon or party.
- Test any new hair color at least eight weeks before the wedding.
- Get your wedding rings from the jeweler.
- Write thank-you notes for shower or wedding gifts as you receive them.

Two Weeks Before
- Confirm your honeymoon reservations.
- Go with your fiancé to get the marriage license.
- Address announcements to be mailed on your wedding day.
- Submit request lists to the photographer, videographer, musicians, et cetera.
- Make the necessary arrangements to have your belongings moved to your new home.
- Visit your hairstylist for a trim and color touch up.

One Week Before
- Supply caterer with a final head count of guests who will attend.
- Stay on top of thank-you notes.
- Have fun at the bridesmaids' luncheon or party you're hosting.
- Confirm with your bridesmaids—again—about the rehearsal dinner's date, place, and time.
- Pack for the honeymoon.
- Buy traveler's checks; inquire with the hotel or bank about ATMs near your honeymoon site.
- Confirm all dates, times, and details with your wedding professionals.

Groom's Twelve-Month Calendar

Twelve Months Before
- Choose and buy your bride's engagement ring (if you haven't already).
- Discuss the wedding plans and budget with your fiancée and each family.
- Select, with your fiancée, a wedding date.
- Choose your ushers (remember, there should be one usher for every fifty guests).
- Decide on the ceremony and reception site with your fiancée.

Nine Months Before

• Find an officiant and schedule a visit with your fiancée. He/she will want to meet you, discuss any prewedding requirements, and go over your ceremony options.

• Begin to compile your guest list. Get input from your fiancée and both families, and combine lists.

• Talk to your fiancée about where you'd like to honeymoon; also consult a travel agent for suggestions.

• Select registry items with your fiancée.

Six Months Before

• Talk to your fiancée about floral details. Traditionally, the groom pays for the bride's bouquet, corsages for the mothers and grandmothers, and the ushers' boutonnieres. Now's the time to arrange to pay for all those things.

• Make honeymoon reservations; purchase any tickets.

• Look into whether you need passports, visa, inoculations, etc., to travel to your honeymoon destination.

Three Months Before

• Finalize your guest list. Give it to your fiancée, along with proper name spellings and correct addresses.

• Select your wedding attire with your fiancée; order what you need for you and your ushers.

• Order your wedding rings.

• If you'll be needing them, start shopping for new honeymoon clothes.

• Talk to your fiancée about lodging selections, then reserve a block of rooms for out-of-town guests.

• Check state requirements for getting prenuptial blood tests (call your local health department).

• Start planning the rehearsal dinner with your parents and formulate your guest list.

Six to Eight Weeks Before

• Help your fiancé write thank-you notes for gifts.

• Look into what's required for getting a marriage license (call your city hall, town clerk's office, or marriage license bureau for details).

• Buy a wedding gift for your fiancée as well as gifts for your ushers.

• Pick up your wedding rings. If there's engraving, take a look at it. Is everything correct?

• Decide upon the rehearsal dinner site and book the space.

Two Weeks Before

• Go with your fiancée to get the marriage license.

• Arrange your transportation from the reception to the airport or your hotel.

• Attend your bachelor party; give them their gifts at the party.

• Confirm all honeymoon reservations; check departing and arriving times and dates on tickets.

• Make the necessary arrangements to have your furnishings and personal items moved to your new home.

• Send out rehearsal dinner invitations.

One Week Before

• Remind your ushers of when and where the rehearsal dinner will take place.

• Get the officiant's fee ready. Entrust it to your best man, letting him know that he should give it to your officiant after the ceremony.

• Give your ushers any special instructions about whom to seat where.

• Buy your traveler's checks; inquire with the hotel or bank about ATMs near your honeymoon site.

• Pack for the honeymoon.

• Confirm the date, times and details with the rehearsal dinner site.

Chapter 2:

FINDING YOUR WEDDING STYLE

A wedding not only speaks of your love and commitment, it tells a story about your personal style, interests, and background. Most weddings fall into four distinct categories (see below). The wedding you ultimately decide upon may not fit into one of these genres exactly, but the definitions will be useful when planning and working with wedding professionals.

SETTING THE TONE

Very Formal

• The ceremony is held in a church, synagogue, or hotel ballroom.

• Two hundred or more guests are invited.

• Invitations are engraved or printed, using traditional wording.

• The bride wears a traditionally styled gown with a long train, such as a chapel or cathedral train (if the wedding is in the daytime, a shorter train is also appropriate). For a unified look, the veil is often the same length as the train.

• Bridesmaids, wearing floor-length dresses, generally number between four and twelve. Other attendants can include flower girls, ring bearers, and pages.

• Groom and ushers are in formal attire (cutaway coats if daytime; white tie and tails, if after six P.M.).

• The reception is elaborate, with a seated meal.

Formal

• The ceremony takes place at a church, synagogue, hotel, club, or private home.

• The guest list tops one hundred.

• Invitations are engraved or printed, using traditional or personalized wording.

• The bride wears a long gown with a chapel, sweep, or detachable train (if the wedding is in the daytime, a shorter dress may be worn). The length of the veil complements the dress.

• The bride is attended by two to six bridesmaids. Dresses can be long or short.

• If an evening wedding, grooms and ushers are in black tuxedos. If daytime, they choose gray strollers, waistcoats, and striped trousers and ties.

• The reception usually includes a seated meal.

Semiformal

• The ceremony takes place in a church, synagogue, hotel, home, or other location.

• Fewer than one hundred guests are invited.

• The invitations are engraved or printed, using traditional or personalized wording.

• The bride has many options. She can wear a floor-length or shorter dress in a white or soft pastel color. Like her dress, her veil may be short or long.

• Bridesmaids usually number just one or two

(for a daytime wedding, it's usually just one honor attendant and no bridesmaids). For an evening wedding, they wear cocktail dresses; for a daytime wedding, a suit or short dress.

• The groom and his attendants wear tuxedos or dinner jackets if it's evening, suits and ties in the day.

• The reception consists of light refreshments, such as cocktails and perhaps a buffet instead of a multicourse meal.

Informal

• The ceremony is held in the daytime, at any number of sites, including city hall, a restaurant, beach, or park.

• Fifty or fewer guests attend.

• The invitations are handwritten or extended personally.

• The bride wears a suit or dress; white is only one option. She may also wear a pastel color.

• Usually, there is only an honor attendant, who wears a suit or short dress.

• The groom and his best man wear a suit or blazer and coordinating trousers.

• The reception is intimate, held at a private home or restaurant.

GETTING FOCUSED

What type of wedding you ultimately say "I do" to will depend upon a lot of different circumstances—your personalities, the time of day you plan on marrying, how many guests you'll invite, and how much money you have to spend. Tradition still reigns supreme when it comes to weddings, with the overwhelming majority of today's couples favoring a formal wedding with a religious ceremony. But these are convention-shattering times, and weddings are not immune. What's the right wedding style for you? You'll need to sort through your options and zoom in on your choices. To help you get started, here are nine points to consider:

1. My wedding budget is:
☐ $1,000 to $5,999
☐ $6,000 to $15,999
☑ $16,000 to $20,999
☐ $21,000 or above

2. I'd like my wedding to be:
☐ Very formal
☐ Formal
☑ Semiformal
☐ Informal

3. I want my wedding ceremony to be held in:
☐ A church, synagogue, or other house of worship
☐ A home
☐ A hotel, club, banquet facility, hall, or restaurant
☑ A garden, park, or beach
☐ An unusual site (a museum, loft, or historic estate)

4. My wedding reception must be held at:
☐ A private home
☑ A hotel, club, banquet facility, hall, or restaurant
☐ A garden, park, or beach
☐ An unusual site (a museum, loft, or historic estate)

5. I intend to have a bridal party numbering:
☑ fewer than ten
☐ more than ten

6. I want to invite:
☐ Just immediate family and very close friends
☐ 100 or fewer guests

☑ 101 to 200 guests

☐ 201 or more guests

7. My wedding will be paid for by:

☐ Me

☐ My fiancé

☑ My fiancé and myself

☐ My parents

☐ My parents, with help from my fiancé's family

☐ All of the above

8. I'd like my wedding celebration to:

☑ Consist of a traditional ceremony and reception

☐ Have ethnic influences

☐ Begin on a Friday, end on a Sunday

☑ Have a theme (nautical, seasonal, Victorian et cetera.)

9. The most important wedding detail to me is:

☐ Inviting as many guests as possible

☐ Serving gourmet food

☐ Having gorgeous flowers

☐ Hiring a top-notch photographer/videographer

☐ Having the reception take place in the most elegant catering hall/ restaurant

☐ Wearing a fabulous gown

☐ Entertaining guests with the best band/DJ money can buy

☐ All of the above

WEDDINGS FOR THE TWENTY-FIRST CENTURY: ALTARED STATES

A church wedding's not your thing? Relax. A wedding is as much an expression of your individuality as it is a celebration of your love. And today, there's no shortage of new, unexpected, creative ways to wed (if you're getting married or holding your reception outside, however, get the proper authorization—call the town hall and see if you need permits—for cooking, an increased noise level, etc.). Here are some suggestions for putting a spin on tradition.

Location, Location, Location: Choosing an Expressive Locale

When choosing an offbeat wedding site, there are practicalities to keep in mind. Is the site large enough to accommodate all your guests? Are the rental cost and security fees prohibitive? Is there room for a dance floor? How about shelter in case of rain? To uncover interesting sites, call the chamber of commerce, historical society, caterers, and wedding planners in the area where you want to have your wedding. The following are some places to consider:

- Flower shop
- Historic mansion
- Ballpark
- Train station
- Ferryboat
- Amusement/Theme park
- Lighthouse
- Spa
- Vineyard
- Art gallery
- Ranch
- Aquarium

A Theme's the Thing

Possibilities include:

Nautical

- Marry on a yacht or in a yacht club.
- Wear a straw boater instead of a veil.

• Use seashells piled together at the base of candles for centerpieces.

Spring

• Carry a hand-tied clutch of freesia, lilacs, and peonies.

• Serve wild asparagus, stuffed pea pods, and roast lamb.

• Give your guests seed packets for wedding favors.

Mystery

• Keep the reception site a secret.
• Have ushers dress in trench coats.
• Give ceremony guests reception clues.

Mardi Gras

• Dance to a zydeco band.

• Feast on gumbo, jambalaya, and crawfish, and have an oyster bar.

• Throw carnival trinkets during the recessional.

Renaissance

• Hire a town crier to announce the start of the wedding to guests.

• Have waiters dress in peasant tunics, with swords at their side.

• Seat guests at tables set with brocade runners, pewter steins, and pewter plates.

CONTEMPORARY CELEBRATIONS: MODERN WAYS TO WED

The Long-Weekend Wedding

A wedding is over in a heartbeat—especially when you're the bride and groom. Between the pictures, the dancing, the cake cutting, and bouquet tossing, there's precious little time to visit with guests. Extending the wedding celebration over a weekend changes that—and gives guests added incentive to come. Start the festivities with a welcome party/rehearsal dinner on Friday night. Invite out-of-town guests to a wedding-day breakfast or luncheon—perhaps at a relative's home. If your wedding will be on Saturday evening, plan a Saturday-afternoon event—a sightseeing trip to points of interest, a touch-football game, a group fishing outing, etc. (consider the age range of your guests and plan accordingly). Bid your guests farewell at a postwedding brunch. Send a schedule of all activities and accommodation information under separate cover. A wedding consultant, party planner, even the hotel manager at the lodge where guests are staying can help you plan the activities.

The Ethnic Wedding

Pledge your love while saluting your heritage. If you're Chinese, consider getting married in a red dress, which symbolizes love and joy. (Still prefer white? Then choose an all-red bouquet or crimson bridesmaid dresses.) A Scotsman might approach the altar in the family's tartan to the sound of bagpipers playing. African American couples might choose to wear wedding clothes made out of African asooke or kente cloth and jump the broom, an age-old custom symbolizing the start of homemaking. Italian American couples could highlight their culture by tying a ribbon across the church door (an old Italian custom representing the bond of marriage), placing sugared almonds on guests' tables (signifying the sweet and bitter aspects of life), and dancing the tarantella. Those of British or Irish ancestry could feast on rich fruitcake instead of the standard white wedding cake. A Greek bride might incorporate the traditional crowning service into her ceremony and carry with her a lump of sugar to ensure a sweet future. To learn more about your nationality's wedding customs, visit your library or bookstore.

The Progressive Wedding

Chances are, you're not marrying the boy next door. Your family—and his—are probably scattered around the country. While that's great for racking up frequent flier miles, it's not so great when you want to get everyone together for your wedding. If a lot of the people close to you will be unable to attend your celebration, consider taking your postwedding festivities on the road, traveling to predetermined spots—visiting your grandparents in Dallas, his college friends in New Orleans—for parties hosted in your honor.

The Fantasy Wedding

Cropping up all over the country are wedding locations that take their inspiration from books, fairy tales, film, and TV. Feel like a true Cinderella and get married in Walt Disney World's Wedding Pavillion. Scarlett O'Hara more your style? Try an antebellum mansion. To find the perfect spot for your fantasy wedding, contact your local or state visitor's bureau or travel or tourism department. Also research theme parks and Renaissance fairs.

The Honeymoon Wedding

Guests are invited to travel with you to a romantic locale. After you exchange your vows, you may choose to stay in the same location and vacation with guests who stay on, or honeymoon elsewhere. Travel expenses of the guests are usually covered by them, though the bride and groom can often find group rates. Your travel agent or a tour operator can help you make the arrangements.

The Sentimental Journey

Take a trip down memory lane and say "I do" in a place that has special significance for you—e.g., the beach where you first met, the restaurant where you had your first date.

The Surprise Wedding

If you're great with a secret, consider hosting a surprise wedding. Send invitations asking your family and friends to attend a party. When they arrive, guests get the unexpected honor of witnessing your vows and joining in your wedding celebration.

Seasonal Weddings

Ask guests to wear costumes to a Halloween wedding; decorate your reception hall with a Christmas tree, evergreen, and well-placed mistletoe for a Yuletide wedding.

The All-Night Wedding

It's the perfect celebration for guests who could have danced all night—given the chance. A late-evening ceremony is followed by cocktails, canapés, a seated or buffet dinner, dancing, and—finally—a breakfast buffet. Give guests the morning paper on the way out.

HOME RULES: A WEDDING WHERE THE HEART IS

There's something comforting about taking the biggest step of your life in a place called home. It's familiar and safe. You're surrounded by fond memories and cherished mementos. And you can get dressed in the room you grew up in.

If you're planning an at-home wedding or a wedding at the home of a close friend or relative, you'll have to think of logistics (given the myriad details, you might want to think about hiring a bridal consultant). The first step: Consider where you'll hold the ceremony and reception—inside, outside, or both? What room or place will be best suited to the wedding? A cozy living room with a roaring fire? A backyard pool or rose garden? (If any part of the wedding will be held outdoors, be sure to rent tents, and have them erected the night before the wedding so the ground stays dry in the event of rain.)

Rental agencies can supply tables, chairs, linens, tents, latrines, heaters, outdoor lighting, and just about anything else you might need (your caterer can supply the waiters, but you might want to look into hiring parking valets for the day). To find rental companies, look in the yellow pages under "Party Supplies." Visit the store's showroom to see the quality of the supplies; ask your caterer for a list of what you might need. If a seated dinner will be served, make sure the tables are situated so waiters have room to circulate. Rearrange furniture to make the most of your space.

As far as your entrance and exit go, you'll probably need to make only a few adjustments. Chairs can be arranged to form an aisle. If there are space constraints, forgo the recessional and simply form a receiving line right at the conclusion of the ceremony.

WEDDING STYLE WORKSHEET

Now that you have some ideas about wedding styles, it's time to envision your wedding. Sit down together and discuss the many aspects of a wedding, listed below. In each case, write down what you want most, even if you're not sure it's available. Don't think about budget yet. The worksheet will help you set priorities so you can then adjust your budget.

Preferred date ___10/3/09_____

Alternate date _____

Time of day ___3 PM_____

Location of the ceremony ___Bentley's At the Barn_____

Transportation to ceremony ___Truck & Car_____

Invitations and announcements (engraved, printed, or a unique design) ___indiv. design___

Officiant _____

What should the ceremony include: Readings? Personalized vows? _readings &_
regular vows

Ceremony musical selections _____

_____

Floral decorations (at ceremony site, reception site) _____

_____

Bridal gown ideas _____

_____

Number of attendants ___1_____

Names of attendants ___Margot_____

_____

_____

Attendants' attire (ideas) _____

_____

Flowers for bride and attendants _____

_____

Rough estimate of number of guests—Hers _____ His _____ Total _____

Reception site ___Bentley's At the Barn_____

Floral decorations _____

_____

Music _____

_____

_____

Beverages for when guests arrive _____

_____

Beverages with meal _____

_____

Beverages for toasts _____

_____

Hors d'oeuvres _____

_____

Main meal _Jumbo Lump Crab Cake & Roast Pork_
c̄ apples

Seated or (buffet?) _____

Desserts _cake & pie_ _____

Other ideas (food stations, oyster bar, make your own sundaes) _fruit & cheese_
bar

Wedding cake (flavor, decorations) _____

Her ideas _____

_____

His ideas _____

_____

Favor ideas _caramel & candied apples_ _____

_____

Other reception needs (tent, lavatory facilities, getaway vehicle) _____

_____

_____

Ideas for personalizing the ceremony and reception (ethnic traditions, reading of poems, wedding
programs, etc.) _Fall theme, pumpkins, gourds_

_____

Honeymoon ideas _Disney World_ _____

_____

_____

THE OUT-OF-TOWNERS: GIVE THEM A WARM WELCOME

Let your out-of-town guests know how much you appreciate all their efforts to get to your wedding by making them feel especially welcome. Here are some tips for red-carpet treatment:

Accommodations

Well before you mail out your invitations, inquire with hotels and inns near your ceremony and reception sites about availability and rates. Reserve a block of rooms (you should be able to get a group rate). Send a reservation form and price list under separate cover. When you know how many rooms have actually been reserved, ask attendants to help you create a welcome basket of fruit, chocolate, bottled water, sunscreen, aspirin, tourist brochures, and perhaps even a baseball cap or T-shirt with your names and wedding date. Also include a list of scheduled activities, rental car information, local maps, directions to the ceremony and reception sites, all pertinent phone numbers (for you, your groom, your families), and a welcome note. Have the hotel staff place a basket in each of your guests' rooms, or ask them to hand them to guests as they check in.

Transportation

Make a master list of arrival schedules for guests coming in by plane, bus, or train (the following chart will help). Then ask local friends, family, and attendants to meet guests and drop them off at their hotels. If a group of guests will be arriving on the same flight, perhaps you could rent a van or bus to transport them to their hotel. The bus rental idea might also come in handy on your wedding day if many guests will be without cars.

Activities

To make guests feel especially welcome and appreciated, line up separate, easy-to-organize events—a sight-seeing trip on Friday, a get-to-know-the-crowd bowling tournament on Saturday—and send out a schedule with the hotel reservation form and price list. Also make note of any points of local interest—shops, parks, beaches, historical sites, etc.—as well as recommended restaurants for out-of-towners who will not be attending the rehearsal dinner. If children are invited (or even just traveling with their parents), plan some activities they'll enjoy as well.

LOGISTICS CHART FOR OUT-OF-TOWNERS

Photocopy this chart so you have one for each family attending.

Name of guest _____   Number in family _____

Address _____

Phone _____   Fax _____

Date and time of arrival _____

How arriving (airplane flight number, train, etc.) _____

Place where staying (name, address, phone, fax) _____

Transportation needs (ride to ceremony, rental car info) _____

Transportation from lodging back to airport, train, bus station _____

Baby-sitting needs _____

Any other special needs (e.g., wheelchair access, dietary restrictions) _____

_____

_____

MARRYING AT THIRTY, FORTY, AND BEYOND

Gone is the child bride. Today, more and more women are choosing to commit to an education and a career before they commit to marriage. Consider this jump: In 1968 the median age of first-time brides was 20.8. In 1994, it was 24.5. Nowadays, it's not uncommon for a bride to wait until her thirties or forties to tie the knot, which begs the question: Can a bride who's old enough to remember bell-bottoms and the Beatles still have the same large, lavish wedding as one who grew up on leisure suits and disco? Yes—with a few minor adjustments. For starters:

Budget/Sponsors

You most likely will contribute—at least partially—to the wedding costs, if not pick up the tab entirely. Your parents could still be listed as hosts of the wedding, or you and your fiancé could do all the inviting and announcing, using wording such as "The honour of your presence is requested at the wedding of Mary Jo Smith to John Paul Adams."

Wedding Parties

As an older bride, you may prefer a coed cocktail or dinner party that includes your fiancé, mutual friends, and their partners in lieu of a traditional shower. Also, since your friends are apt to be older and more financially secure than those of younger couples, be prepared to have several parties thrown in your honor.

Gifts

If you already have a home established—either together or individually—consider registering for the finer things in life: crystal, china, and silver. If your home is composed of mish-mashed, hand-me-down, second-time-around pieces, register for new sets of things you need. And in either case, broaden your horizons. Wine, books, sports equipment, and electronics are all registry items these days; you can even register at some mortgage firms (for a down payment on a house) or travel agencies (for your honeymoon). If you'd like to receive money, be discreet. Have close friends, family, and attendants spread the word orally; never indicate that you have a preference for monetary gifts on invitations.

Dress

A long, formal gown is as appropriate for an older bride as for a younger one. However, if you'd like something more understated, there's plenty to choose from. Bridal salons carry dresses in a wide variety of styles, lengths, and colors. You might even consider a bridesmaid's dress in white. Depending on your gown, you might choose a veil—or opt for a hat, flowers, or satin headband.

I DO (AGAIN): ETIQUETTE FOR REMARRYING

As divorce becomes more commonplace, so, too, do second marriages. In fact, the majority of women who divorce in this country eventually remarry, on average within four years of when their last marriage ended. If you're saying "I do" again—because you've been either divorced or widowed—here's what you should know.

The Ring

• A diamond engagement ring is a symbol of love, regardless of whether it's your first. Sixty percent of repeat brides receive one, according to the Diamond Information Center in New York City.

Announcements

• Let any of your children know about the marriage first; next, tell your parents.

• If you're recently divorced or widowed, it's customary to wait until after the wedding to announce your marriage. Otherwise, go ahead and place an announcement of the engagement in the newspaper.

• Your parents may officially make the announcement (even if they won't be paying for the wedding), or you and your fiancé can do it yourselves.

The Invitations

• Send out printed invitations if you're inviting fifty or more guests. For smaller weddings, you can write an informal note or just phone family and friends.

• If you're inviting many people to the reception but just a few to the ceremony, send out formal reception cards to guests. Include handwritten ceremony cards in the invitations of those you're inviting to both.

Gifts

• If there are gifts you'd like to receive—be it china or CDs—then feel free to register for them. Even though it's a second wedding, guests will want to celebrate your happiness by giving you a present—and registering makes it easier for them to pick out something you really want.

The Clothes

• White is the color of joy—it's been that way since ancient Roman times; it's just as appropriate for a second-time bride as for a first-time.

• Pastels—lavender, peach, melon, platinum— are other pretty options. Take a look at the offerings at bridal shops.

• Skip the long train and veil—both represent virginity and are the prerogative of the first-time bride. Instead, consider a hat, flowers, an embellished hair barrette, or a headband.

The Ceremony

• Consider your first wedding. If you got married in a big church wedding the first time around, would you prefer something smaller and more intimate this time? Was your first wedding more your mother's affair than yours? Plan a celebration that *really* reflects your tastes and uniqueness as a couple. One caveat: Don't make it too similar to your last wedding. Hold the reception in a different place; write new vows; pick a song special to the two of you for your first dance. This should be a fresh start, not a repeat of a prior event.

• Second-time couples marry everywhere that first-time couples do—in churches, synagogues, hotel ballrooms, city hall, and on the beach at sunset.

• Find roles for your children—as attendants, readers, escorts, and greeters.

• Don't invite your ex-spouse or ex-in-laws, even if you're still the best of friends. Even if they don't feel uncomfortable, your fiancé or his family very well may.

• If your father is no longer living, consider walking down the aisle alone; having your mother, a brother, older child, or close friend escort you; or even entering on the arm of your groom.

The Honeymoon

• If you have children, think about leaving them with friends and relatives. Creating a sense of family is important, but so is spending time alone together, especially after the whirlwind of wedding planning.

• Explore a place neither of you has been before so you have the thrill of experiencing something new together.

DO YOU NEED A WEDDING CONSULTANT?

They've been dubbed "miracle workers" by many a bride—and for good reason. A bridal consultant is someone who can scour reception sites for you, haggle with the caterer about the virtues of salmon mousse versus butterflied shrimp, and even get your mom to calm down. But do you really need one to plan the wedding of your dreams? No— and yes, depending on how much time and energy you want to devote to planning your wedding. Here is how a consultant can help you pull off the wedding of a lifetime, plus tips on finding one should you decide you need professional help.

The Wedding Consultant: A Résumé

Responsibilities include:

• **Mapping it all out.** A consultant will help you pinpoint your wedding goals, offer you suggestions for getting there, and then devise a plan of attack.

• **Start-to-finish wedding planning.** If you like, you can hire a consultant for full-service wedding planning. She/he will scout out the best photographers, florists, caterers, then present you with names of those who will do the best job in your price range. This is particularly helpful if you're planning your wedding long-distance. Don't worry about relinquishing control. The consultant does all the background work, but you make all the hiring and buying decisions.

• **Day-of-wedding service.** Think of your wedding as a movie, and the consultant its director. If you hire a consultant just for your wedding day, you'll do all the planning—but she/he does all the last-minute orchestrating, telling the caterer when to start serving, the DJ or band where to set up, etc.

• **Saving the couple money.** Granted, a consultant typically costs money—usually it's a percentage of the total wedding cost, or she'll bill you per hour or charge a flat fee—but she can also help you save money by showing you cost-cutting moves (using ribbon as napkin rings, for example) and inding the right professionals for your budget and wedding style. Since they're counting on your consultant for repeat business, they'll aim to please.

• **Being the peacemaker.** She'll do her best to help settle wedding-related battles between you and your fiancé, you and your families, and you and the wedding professionals you hire.

Where Oh Where: Finding a Consultant

• Ask friends, family, and recent brides you know for recommendations. Ask the consultants for references.

• Before you settle on a consultant, look at how much experience she/he has—the consultant should have planned a minimum of twelve weddings.

• Ask other wedding professionals whose work you respect—caterers, photographers, florists, etc.—if they have names to suggest.

• Call the Association of Bridal Consultants in New Milford, Connecticut; June Wedding Inc., in Temple, Texas; and the Association for Wedding Professionals in Sacramento, California, for referrals in your area.

• As a last resort, look for names under "Wedding Consultants" or "Party Planners" in the yellow pages. Be sure to check references.

WEDDING CONSULTANT/ PARTY PLANNER WORKSHEET

Estimate #1

Name _____

Address _____

Phone _____ Fax _____

Recommended by _____

Services/Ideas/Notes _____

Cost _____

Estimate #2

Name _____

Address _____

Phone _____ Fax _____

Recommended by _____

Services/Ideas/Notes _____

Cost _____

Estimate #3

Name _____

Address _____

Phone _____ Fax _____

Recommended by _____

Services/Ideas/Notes _____

Cost _____

Final selection (name, address, phone, fax) _____

_____

_____

Contract signed   Deposit paid/date   Balance due/date

_____

Chapter 3:

YOUR WEDDING PARTY

THE WEDDING PARTY: A CHOICE DECISION

They smooth your train and calm your jitters. They pick up wedding planning slack as well as friends and family at the airport. They not only get your groom to the church on time but also get the tuxedos back to the rental shop before you're charged a late fee.

The friends and family you choose to be your attendants stand up for you, in more ways than one. Before you select the people who will be members of the wedding, get a handle on what they're required to do. Here is a roster of the key players:

Honor Attendant

• **She's usually a very close friend or sister**, although some brides may want to recognize and honor the special relationships they have with their **mothers, aunts, grandmothers,** or **grown daughters.**

• **What if a man is your closest friend?** Then give him the distinction of being the bride's best man. Just be sure to inform your wedding professionals (photographer, band leader, etc.) who your person-of-honor is. Also, don't ask your best man—who should wear whatever the ushers are wearing—to do anything that might make him feel uneasy, be it attending your bachelorette party or ducking into the ladies' room with you to adjust your gown.

• **The honor attendant usually hosts or cohosts a bridal shower and helps you with prewedding duties** such as addressing invitations, shopping for a gown, etc.

• At the ceremony, **she fluffs your train and adjusts your veil, holds your bouquet,** and **carries the groom's ring.** She also helps make everything official by **signing the marriage certificate** as a witness.

• At the reception, **she'll help you bustle your train, change into your going-away clothes,** and **look after your gown** and **see that any wedding gifts** guests may have brought with them are transported to your parents' home or your new home. She may be asked to offer a toast along with the best man.

Bridesmaids

• **They can number from zero** (you may choose to simply have one honor attendant and no bridesmaids) **to twelve** for a large, lavish wedding.

• **Junior bridesmaids are between nine and fourteen years of age.** Because of their younger age, they should wear a less mature, less revealing version of the bridesmaids' dresses—or a more sophisticated version of the flower girl's dress.

• Like the honor attendant, **bridesmaids help the bride with a variety of wedding planning tasks.** They may address invitations, accompany the bride as she shops for her gown, and offer to house out-of-town guests in their homes. They also **cohost a bridal shower and bachelorette party.**

Best Man

• **Traditionally, he's a brother, close friend, relative, or the father of the groom.** A **sister or other close female relative** or friend could also act as a "best woman."

• The best man **makes sure the groom and ushers are at the ceremony on time.** He also **holds any envelopes containing fees/tips** (i.e., for the officiant, altar servers) for the groom, **carries the bride's wedding ring down the aisle,** and **signs the marriage license.**

• **It's also the best man's responsibility to propose the first toast to the couple at the reception** and **read any congratulatory telegrams.**

• If the couple needs **a ride to the airport or hotel**, he's the one to provide it.

• He also organizes **the return of all rented formalwear.**

Ushers

• As a rule of thumb, **you'll need one usher for every fifty guests** (to assist in seating guests for the ceremony), but you may have more.

• Ushers are generally **the groom's brothers, cousins, future brothers-in-law, and friends**.

• **Junior ushers (ages nine to fourteen)** can stand near the entrance of the ceremony site to **distribute programs** and **seat late-arriving guests**.

• **Besides seating guests** at the ceremony, **unrolling the aisle runner** prior to the procession, and making sure all **guests have rides and directions to the reception, ushers may throw a bachelor party** for the groom.

• **If it's raining, umbrella-holding ushers escort guests to their cars** after the ceremony. They also **give the ceremony site a once-over**, making sure the bride and groom haven't left behind any personal belongings.

• As a parting gesture, they might **decorate the getaway car.**

• The groom may appoint a **head usher to supervise special arrangements, such as seating divorced parents or disabled guests.**

Child Attendants

• In general, **child attendants are between four and eight years old.** You may be tempted to have younger children in your party, but weigh the pros and cons. While younger children can look adorable, they often can't be expected to perform predictably in front of a crowd, or to sit and stand quietly during a ceremony.

• **Flower girls carry a basket of flowers** (often rose petals) to strew in the bride's path, ensuring her a beautiful route ahead. If you are concerned that flower petals on an aisle runner can create slippery conditions, have the flower girl carry a basket of posies or a tiny nosegay.

• **The ring bearer**, traditionally a boy, **carries a satin pillow with rings tied or sewn onto it.** Usually these are symbolic rings; the honor attendants hold the actual rings.

• **Pages or train bearers** may be appointed at a very formal wedding to **carry a lengthy train down the aisle.** Traditionally, two boys of about equal height are chosen, but you may also have two girls.

• **Candle lighters** are often children from either family who **light candles just before the mother of the bride is seated.** They dress similarly to junior bridesmaids/ushers and **extinguish the candles** at the ceremony's end.

HOW TO CHOOSE ATTENDANTS WITHOUT MAKING ENEMIES: SOME STICKY SITUATIONS

• **Can't decide which of your two sisters to have as honor attendant?** Choose them both. Divide the maid-of-honor responsibilities—one can fix your train, for example, and the other can hold your bouquet during the ceremony.

• **Instead of your sister, you'd rather ask your best friend, to whom you're closer, to be your maid of honor.** Should you? Ultimately, it's your decision, but you do have options. Split the maid-of-honor duties, or if your sister is married, ask her to be your matron of honor. If your sister is quite a bit older than you, she might feel more comfortable taking a different role in your wedding. Ask her to perform some other important task, such as reading a piece of Scripture at your ceremony.

• **You've chosen three bridesmaids while your fiancé has rounded up four ushers. Can you have an odd number of attendants?** Absolutely. Just make sure you have one usher for every fifty guests. In the recessional, have two ushers escort one bridesmaid.

• **Do you have to include all your fiancé's sisters in the bridal party?** It's a nice gesture, but not mandatory. Unless your families expect all of your respective siblings to be in the bridal party, just ask those you're closest to.

HONORING FRIENDS AND FAMILY WHO AREN'T ATTENDANTS

You can only choose so many people to be bridesmaids and ushers. But you can still honor important people in your life by giving them a special wedding role. For instance:

• **Ask young nieces, nephews, sons, and daughters** to **pass out yarmulkes** or **wedding programs**, or **flower petals** to toss at the bride and groom after the ceremony.

• **Have a relative, sibling, or close friend read a poem or Scripture at your ceremony.** You can involve several people by asking them to split up one reading. Musically talented friends also may be invited to play or sing.

CONDUCT UNBECOMING: HOW NOT TO TREAT YOUR BRIDESMAIDS

Wedding planning is stressful. Tensions can run high. Still, that's no excuse for turning into the bride of Frankenstein. Here are some common problems brides have with their attendants—and how to sidestep them:

• **The number one source of conflict between a bride and her bridesmaids is what they wear.** While it's ultimately up to you to choose the style and color you like best, listen to your attendants' suggestions. Let them know you're concerned about their feelings and will be open-minded. Although their outfits should complement one another, remember that it's not essential that attendants dress alike.

• **Don't expect your attendants to share your excitement completely.** The harsh truth is that there's life outside your wedding plans. While bridesmaids have responsibilities, you need to respect their schedules and financial constraints. As you choose your attendants, be up-front about the time and money commitments involved. If a friend declines to be a part of your wedding party, don't take it personally. If she's extremely close to you, you might offer to pay for her dress—but keep it quiet.

• **If someone seems unhappy—constantly complaining, refusing to attend the rehearsal dinner—talk to her.** She may be dealing with small concerns, such as how she can walk gracefully down the aisle in three-inch heels, or bigger ones, such as how the marriage will affect your friendship.

• **Give thanks where thanks is due.** Your bridesmaids will play every role from planning assistant to relationship counselor. Let them know how much they mean to you, and remember to thank each one with a special gift and personalized note.

WEDDING PARTY CHART

My maid of honor Margot James
Address 950 Harney Rd
Phone 359 8156
Cell
Fax

My matron of honor
Address
Phone
Fax

1. Bridesmaid
Address
Phone
Fax

2. Bridesmaid
Address
Phone
Fax

The best man Lewis Buckley
Address 640 White Church Rd
Phone
Cell
Fax

The head usher
Address
Phone
Fax

1. Usher Jesse Firestone
Address
Phone
Fax

2. Usher Aaron Conklin
Address
Phone
Fax

3. Bridesmaid _____
Address _____
Phone _____
Fax _____

4. Bridesmaid _____
Address _____
Phone _____
Fax _____

5. Bridesmaid _____
Address _____
Phone _____
Fax _____

6. Bridesmaid _____
Address _____
Phone _____
Fax _____

7. Bridesmaid _____
Address _____
Phone _____
Fax _____

8. Bridesmaid _____
Address _____
Phone _____
Fax _____

9. Bridesmaid _____
Address _____
Phone _____
Fax _____

10. Bridesmaid _____
Address _____
Phone _____
Fax _____

11. Flower girl _Sarah Kiehl_
Address _760 Flhorhs Chuuch Rd_
Phone _____
Fax _____

Other helper _____
Address _____
Phone _____
Fax _____

3. Usher _____
Address _____
Phone _____
Fax _____

4. Usher _____
Address _____
Phone _____
Fax _____

5. Usher _____
Address _____
Phone _____
Fax _____

6. Usher _____
Address _____
Phone _____
Fax _____

7. Usher _____
Address _____
Phone _____
Fax _____

8. Usher _____
Address _____
Phone _____
Fax _____

9. Usher _____
Address _____
Phone _____
Fax _____

10. Usher _____
Address _____
Phone _____
Fax _____

11. Ring bearer _Michael Kiehl_
Address _760 Florhes Chuuch Rd_
Phone _____
Fax _____

Other helper _____
Address _____
Phone _____
Fax _____

Chapter 4:

PLANNING YOUR CEREMONY

Your ceremony is the heart and soul of your wedding. It seals your union and joins your fates. It marks the end of one journey and the start of another. It gives you strength and courage—to merge your lives and mingle your toothbrushes—for better or for worse.

CHOOSING YOUR OFFICIANT

Before you can have a ceremony, you have to have an officiant. Don't rely on divine inspiration. Here are pointers for selecting one:

• **If you'll be having a religious ceremony,** contact your house of worship and ask who might be available to perform your ceremony. Meet with that person(s) to get a sense of his/her style. Most couples want an officiant who's warm and uplifting—look until you find a good match.

• **If you're unaffiliated or planning your wedding from afar,** ask friends, relatives, clergymembers, and wedding consultants who are familiar with the area in which you're getting married to recommend officiants. Once you have a list, do some interviewing. If you're looking for a church/synagogue as well as an officiant, you can also look through the business listings in the phone book for houses of worship in your faith—or again, ask friends and family for recommendations.

• **If you're planning a civil ceremony,** contact the town hall in the town where you'll be married and ask for the office that issues marriage licenses. They can tell you who in that area is qualified to perform ceremonies, be it judges, Justices of the Peace, mayors, etc. Again, interview the prospective officiant to determine if he or she seems appropriate for your wedding.

• **If you're having an interfaith ceremony,** your first step is to check with your own houses of worship to see if there are clergy who are willing to marry you. You may be asked to make some concessions, for example, holding the ceremony on neutral territory such as in a catering hall. Can't get anywhere with local clergypeople? Go higher. If you're Catholic and he's Jewish, for instance, you can inquire with your archdiocese for help in locating a priest willing to marry you. He might look outside his branch of Judaism for a rabbi. Generally, Reform rabbis are more apt to perform interfaith ceremonies than Conservative or Orthodox ones. Another good lead: asking friends, family, and any interfaith couples you know for recommendations. Many interfaith couples also turn to the Unitarian Church, an ethical cultural society, or the ministry office of a local university, all of whom may be willing to marry you and offer suggestions for nondenominational sites (e.g., a hotel ballroom, public building, etc.) in which to hold the ceremony. Again, before you settle on an officiant, arrange a meeting to get a sense of his/her personality.

MEETING WITH YOUR CLERGYPERSON

Just as you want to make sure that your clergyperson is up for the job of marrying you, he or she will want to make sure that you're up for the job of marriage. Your clergyperson is looking at your wedding from a religious perspective and needs to make sure you're committed to marriage in a spiritual context. Consequently, you may be asked some questions about why you want to marry, your feelings on important issues such as money and children, and the extent of your religious participation.

You may also be asked for certain papers, for example:

- **certificates of baptism and confirmation,**
- **a letter attesting to the marital** or **religious status** of each of you,
- **a special dispensation** if you are of different faiths, and
- **a signed "letter of intention to marry"** or similar document, which usually states that you will participate in premarital counseling with a clergymember.

QUESTIONS FOR YOUR CLERGYPERSON

Checklist for Your Initial Meeting

- Are the date and time we've chosen available? If not, what alternate dates and times are free?

- Must we be members of this church or synagogue, or know members, to be married here? If we're not members, must we pay special fees?

- Are we required to go through premarital counseling? If so, how many sessions? What topics will be covered?

- Will you marry us if one of us is divorced? What special arrangements does a remarriage require? (Permission from a religious authority? Proof of divorce?)

- Will you marry us if we are of different faiths? On what conditions? Will one partner have to convert? Will we have to agree to raise any children in one religion over another? Will you perform the ceremony with a clergymember of a different faith? How do you usually share officiating duties?

- During which holidays or liturgical seasons are weddings prohibited? Is any time of day inappropriate? (Judaism prohibits weddings before sundown on the Sabbath; some pastors encourage

Saturday morning nuptials so as not to interfere with regular Saturday afternoon or Sunday services.)

- What are the fees for using the synagogue or church and for your services, the organist, and the services of your staff? Who is usually tipped? About how much? When?

- Will you marry us at a nonreligious site, such as a hotel or a private home?

- Are there any restrictions on ceremony dress? (For example, must the men wear yarmulkes? Should the bride's and bridesmaids' shoulders be covered?)

- Can we write our own vows? Personalize our ceremony? Are there any restrictions or guidelines?

- Must readings be religious in nature? At what point in the ceremony are they performed?

- Is a kiss permitted at the end of the ceremony?

- Are other weddings scheduled on our date? How much time will be devoted to our ceremony? Is there leeway so we won't feel rushed? Can we share flowers with another bride and groom?

- What's the seating capacity of the sanctuary? How big a wedding party fits comfortably on the altar? If there's a center aisle, how many can walk down it abreast? Can the side aisles be used for a procession?

• Is the church/synagogue wheelchair accessible?

• Is there a changing room for the bride and her wedding party?

• Does the synagogue or church have space available for receptions?

• Are there food requirements (e.g., only serving Kosher foods)? Can alcohol be served?

• Is there adequate parking for all our guests? On-site? Off-site? Will they be charged?

• Is there air-conditioning in the summer? Adequate heat in the winter?

Checklist for Your Second Meeting

• When will you give us our marriage license? How many witnesses should sign it? Can we include signing it in the ceremony?

• Are photographers permitted to use flash attachments during the ceremony? How close to the altar may they stand?

• Are there any restrictions on lighting candles? Throwing rice or flower petals? Other items?

• When can we gain entry to the synagogue or church on our wedding day before the ceremony?

• Is there a recommended area in which to position the receiving line?

• Must we use the staff organist and/or cantor? Are instrumentalists permitted? Is secular music permitted? Must music selections be approved? Is there an approved list?

• Do you have samples of wedding programs? How are they usually passed out?

• Can we preview the wording of the service and rewrite dated language?

• How long will the ceremony last? Will you be offering a welcoming prayer? Giving a homily? Can we preview these things in advance?

• Can we reserve family-only seats?

• Which accessories are provided (i.e., chuppah, aisle runner, etc.)?

• Can you suggest ceremony roles for children from a previous marriage? Can young relatives from a different congregation be altar servers and candle lighters?

• Do you have any suggestions for incorporating ethnic traditions into our ceremony?

• When is the rehearsal held? Who should be invited to the rehearsal? What if an out-of-town wedding party member cannot attend? Will there be music at the rehearsal? Will you coordinate a processional and recessional? Will you and your spouse attend the rehearsal dinner?

• Will you and your spouse attend the reception? Will you bless the meal?

• Will you arbitrate between divorced parents? Feuding in-laws?

CLERICAL ERRORS: CHECKING THE AUTHORITY VESTED IN HIM OR HER

When it comes to unscrupulous behavior, not every clergyperson is without sin. One bride, for example, had to change officiants at the last minute after learning that the priest she booked for her ceremony was really an *ex*-priest. While

her marriage would be sanctioned by the state, it wouldn't be sanctioned by the Catholic Church. Other clergy are really nothing more than mail-order ministers. While some states will recognize the marriages they perform, others may apply more scrutiny. And even secular sources can be suspect. For example, it's a good idea to check out the credentials of a ship's captain who claims to be able to perform wedding ceremonies; captains without credentials are no longer allowed to conduct weddings. Here are more pointers:

• **If you have doubts about a clergyperson's credentials,** call the national organization for the faith he/she is ordained in. You should be able to find out if he/she is a member in good standing.

• **If you're asked for a deposit,** don't put down more than 50 percent.

• **Ask for references,** then follow up on them.

• **If possible, attend a ceremony, mass, or service he/she is officiating.** Do you like his/her manner? The way he/she relates to the couple and the congregation?

PERSONALIZING YOUR CEREMONY

Your relationship isn't cookie-cutter, so why should your wedding be? Here are ways to add uniqueness and individuality to a wedding ceremony, without throwing tradition totally to the wind.

Set the Groundwork

• **Do your homework.** Talk to your clergymember and find out what parts of the traditional ceremony must be included. Your clergymember has probably helped many other couples personalize their ceremonies, and is an excellent source of ideas.

• **Analyze what you like and don't like about a traditional ceremony.** For example, having your father "give you away" may seem outdated to you. If that's the case, consider walking down the aisle alone but giving each parent a kiss before meeting your groom at the altar.

• **Scour religious as well as secular sources for inspirational, meaningful readings** (after asking if your clergyperson has any objections to using nonreligious material in your ceremony).

• Before you set your heart on any ceremony change/addition, **check it out with your offi-ciant.** He or she may first have to approve your choices.

Setting

• Select an **outdoor** or **at-home setting.**

• Reverse positions with the clergymember so that **you and your groom face the guests.**

• Eliminate seats at a small wedding and **gather everyone in a semicircle around you.**

Arrival

• **Have your attendants** or **close friends welcome guests** as they arrive.

• Have **ushers hand guests flowers, candles,** and **yarmulkes** as well as **rice** and/or **birdseed** or **flower petals** to throw as you exit the ceremony site if allowed.

• **Set the mood *outside* the church.** Hire a classical guitarist, bagpiper, or other musician to serenade guests as they arrive.

• Designate a friend or relative to **distribute wedding programs listing the names of all wedding participants.** Include a list of all musical, poetry, and prose selections. A nice touch: adding a welcoming note to guests, a thank-you message to parents, or your personal reflections on love and marriage.

Processional

• **Include both sets of parents in the procession.** It's a Jewish custom that can be used by those of other faiths as well.

• **Give each mother a kiss, flower, or handkerchief embroidered with your names and wedding date** when you reach the first pew.

• Walk down the aisle alone or **have your groom walk with you down the aisle** or **meet you halfway.**

Giving the Bride Away

• Instead of having your clergyperson ask "Who gives this woman away?" have him or her ask **"Who rejoices in this union?" Both sets of parents can answer "We do."**

• **Have your father escort you down the aisle to the point where his seat is located.** There, you can give him a kiss, then proceed the rest of the way alone to meet your groom.

Before the Vows

• **Have special people perform readings.** A brother or sister could offer a quote on the meaning of families; a good friend could speak on the importance of being friends and partners.

• **Read lines from a favorite poem or song** to each other and to the congregation.

• **Write a prayer,** and print it in your wedding program. Have your clergyperson invite the congregation to say it with you.

• **Ask a sibling from each family to extend welcoming remarks to the other.**

• **Include a Unity Candle in your ceremony.** Have three candles placed on the altar prior to your ceremony—one in the center and two smaller ones on either side. The bride, her parents, or the whole family walks up and lights the candle on the left; the groom, his parents, or the whole family lights the right candle. After exchanging your vows, you two light the center candle together, using the two family candles.

During the Vows

• **Give each bridal party member a candle,** dim the lights, then light the candles in succession; have the attendants form a semicircle around you as you recite your vows.

• If you like the wording of traditional vows but don't think they express all there is to say about your love and commitment, **exchange two sets of vows**—the standard ones as well as ones you've written yourselves.

• **Have parents affirm their wedding vows** after you say yours.

After the Vows

• **Kiss your spouse, then kiss your parents** and grandparents, reaffirming the family bond.

• **Include a short period of silence** so you and your guests can contemplate the significance of your words.

• **Have a "sign of peace"**—a handshake or kiss passed from your clergymember to you to your attendants to your guests.

The Recessional/Getaway

• **Stop at each pew** to greet guests.

• Instead of throwing rice (most churches ban it, unless it's biodegradable), have ushers **give guests small bells to ring,** bottles of **soap** (wrapped in tulle or lace) **to blow bubbles,** even boxes of **butterflies to release** (or fireflies, if it's nighttime). Call novelty suppliers and butterfly farms for details. Still want to throw something? Try packets of **potpourri, rose petals, birdseed,** or **safflower seeds** (check with your ceremony site, however, to see if there are any restrictions).

• Consider **unique transportation** to and from the wedding site: a horse-drawn carriage or sleigh, a vintage or classic car (a '57 Chevy, say, with piles of chrome). The more adventurous might think about a motorcycle, a convertible, even a bicycle built for two—provided you can maneuver one in your dress.

• **Walk to your reception site,** if it's nearby. Attendants and guests follow you, creating a wedding parade. It will give your wedding an old-world flavor.

WHEN PARENTS ARE DECEASED OR DIVORCED

If your parents have divorced and remarried, or if one or both parents have passed away, you'll need to rework elements of your ceremony.

Processional

• If your father is deceased, ask your mother to escort you down the aisle. If she's uncomfortable with that, or if she's deceased as well, ask a sibling, relative, or close friend to do the honors. If your mother has remarried, your stepfather may appreciate having the honor.)

• If your parents are divorced, it's still acceptable to honor your father by asking him to escort you down the aisle.

• If your parents are divorced and your mother is remarried, you may want to include your stepfather. Consider having both your father and stepfather escort you down the aisle if they're on friendly terms. Or one can escort you halfway down the aisle, the other the rest of the way. A third option is to choose one of your fathers to escort you, the other to perform some role of distinction, such as dancing the first father-daughter dance with you.

• It's perfectly acceptable to have both divorced parents escort you down the aisle. The same goes for your groom and his divorced parents.

• Is the decision causing a lot of friction? Opt to walk down the aisle alone or with your groom.

The Ceremony

When parents are divorced, not remarried, and still on friendly terms, they may sit together in the front pew. If your parents are not on good terms and/or are remarried, the parent who raised you should sit in the first pew (with his/her spouse); your other parent should sit in the third pew (behind siblings and grandparents), with his/her spouse.

• In a Jewish ceremony, both divorced parents may stand under the chuppah; stepparents sit in the second and third pews.

• If one parent is widowed, you may ask a close family member or friend to fill in for the deceased parent. If your mother is deceased, for example, your aunt can sit in the front pew with your father.

CIVIL CEREMONIES

A civil ceremony can be big or small, with varying degrees of formality. It can include a processional and recessional. What it probably won't include are any references to God.

Finding an Officiant

• Call the marriage license bureau of the town where you'll be married and ask for referrals.

• Ask family and friends for recommendations. Your ceremony will have a warmer note if the officiant is someone you know or comes personally recommended.

Ceremony Sites

• The sky's the limit. While many civil ceremonies are performed in a judge's chambers, a courthouse, or the office or home of the officiant, you can hold yours in your own home, a hotel ballroom, a restaurant, historic mansion, park, etc.

Dress

• Let the mood of the ceremony dictate. If you're holding it in a judge's chamber and inviting only a few guests, wear a suit or stylish dress. For a large wedding at a formal location, wear a traditional wedding dress.

HOW TO VOW 'EM: WRITING YOUR OWN VOWS

Think of your vows as the pièce de résistance of your wedding ceremony. If traditional wording doesn't fully express the love and devotion you feel for each other, then improvise. Here are some tips on writing your own vows:

1. Talk to your officiant. He or she can give you some suggestions on how to personalize your vows. If you're planning a religious ceremony, your officiant can also offer you guidelines on what is and what is not acceptable in the eyes of your faith.

2. Look at traditional vows and decide what concepts are particularly meaningful to you—love, fidelity, unwavering support, etc. You can keep the same wording but expound on issues that are really important to you.

3. Read up. For meaningful passages on love and marriage, look through the Bible, love poems (try Shakespeare, Elizabeth Barrett Browning, Pablo Neruda, e. e. cummings, and others), novels (e.g., D. H. Lawrence's *Women in Love* or E. M. Forster's *A Room with a View),* and inspirational reading (Kahlil Gibran's *The Prophet*).

4. Think about what marriage—and everything it signifies (e.g., lifelong love, partnership, trust, and forgiveness)—**means to you.**

5. Write vows that illustrate what's unique about you as a couple, be it your differing ethnic or religious backgrounds, your love of the outdoors, etc. One caveat: Don't get *too* personal. No one wants to hear about your sex life or other intimate details.

6. Honor any children from a previous marriage by pledging your love for them as well.

7. Remember decorum. Your vows are not the place for remarks about old boyfriends/ girlfriends, money issues, or controversial political ideals.

8. Keep it short. The vows themselves should take about one to three minutes.

9. Practice makes perfect. Try reciting your vows in front of a mirror. It will allow you to get comfortable with the words and to see if what seems to flow on paper flows when spoken.

10. Consider making your vows different from his. While it's perfectly acceptable to recite the same vows, it's also okay to recite completely different ones.

11. Put your vows on paper—and give a copy to your officiant. If it's a religious ceremony, your officiant will need to approve the vows before you recite them. In any case, it's a good idea if he/she holds a copy during your ceremony so you can be cued in case you forget the words.

READINGS THAT SAY IT ALL

"I do" aren't the only important words that will be spoken during your ceremony. If you're like a lot of couples, you'll want to give your ceremony life, meaning, and personality by incorporating various readings into it. Speak to your officiant first. Besides being able to offer ideas, he or she will fill you in on whether or not there are restrictions about what kind of material can and cannot be used (e.g., some religions discourage the use of secular readings). With that done, visit your library or local bookstore (head to the wedding-planning section) and look for compendiums of wedding ceremony readings. Other sources of inspiration: the Bible (read different versions to find one with a translation you like), love poems, romantic literature, and philosophical works. Here are some contemporary and traditional suggestions for a variety of ceremonies:

Civil Ceremonies

Generally, when it comes to readings for a civil ceremony, there are no constraints. You can choose many or just a few; they can come from the Bible or ancient Chinese proverbs. Examples:

   • The poetry of Emily Dickinson, Juan Ramón Jiménez, Pablo Neruda, or William Carlos Williams

   • The Book of Psalms
   • Rainer Maria Rilke, *Letters to a Young Poet*

Jewish Ceremonies

Readings typically come from the Hebrew Bible or secular sources. Some possibilities:
   • Book of Proverbs, 31
   • Song of Songs 8:7
   • Marge Piercy, "The Chuppah"

Christian Ceremonies

With your minister's approval, readings may be selected from the Bible as well as secular sources (some religions, such as Roman Catholicism, often prohibit the use of secular material).
   • Genesis 2: 18–24
   • Corinthians 12: 31–13:8a
   • Ecclesiastes 4: 7–13

Interfaith Ceremonies

In most cases, readings can be selected from Scripture or from secular sources. Consider some of these:
   • Colossians 3: 12–14
   • Apache Wedding Song
   • Wendell Berry, "The Country of Marriage"

GETTING PROGRAMMED: HOW TO WRITE A WEDDING PROGRAM

Help your guests follow the sequence of events and identify key participants with a wedding program. Here are the how-tos:

Determine the Style

Your wedding program can be simple or detailed. It can be typed and photocopied, computer generated, or professionally printed—the choice is yours. You might want to color-coordinate the paper to your wedding hues and/or reproduce a photo of yourselves or the ceremony site on the cover.

What Information to Include

Your guests will want to know the names of your attendants, parents, officiant, and musicians, so list all of them. Also cite any readings and musical compositions (if you have room, print the words to encourage your guests to follow along). In addition, explain the meaning of any religious customs or ethnic traditions (the breaking of the glass in a Jewish ceremony, for example, or the crowning of the couple in a Greek Orthodox church), so guests who aren't familiar with them can appreciate their significance. A program is also a nice place to acknowledge deceased relatives and to formally thank your parents for their help and support.

Passing Pointers

You could have ushers place a stack on both sides of each pew or put one on each seat. Another option is to ask the ushers or a special friend, relative, even a child guest, to hand one to each person as she/he enters.

CEREMONY WORKSHEET

Site reserved _Bentley's at the Barn_ Cost, if any $ _c̄ reception_

Date _Oct 3, 2009_ Ceremony time _1500_ to _1600_

Name and telephone number of clergyperson/officiant _Sally Daminger_

_____

Clergymember/officiant's fee, if any $ _____

Name and telephone number of other church/court/government official (secretary, etc.) _____

_____

Ideas for making the procession, ceremony, recessional unique _____

_____

_____

Procession (names of participants and their order) _____

_____

_____

Giving away/family gesture ideas _____

_____

_____

Reading or prayer ideas _____

_____

_____

Reader _Carol, Granny, Stacy_____

_____

Bride's vows _____

_____

Groom's vows _____

_____

_____

Exchange of rings _____

_____

_____

Pronouncement of marriage _____

_____

Benediction and blessing _____

_____

Recessional (names and order) _____

_____

Other ideas—programs, Unity Candle, etc. _____

_____

YOUR CEREMONY MUSIC

Music is a mood maker. Consider how a soloist's high notes can raise a spirit, lift a soul. Here are tips on choosing your wedding ceremony music.

What You'll Need: Songs for Your Ceremony from Prelude to Postlude

The Prelude

For a traditional religious ceremony, the music usually begins about thirty to fifteen minutes before the ceremony with a prelude. If you want a longer prelude, you might have to pay extra (consider whether it's worth it—about the only person likely to benefit by the music played an hour before your ceremony is your florist, setting up pew markers).

While guests are being seated and after the bride's mother has been seated (to prelude music), an organist, a soloist or choir may perform.

- "O Perfect Love," Burleigh
- "Chant de May," Jongen
- "The Lord's Prayer," Malotte
- Adagio, Albinoni
- "Siciliano for a High Ceremony," Howells
- "Wedding Day at Trolhaugen," *Lyric Pieces*, Grieg
- Largo, *The New World Symphony*, Dvorak
- "Benediction Nuptiale," Saint-Saëns
- "Songs without Words," no. 48, Mendelssohn

The Processional

You and your wedding party walk down the aisle to a joyous processional.

- Trumpet Voluntary, Clarke
- "Prince of Denmark's March," Clarke
- Allemande, G Major Suite, Pachelbel
- "Spring," *The Four Seasons*, Vivaldi
- "Apotheosis," *Sleeping Beauty*, Tchaikovsky
- "Music for a Royal Occasion," Handel
- Air and Bourrée, *Water Music*, Handel

- Canon in D, Pachelbel
- "Wedding March," *A Midsummer Night's Dream*, Mendelssohn
- "Wedding March," *The Marriage of Figaro*, Mozart
- "Wedding March" (a.k.a. "Here Comes the Bride"), *Lohengrin*, Wagner

The Ceremony

There may be additional solos or choral numbers performed during the ceremony—say, between readings, during a communion service—or the congregation may be invited to sing a hymn.

- "Jesu, Joy of Man's Desiring," Bach
- "Ave Maria," Gounod or Schubert
- "Ode to Joy," Beethoven
- "Sheep May Safely Graze," Bach
- "The Wedding Song," Stookey
- "One Hand, One Heart," *West Side Story*, Bernstein and Sondheim

The Recessional

You and your wedding party leave the ceremony to the strains of a triumphant recessional.

- "Priests' March," *The Magic Flute*, Mozart
- Toccata, Organ Symphony no. 5, op. 42, Wildor
- "Trumpet Tune," Stanley
- Rondo (a.k.a. *Masterpiece Theater* theme), *Fanfares for Violins, Oboe, Bassoon, Trumpets, and Percussion*, Mouret
- "Bridal March," Hollins
- March no. 4 (a.k.a. "Pomp and Circumstance"), Elgar
- "Radetzky March," Johann Strauss, Sr.
- "Benedictus," Simon and Garfunkel

The Postlude

Your musician(s) continue playing a postlude as your guests file out. Consider pieces from *The Prelude* list.

Planning

• Start by talking with your officiant and/or the music director of your house of worship. Does he/she object to secular music? (Some religions prohibit it.) If you'll be having a ceremony in a house of worship, ask what musicians are available to you. A choir? An organist? What are their fees? Are you required to pay him/her a fee if you use an outside musician? Are you charged extra if the ceremony goes over the allotted time? Must you reimburse musicians for expenses incurred, such as buying sheet music for pieces you ask them to play? Tip musicians 15–20% for extra-special service.

• For an informal civil ceremony, you can still have a prelude, processional, recessional, and postlude (depending on the number of guests). Incorporate music into areas of your ceremony where it seems relevant—before the reading of a poem, for instance, or after you exchange your vows, as a moment of reflection.

• With your fiancé, discuss what mood you're aiming to achieve. Do you want the music to evoke the solemnity of a traditional religious service? Would you like to give your ceremony a contemporary feel by adding secular songs?

• Organ music is traditional at a religious wedding ceremony, but it's not your only option. With your officiant's approval, you could have woodwinds, violins, a harp, a classical guitar, and other instruments. Remember, though, that certain pieces may be written for certain instruments. Music written for strings, for example, will sound different when played on an organ. Locate musicians through friends or local schools or symphonies.

• If you can't audition the musicians in person, ask for a tape.

• Book early—about the same time you book your ceremony site. Schedule a meeting at least a month before your wedding date to go over music selections.

• Listen to tapes and CDs of wedding music to get a sense of what you like. Also speak with the musicians who will be performing for some suggestions.

• If you have musically gifted friends and family, ask them to perform at your wedding (check it out first with your officiant).

• Prepare a list of songs for your musicians. Supply sheet music early if they must learn a new song. Invite relatives/friends who will perform to the rehearsal (professionals most likely will *not* attend).

CEREMONY MUSIC CHECKLIST

Ceremony Moment	Performance Time	Selections
Prelude	_____	_____
		_____
		_____
		_____
		_____

First solo _____   _____

Second solo _____   _____

Processional _____   _____

Other _____   _____

Recessional _____   _____

Postlude _____   _____

_____

_____

_____

Organist or main instrumentalist _____   Cost $ _____

Phone _____   Fax _____

Soloist _____   Cost $ _____

Phone _____   Fax _____

Ensemble or choir leader _____   Cost $ _____

Phone _____   Fax _____

Ensemble members _____

_____

Total ceremony music cost $ _____

Chapter 5:

PLANNING YOUR RECEPTION

Your reception is the party of a lifetime and possibly the biggest celebration you have ever planned. You'll want to please your guests and your family, your new husband, and yourself. Here are some tips for general planning.

PLANNING POINTERS

• Start early. Popular caterers, photographers, and other wedding professionals are sometimes booked a year ahead. Begin searching the market for service personnel well in advance of your wedding date to secure the best people at the best price. The more time you have, the more you can meet with your professionals to get all the details about your wedding straight—and to change a service person if things aren't working out between you.

• Cruise the Internet, too, for party planning tips.

• Be assertive, but not unbending. Ask your service professionals for opinions, but remember that they are working for you. Make the final decisions based on *your* likes and dislikes.

• Have a budget in mind. Know approximately what you can spend in each particular area. Before meeting with a service provider, call three or four in your area to get rough estimates.

• Specify all details in writing. When things are left unclear, you're left unprotected. A different band shows up; flowers that don't resemble what you ordered arrive; the photographer leaves before the cake is cut. To make an agreement enforceable, you have to specify the terms and sign it along with your wedding professional. Never sign a contract until you've read it carefully, understand the language, and are comfortable with the contents.

FINDING THE PERFECT RECEPTION SITE

When it comes to your reception site, there's a smorgasbord to choose from. Traditional choices are banquet halls, hotels, clubs, and restaurants. Community centers or church/synagogue meeting rooms may offer space for an inexpensive rental fee. And there's no shortage of imaginative places—a winery, lighthouse, or historical building.

How do you find the perfect site? Focus on what you want, be it a grand ballroom, cozy restaurant, elegant mansion, or romantic garden. Spend time viewing only those sites that meet your specifications. Look for site information in the party-space classifieds in city or regional magazines (special wedding sections are especially useful), advertisements in bridal magazines, and the yellow pages. If you live in a major metropolitan area, check bookstores and the library for reference books that list local event sites. Wedding consultants and recent brides can also help, as can historical societies, chambers of commerce, and tourist boards (especially for off-beat site recommendations).

But before you book, know the scoop. Here are questions to ask:

When You're Checking Out a Site

1. What is the rental fee and what does it include? Must the site be booked for a certain number of hours? Are there extra fees for groundskeepers, janitorial staff, etc.?

2. Are there any additional charges for other services (e.g., doormen, coat-check people, etc.)? What are these charges?

3. Is adequate parking at the reception site available for my guests? Will they be charged?

4. How many people can the room fit and for what type of reception? A buffet? Seated dinner?

5. Is another wedding booked that day? How are the facilities divided? How is privacy ensured?

6. How many hours does the rental fee cover? When do they begin? Are there charges for overtime? Is there a grace period before overtime is charged?

7. Are there any times the site is not available?

8. Are there any price reductions for certain time periods or days of the week?

9. Do you have a piano or other musical instruments on the premises? Is there any charge for their use?

10. Are there any restrictions on the type of music that can be played, the number of musicians who can perform, or the duration of the music?

11. Are there any regulations on decorations, candles, flowers, or photography?

12. Is the site air-conditioned (for warm-weather weddings)? Is there adequate heat (for cold-weather weddings)?

13. Do you have an in-house caterer or preferred list of caterers? Can I bring in the caterer of my choice?

14. Do you have liability insurance in the event that a guest is injured?

15. Are the kitchen facilities adequate? (A caterer may add surcharges for appliances brought in, such as a stove, refrigerator, etc.)

16. Can the site be used for the ceremony?

17. Is dancing allowed? Is there a dance floor? Where? How many people can fit on the dance floor at one time?

18. What is your cancellation policy? Is the deposit refundable?

When You're Ready to Book

1. Will you confirm the reservation in a letter that will outline all the details and prices? (Most reputable places will have no problem doing so. If they put up a fight, look elsewhere.)

2. Are there rooms available where I, my groom, and our attendants can change clothes?

3. Is there a comfortable area for guests to await our arrival from the ceremony site? Will hors d'oeuvres and drinks be served?

4. Where's the best place to set up the receiving line?

5. Will the banquet manager be on hand the day of my wedding? If not, who will be in charge?

6. Is a security deposit for furniture, decor, or artwork required? When will it be refunded?

AVOIDING RECEPTION RIP-OFFS

Some caterers and reception sites have been known to take your down payment and go out of business. Or they book another wedding for the same date and time as yours, then ask *you* to switch rooms. Don't get rooked. Here are surefire strategies for avoiding reception rip-offs:

• Find out if your caterer will take responsibility for anyone he/she subcontracts. For example, if the florist you're required to use because he/she works exclusively with your caterer goes out of business before your wedding, will your caterer refund any deposit money you put down?

• Ask for references, then call them.

• Call the Better Business Bureau in your area. See if there have been any complaints lodged against the people you're thinking of using and what the outcome was.

• Pay with a credit card (deposits, too). If your wedding service personnel reneges on a service, you may have some recourse with the credit card company.

FOOD FOR THOUGHT: HIRING A CATERER

A caterer puts together some of the most important elements of your reception: food, drink, and sometimes the site and its decorations. When planning a wedding, "caterer" is the first thing many people think of.

Actually, the term "caterer" can mean many things—from a person who prepares specialty foods to an entire company that provides a wedding site, waiters, tables, linens, food, even bands or photographers. Find out exactly what various caterers provide and what they charge.

You may work with one banquet manager who will take care of the entire site, food, and drink. If so, find out as much as you can about the facilities: Is the site large enough for all your guests? Will you be sharing the facilities with other bridal parties?

On the other hand, the wedding you plan may involve many specialists. For example, at a wedding in a historic mansion, you first contact the person responsible for renting the space. Then you hire a caterer, bartenders, waiters, and a rental company to supply everything from the dishes and tables to a dance floor.

Here are some more questions to ask:

When You're Checking Them Out

1. What's the estimated cost per person for a seated dinner? Buffet? Cocktail reception? Open bar? What does the cost include?

2. What is the staff-to-guest ratio? (For a seated meal, it's usually one waiter per eight to ten guests.)

3. Have you ever worked at my prospective reception site?

4. Do you have a set menu? Can it be modified?

5. Can the kitchen staff adhere to special dietary restrictions for some guests who may be diabetic, kosher, or vegetarian?

6. Can you supply me with a list of references? (Call them.)

7. How far in advance must I give you a head count?

8. How can I arrange to view the catering of another reception to check out the food display? (Also ask to taste the foods on the menu suggested by the caterer.)

9. Do you provide tables? Linens? Order floral arrangements? Coordinate the activities? (Some caterers do, others don't.)

10. What's the policy for payment and tipping? (Some caterers request checks, others credit cards, others cash; some include gratuities in the base price, others don't.)

11. Can I expect any charges besides those for food, beverages, and rental items?

12. Are you state licensed? Do you carry liability insurance (including liquor liability insurance) in the event a guest chips a tooth, gets food poisoning, or has an accident after leaving the reception intoxicated?

When You're Ready to Book

1. How much time will it take you to set up?

2. Will you send me a confirmation letter including the wedding date, time, names of the service help, tipping policy, decorating details, menu, and cost per person?

3. May I see available linens, china, and flatware? What is the rental charge?

4. Will the hors d'oeuvres be butlered or on a buffet table?

5. How much are your overtime and cancellation charges?

6. Will you give me a ceiling on anticipated menu price increases? (Your caterers will quote you final prices a few weeks to several months before your wedding. Because food prices fluctuate, be prepared for an increase.)

7. Can you provide the wedding cake? When will it be delivered?

8. Where will the head table be? Will it be round? On a dais?

9. How many drinks does each bottle of liquor provide? Is there an opening fee per bottle of champagne?

10. Will you feed the photographer and/or musicians? Are they included in the final head count?

11. How many guests must I guarantee?

FIVE WAYS TO AVOID CATERING CALAMITIES

1. Reserve your caterer or banquet hall twelve months before your wedding date. (The best ones book early.)

2. If other events will take place at the banquet hall during your wedding, be sure there is an empty room or hallway between the parties. You don't want someone else's music to drown out your reception band.

3. Get a detailed list of what's included in your package.

4. Never pay for the entire reception months in advance. It's customary to pay part of the total up front, then the balance a few days before your wedding day.

5. Read your contract thoroughly and question what you don't understand *before* signing. The contract should include your wedding date, prices, cancellation and refund policies, and all oral agreements.

RECEPTION HALL/HOTEL/CLUB WORKSHEET

Estimate #1

What's provided and cost

Name _____

Food _____

Address _____

_____

Telephone _____

_____

Fax _____

_____ Cost $ _____

Contact _____

Beverages _____

_____ Cost $ _____

Cake _____

_____ Cost $ _____

Waiters/Bartenders _____

_____

_____ Cost $ _____

Flowers/Decorations _____

_____

_____ Cost $ _____

Band/DJ _____

_____

_____ Cost $ _____

Photographer _____

_____

_____ Cost $ _____

Limousines _____

_____ Cost $ _____

Coat check _____

_____ Cost $ _____

Parking _____

_____ Cost $ _____

Changing rooms _____

_____ Cost $ _____

Other _____

_____ Cost $ _____

Total cost $ _____

Estimate #2

What's provided and cost

Name _____

Food _____

Address _____

_____

Telephone _____

_____

Fax _____

_____ Cost $ _____

Contact _____   Beverages _____

                            _____   Cost $ _____

                            Cake _____

                            _____   Cost $ _____

                            Waiters/Bartenders _____

                            _____   Cost $ _____

                            Flowers/Decorations _____

                            _____   Cost $ _____

                            Band/DJ _____

                            _____   Cost $ _____

                            Photographer _____

                            _____   Cost $ _____

                            Limousines _____

                            _____   Cost $ _____

                            Coat check _____

                            _____   Cost $ _____

                            Parking _____

                            _____   Cost $ _____

                            Changing rooms _____

                            _____   Cost $ _____

                            Other _____

                            _____   Cost $ _____

                                                                 Total cost $ _____

Estimate #3   *What's provided and cost*

Name _____   Food _____

Address _____   _____

Telephone _____   _____

Fax _____   _____   Cost $ _____

Contact _____   Beverages _____

                            _____   Cost $ _____

                            Cake _____

                            _____   Cost $ _____

                            Waiters/Bartenders _____

                            _____

                            _____   Cost $ _____

Flowers/Decorations _____

_____

_____ Cost $ _____

Band/DJ _____

_____

_____ Cost $ _____

Photographer _____

_____

_____ Cost $ _____

Limousines _____

_____ Cost $ _____

Coat check _____

_____ Cost $ _____

Parking _____

_____ Cost $ _____

Changing rooms _____

_____ Cost $ _____

Other _____

_____ Cost $ _____

Total cost $ _____

Final selection—name, address, phone, fax, contact ___Bentley's at the Barn___

_____

_____

Contract signed   Deposit paid   Balance due

__10/3/2007__ $ _500_____ $ _____

Date final guest count needed _____

Notes _____

_____

_____

_____

AT-HOME/OUTDOOR/OTHER SITE RECEPTION WORKSHEET

Site: Estimate #1

Name and address of site _____

_____

Description _____

Contact name, phone, fax _____

_____

Rental costs $ _____

_____

Site: Estimate #2

Name and address of site _____

_____

Description _____

Contact name, phone, fax _____

_____

Rental costs $ _____

_____

Site: Estimate #3

Name and address of site _____

_____

Description _____

Contact name, phone, fax _____

_____

Rental costs $ _____

_____

Caterer: Estimate #1

Name and address of caterer _____

_____

Description of services (e.g., waiters, bartenders) provided _____

_____

Menus provided _____

Contact name, phone, fax _____

_____

Cost $ _____

Caterer: Estimate #2

Name and address of caterer _____

_____

Description of services (e.g., waiters, bartenders) provided _____

_____

Menus provided _____

Contact name, phone, fax _____

_____

Cost $ _____

Caterer: Estimate #3

Name and address of caterer _____

_____

Description of services (e.g., waiters, bartenders) provided _____

_____

Menus provided _____

Contact name, phone, fax _____

_____

Cost $ _____

Rental Needs: Estimate #1

Tent	$ _____
Dance floor	$ _____
Additional tents for food preparation,	
other needs	$ _____
Tableware	$ _____
Tables	$ _____
Chairs	$ _____
Linens	$ _____
Lighting	$ _____
Power generator	$ _____
Other	$ _____
Total cost	$ _____

Rental Needs: Estimate #2

Tent	$ _____
Dance floor	$ _____
Additional tents for food preparation,	
other needs	$ _____
Tableware	$ _____
Tables	$ _____
Chairs	$ _____
Linens	$ _____
Lighting	$ _____
Power generator	$ _____
Other	$ _____
Total cost	$ _____

Rental Needs: Estimate #3

Tent	$ _____
Dance floor	$ _____
Additional tents for food preparation, other needs	$ _____
Tableware	$ _____
Tables	$ _____
Chairs	$ _____
Linens	$ _____
Lighting	$ _____
Power generator	$ _____
Other	$ _____
Total cost	$ _____

FINAL CHOICES

Site—name, address, phone, fax

_____

_____

Total cost   Contract signed   Deposit paid/date   Balance due/date

_____

Caterer—name, address, phone, fax

_____

_____

Total cost   Contract signed   Deposit paid/date   Balance due/date

_____

Rental Company—name, address, phone, fax

_____

_____

Total cost   Contract signed   Deposit paid/date   Balance due/date

_____

A LOVE FEAST: FOOD FOR YOUR RECEPTION

A surefire way to win raves from guests is to feed them—well. Menu options and food preparation selections are plentiful at today's wedding receptions. Beef is making a comeback as the dinner entrée of choice at wedding receptions, surpassing the ubiquitous chicken. Veal and salmon are also popular entrées. And no politically correct wedding would be complete without a vegetarian meal choice. Another new reception trend: dinner by the bite. Guests enjoy a mix of hot and cold passed hors d'oeuvres and visit carving stations, pasta bars, sushi setups and other buffet tables filled with bite-size food. Appetizer-only and cocktail-and-canapé parties are another new idea, popular with couples who want to give their reception the feel of a big party. (An added bonus is that they can be tailored to nearly any budget.) Guests like them, too, because they're free to mix and mingle. Consider a theme. For an Italian canapé party, serve bruschetta, grilled peppers, stuffed baby vegetables, and, of course, pasta. But before you decide on a menu, think about this:

• **Time of day.** Serve a breakfast or brunch after a morning wedding; a seated lunch after a noontime ceremony; tea sandwiches, cake, and beverages after an early afternoon ceremony; hors d'oeuvres after a midafternoon ceremony; a seated, buffet, or dinner-by-the bite reception after a late afternoon or evening ceremony.

• **Local style and trends.** What's the norm for wedding receptions in your area—a seated meat-and-potatoes dinner? Hors d'oeuvres and champagne? If you want a wedding reception that's completely different from the ones typically hosted in your area, you might consider keeping some familiar elements while adding some new ones so as not to bewilder guests.

• **Season.** Serve light fare in the summer, heartier meals in the winter. Also consider the seasonal availability of fruits and vegetables. For example, you might serve fresh asparagus with a vinaigrette as a first course in late spring or summer, a filling ratatouille in the colder months.

• **Budget and taste.** A good caterer can put together a menu that reflects your personal taste and still adheres to your budget. Ask to sample foods made by your caterer or by the hotel or restaurant where you're considering having your reception, and check photographs of past events to see if the food is attractively presented and served. Brides are also combining different types of service. For example, the main course may be served by waiters, but guests serve themselves at a dessert buffet. You can help personalize your wedding by incorporating into your menu foods that have particular meaning to you. If you and your groom make it a ritual of stopping for cappuccino and cannoli every Saturday night, consider having a wedding cake made with cannoli filling. If you're British, you might want to salute your heritage by serving a sampling of English cheeses.

MENU WORKSHEET

Style

☐ Seated

☑ Buffet

☐ Punch and cake

☑ Hors d'oeuvres/cocktails

☐ Food stations/dinner-by-the-bite

☐ Other

Hors d'oeuvres _____

_____

Salads _____

_____

Food stations _____

_____

Main course _Jumbo Lump Crab Cake & Roast_
Pork c̄ apples

Other dishes _green beans c̄ onions & peppers,_
roasted potatoes

Desserts _pie_ _____

_____

Wedding cake _____

_____

Other ideas (ethnic foods, sundae bar, etc.) _____

_____

FOR A SWEET ENDING: CREATIVE WEDDING CAKES

The tradition of serving wedding cake began in Roman times when a bun or wheat cake was broken over the bride's head. The crumbs that landed were a symbol of good luck and fertility. In the seventeenth century, a sweet-toothed French baker stacked buns and coated them with icing, creating the first tiered wedding cake that was eaten by the bride, groom, and guests.

Personal touches make the cake especially memorable. Talk to your caterer or baker about what can be done to reflect what's important to you and your groom. Maybe it's pearl-like piping, lacework icing, or candied bows that resemble those on your wedding gown. Or perhaps it's a spun sugar bird's nest topper to reflect your love of nature. If you have a passion for music, consider putting a gilt miniature violin on top of a cake embellished with musical notes.

Traditional wedding cakes are made of white or yellow sponge cake and frosted in white, but white cake with white icing is only one option. Get your guests' mouths watering with an almond cake and raspberry filling, mocha espresso cake filled with praline crunch, even cheesecake.

Here are some other points to consider when ordering a wedding cake:

- **Shape.** Possibilities include a heart or Bible shape, a cake shaped to resemble your city's skyline, or even a ski slope.
- **Cake toppers.** Traditionally, a plastic or porcelain bride and groom top the cake. If you prefer to be nontraditional, think about topping your cake with cherubs, wedding bells, a music box, animal figurines, or fresh flowers. Or keep the figures and personalize them with outfits that reflect your interests and hobbies—scuba gear, tennis outfits, etc. Consider, too, an heirloom topper—one that donned your parents' or grandparents' wedding cake, for example.

- **The groom's cake.** The groom's cake may be brandied fruit, chocolate, or some other favorite flavor of the groom's. It can be baked in a creative shape such as a top hat or champagne bottle. It may also be a whimsical representation of the groom's favorite hobby or sport. In some areas of the country, the groom's cake may be cut and served at the rehearsal dinner, but traditionally, guests are given a small box with a slice to take home from the wedding reception. Legend has it that a woman who puts a piece under her pillow will dream of the man she'll marry.

Hiring a Cake Maker: A Recipe for Success

While some caterers will create the cake for you, others won't—you'll have to hire an independent baker. Friends, family, recent brides, and caterers can offer recommendations. Once you get the names, you'll have to do a little probing to make sure the people suggested to you are reputable (also check out their status with your local Better Business Bureau). Look through magazines for ideas and bring these pictures with you when you meet with the baker. Here are questions to ask a prospective baker (or your cake-making caterer):

1. What flavors of cake and icing are available? Can I sample them?

2. How can you decorate the cake? With spun-sugar flowers? Icing that looks like wedding-dress lace? Can I see samples of different decorating techniques?

3. Do you have a price list for flavors, icings, and decorations that I can take with me?

4. Can each decorated tier of the cake be a different flavor? What are some options?

5. Can I order a supplemental sheet cake(s) if the decorated cake will not be enough to serve all my guests? What will that add to the cost?

6. Can you make a personal statement about us (our careers, our honeymoon destination) with the shape of the cake and its decorations?

7. Can I also order my cake topper from you?

8. What ideas do you have for the cake topper?—Fresh flowers? Figurines? Symbols?

9. Can I order personalized cake-slice boxes from you? What will that add to the cost?

10. Do you make groom's cakes or personalized favors?

11. What time—and where—will the cake(s) be delivered? Will they cut and serve it?

12. What is the cost of the wedding cake? The groom's cake?

13. When must the deposit and total bill be paid?

Wedding Cake Shopping Tips

• Start shopping about three months before the wedding.

• Ask to see photographs of other wedding cakes the baker has created; taste some samples.

• Get the baker's recommendations on what types of cake, frostings, and shapes will hold up best for your reception—especially if it will be a lengthy one or held outside during warm weather.

• Arrange for the baker to work with the banquet manager to make sure that the cake is properly assembled and displayed.

• Ask that the baker work with the florist as well, to coordinate any floral decorations on the cake.

• Inquire about extra fees for delivery and setup.

• To cut down on cost, see if your baker can make you a small wedding cake for display and a larger sheet cake with identical icing (left in the kitchen) for serving.

• Put everything in writing. Describe the size, shape, flavor, and color of the cake. Include details about your wedding date and time, delivery information, and payment schedule.

BAKER'S WORKSHEET

Estimate #1

Name _____

Address _____

Phone _____

Fax _____

Recommended by _____

_____

Description and comments

_____

_____

_____

_____

_____

Cost $ _____

Estimate #2

Description and comments

Name _____   _____

Address _____   _____

Phone _____   _____

Fax _____   _____

Recommended by _____   _____

_____   Cost $ _____

Estimate #3

Description and comments

Name _____   _____

Address _____   _____

Phone _____   _____

Fax _____   _____

Recommended by _____   _____

_____   Cost $ _____

Final choice—name, address, phone, fax _____

_____

_____

Cake description _____

_____

Contract signed   Deposit paid/date   Balance due/date

_____

WEDDING CAKE CHECKLIST

Number to serve _____

Size of cake _____

Shape _____

Cake flavor _____

Filling flavor _____

Icing flavor and color _____

Decoration description _____

_____

Cake topper description _____

_____

Cake knife included?   Yes _____ No _____

Cutting instructions _____

_____

_____

                                    Cost $ _____

Groom's cake?   Yes _____ No _____

Description _____

How many boxes? _____

                                    Cost $ _____

Reception site address (for delivery) _____

_____

Phone _____   Fax _____

Person to see _____

Date of delivery _____   Time _____

                          Total cake cost $ _____

Preserving Your Cake

In early American times, it was considered good luck and an omen for a long life together if a newly married couple saved the top tier of their wedding cake to eat on their first anniversary or after the christening of their first child.

You too can carry on this tradition by freezing it. Just follow these easy steps.

1. Encase the cake tightly in plastic wrap, then aluminum foil.

2. Put the wrapped cake in a plastic container and seal tightly. Because air breaks down flavor, you want to make the container as airtight as possible.

3. Place the cake in the back of the freezer— where the temperature is constant (temperature fluctuations can cause deterioration).

RECEPTION BEVERAGES

Caterers or banquet facilities often provide beverages as part of their packages. But look carefully at the pricing policies—they can vary (and may be determined by state law). They may charge per drink, per bottle, per person, per hour, or some combination thereof (about $4 per person, per hour). Decide if you want name-brand alcoholic beverages or vintage wines. Ask if you can supply your own liquor (which you can buy at a discount outlet) and have the wait staff serve it. Discuss any other liquor costs, such as a "corkage fee" for each bottle of champagne or wine opened.

To see if the price you've been quoted seems fair, talk to several caterers/banquet hall managers in your area, then compare prices. If you need to conserve funds, discuss options with your caterer. Can some liquors be eliminated from the bar to save money? Can the hours which it is opened be limited? Consider the tastes of your guests. If you know many of them like beer, for example, buying a keg may be the best value.

Alcoholic Beverages: How Much Will You Need?

If you'll be buying your own liquor for your reception, use the following guide. Remember to consider the tastes of your guests and the time of year (people tend to drink lighter drinks in summer, heavier ones in winter). On average, allow one drink per adult per hour. Plan for slightly more consumption if the wedding is in the evening or summer. Remember, it's better to order too much than to run out (and unopened bottles may be returnable—check out the policy with your liquor store).

• One bottle of wine = six to eight partially filled glasses

• One quart of hard liquor = twenty one-and-a-half-ounce drinks

• One twenty-six-ounce bottle of champagne = eight servings (one case of twelve bottles gives one hundred guests one glass each)

• Half a keg of beer = 260 eight-ounce glasses

Nonalcoholic Beverages

Your guests will appreciate a wide selection of nonalcoholic drinks such as

• punches, which can be presented beautifully with flower-embedded ice and fresh fruit, and placed in a stunning punch bowl;

• sparkling apple cider for toasts;

• a water bar stocked with a selection of mineral waters, carbonated and still; and

• a variety of soft drinks, juices, coffees, and teas (decaffeinated, too). For tips on acquiring the right amounts, consult your caterer or party-planner, or party-planning books in your library or bookstore.

BAR CHECKLIST

Number of guests _____   Cocktail hours _____ to _____
Champagne toast _____ Time _____ Wine with dinner _____ Punch bowls _____

LIQUOR

Item	Quantity	Brand	Cost
Champagne	_____	_____	$ _____
Bourbon	_____	_____	$ _____
Whiskey	_____	_____	$ _____
Gin	_____	_____	$ _____
Rum	_____	_____	$ _____
Scotch	_____	_____	$ _____
Tequila	_____	_____	$ _____
Vermouth	_____	_____	$ _____
Vodka	_____	_____	$ _____
Red wine	_____	_____	$ _____
Rosé wine	_____	_____	$ _____
White wine	_____	_____	$ _____
Punch	_____	_____	$ _____
Beer	_____	_____	$ _____
Aperitifs	_____	_____	$ _____
Brandy	_____	_____	$ _____
Assorted liqueurs	_____	_____	$ _____

Total liquor cost $ _____

MIXERS/NONALCOHOLIC DRINKS

Item	Quantity	Brand	Cost
Collins mix	_____	_____	$ _____
Cola	_____	_____	$ _____
Diet cola	_____	_____	$ _____
Ginger ale	_____	_____	$ _____
Club soda	_____	_____	$ _____
Tonic water	_____	_____	$ _____
Orange juice	_____	_____	$ _____
Tomato juice	_____	_____	$ _____
Grapefruit juice	_____	_____	$ _____
Cranberry juice	_____	_____	$ _____

Pineapple juice _____ _____ $ _____

Sparkling grape/
   apple juice _____ _____ $ _____

Nonalcoholic
   punch _____ _____ $ _____

Bottled mineral
   water
   (carbonated,
   still, imported)_____ _____ $ _____

Lemon-lime
   soda _____ _____ $ _____

Diet lemon-
   lime soda _____ _____ $ _____

Other sodas
   (orange, root
   beer) _____ _____ $ _____

Iced tea _____ _____ $ _____

Hot tea/
   decaffeinated
tea/herbal tea _____ _____ $ _____

Coffee/
   decaffeinated
   iced coffee _____ _____ $ _____

Sparkling water_____ _____ $ _____

Bottled water _____ _____ $ _____

Other _____ _____ $ _____

Total mixer/nonalcoholic drinks cost $ _____

DRINK INGREDIENTS

Item	Quantity	Brand	Cost
Angostura bitters	_____	_____	$ _____
Cocktail olives	_____	_____	$ _____
Cocktail onions	_____	_____	$ _____
Ice	_____	_____	$ _____
Lemons/ lemon peel	_____	_____	$ _____
Limes	_____	_____	$ _____
Cherries	_____	_____	$ _____

Superfine sugar _____ _____ $ _____

Tabasco sauce _____ _____ $ _____

Other _____ _____ $ _____

_____ _____ $ _____

_____ _____ $ _____

Total drink ingredients cost $ _____

BAR EQUIPMENT

Item	Quantity	Item	Quantity
Bottle openers	_____	Pitchers	_____
Can openers	_____	Drink recipes	_____
Cocktail shakers	_____	Cocktail napkins	_____
Corkscrews	_____	Swizzle sticks	_____
Ice buckets	_____	8-oz. glasses	_____
Ice tubs	_____	4-oz. glasses	_____
Knives	_____	Champagne flutes	_____
Spoons	_____	Wineglasses	_____
Strainers	_____	Serving trays	_____
1 1/2 oz. jiggers	_____	Blender	_____
Other	_____	Other	_____
		Total equipment cost	$ _____
		TOTAL BAR COST	$ _____

STRIKE UP THE BAND: YOUR RECEPTION MUSIC

Music sets the tone of your reception. Have the band play only classical waltzes, and your reception will be formal and romantic. Get them playing some popular rock music, and the reception takes on a lively note. Consider the following when choosing your reception musicians:

• **Size of the reception site.** A soft trio would be lost in a big hall; a loud band would overwhelm a reception in a small room.

• **Taste of guests.** Consider bands that play a variety of music to satisfy the different ages and preferences of your guests.

• **Extra services.** Some bands provide children's entertainment, others use professional staging and lighting effects.

When Checking Bands Out

• Get word-of-mouth references from friends, and relatives, or contact your local musicians union. Then check them out with the local Better Business Bureau.

• Find out how many musicians are in the band and what instruments they play. Request an audition tape if you haven't heard them play before. Better yet, arrange to hear them play at another wedding/event.

• Ask what type of music they perform best. Do they play the type you like? Can they perform the ethnic selections you want? If not, are they willing to learn?

When You're Ready to Book

• Inquire about breaks—how many will the band take and for how long?

• Are you required to provide the band with food? Most will not expect a full meal, but given the amount of time they'll be at your wedding, it's a nice idea to provide light refreshments.

• Will they play special requests? Can you provide them with a list of must-play songs?

• Ask if the bandleader will be present for your reception; specify that his/her name appear in your contract, along with the name of the group's lead vocalist and all other musicians to ensure that you get the sound you heard at the audition.

• Discuss with the bandleader how active you want him/her to be in making announcements. Should he/she announce your first dance and the cake cutting only? Do you want the members of the bridal party introduced?

• Request that the musicians dress in a style and level of formality suited to your wedding.

• Request that a representative of the band visit your reception site beforehand to determine if there's adequate room for equipment and enough electrical outlets.

• Get a contract. Specify the names of the musicians and the hours they will be performing. Include any overtime rates in writing. You'll probably be required to pay a 50 percent deposit up front, with the remainder due on the day of the wedding (generally, bands do not expect tips). If the group doesn't perform as promised (a vocalist you requested doesn't show up), then consider withholding your final payment until you renegotiate a fee.

HIRING A DJ: THE HOW-TOS

Prefer to hear your reception songs performed by the original artists? Then hire a DJ. The advantages are that the music sounds just the way it's supposed to (no off notes or wacky interpretations), a wider variety of music can be played (as talented as they may be, few bands can play rhythm and blues, classical, folk, country, *and* hard rock—or at least play it well), there are fewer breaks, the volume can be adjusted, DJs need less space to set up and perform, and are usually less expensive than a live band. The downside is that if you're planning a very formal, traditional wedding, a DJ just won't give you the ambience of a big band or orchestra.

You can find disc jockeys listed in the yellow pages, or get referrals from friends, family, and even your other wedding professionals.

Here are some pointers:

When Checking DJs Out

• Ask for references—and call them.

• See if a complaint has ever been lodged against the DJ with the Better Business Bureau.

• Check out the DJ's playlist and determine if he/she plays a lot of the music you like.

• Ask if the DJ has any wedding experience.

Performing at a New Year's Eve party is vastly different from performing at a wedding.

When You're Ready to Book

• Inquire not only about the fee but also about overtime rates.

• Get the particulars. Ask how many breaks the DJ will take—and for how long. Will he or she act as the master of ceremonies? Must you supply the DJ with a meal? Suggest including all these specifics in the contract.

• See if the DJ is agreeable to playing special requests. Also ask if he/she will play songs you like that are not on his/her playlist. Supply him with the CDs if necessary.

• Ask what the DJ will wear—it should match the formality of your wedding.

• Question the DJ about his/her equipment. Quality CDs are preferable to scratchy cassette tapes.

• Meet in person. Have the DJ show you a videotape of a wedding he/she has worked. Meeting in person also gives you the opportunity to go over your song selections and set up the timetable for your wedding (when you'll have your first dance).

• Establish how many breaks he/she will get during the event.

• Be sure to get everything you have discussed in writing.

RECEPTION MUSIC WORKSHEET

Estimate #1

Name _____

Address _____

Phone _____ Fax _____

Number of musicians _____ _____

Type of music they play _____

Heard in person or heard audition tape?

Yes _____ No _____

Thoughts on their music _____

_____

Recommended by _____

_____

Cost $ _____

Estimate #2

Name _____

Address _____

Phone _____ Fax _____

Number of musicians _____

Type of music they play _____

Heard in person or heard audition tape?

Yes _____ No _____

Thoughts on their music _____

_____

Recommended by _____

_____

Cost $ _____

Estimate #3

Name _____

Address _____

Phone _____ Fax _____

Number of musicians _____

Type of music they play _____

Heard in person or heard audition tape?

Yes _____ No _____

Thoughts on their music _____

_____

Recommended by _____

_____

Cost $ _____

Final selection—name, address, phone, fax

_____

Hours of music _____ to _____

Continuous music   Yes _____ No _____

Number of musicians _____

Overtime rate _____

Contract signed   Deposit paid/date   Balance due/date

_____

SONGS TO GET 'EM DANCING: NEW CHOICES AND OLD FAVORITES FOR YOUR RECEPTION

First Dance

- "After the Lovin'," Engelbert Humperdinck
- "Can You Feel the Love Tonight," Elton John, from _The Lion King_
- "Can't Help Falling in Love," Elvis Presley
- "Cheek to Cheek," Tony Bennett
- "Embraceable You," Nat King Cole
- "Fields of Gold," Sting
- "Forever and Ever, Amen," Randy Travis
- "Have You Ever Really Loved a Woman," Bryan Adams, from _Don Juan DeMarco_
- "I Can Hear Music," The Beach Boys
- "I Get a Kick Out of You," Frank Sinatra
- "If Tomorrow Never Comes," Garth Brooks
- "In Your Eyes," Peter Gabriel
- "It Must Be Love," Madness
- "It's Not Unusual," Tom Jones
- "Let It Be Me," The Everly Brothers
- "Love Song," The Cure
- "Mad About You," Belinda Carlisle
- "Save the Best for Last," Vanessa Williams
- "Slave to Love," Bryan Ferry, from _9 1/2 Weeks_
- "Somebody," Depeche Mode
- "Somewhere," from _West Side Story_
- "Stand by Me," Ben E. King
- "Stand By My Woman," Lenny Kravitz
- "Thanks Again," Ricky Skaggs
- "(They Long to Be) Close to You," The Carpenters
- "True Companion," Marc Cohn
- "The Way You Look Tonight," Frank Sinatra

- "Unchained Melody," The Righteous Brothers
- "What a Difference You've Made in My Life," Ronnie Milsap
- "When a Man Loves a Woman," Percy Sledge
- "A Whole New World," Peabo Bryson and Regina Belle, from *Aladdin*
- "You're in My Heart," Rod Stewart
- "You're My Home," Billy Joel

Father-Daughter Dance

- "How Sweet It Is (to Be Loved by You)," Marvin Gaye
- "My Girl," The Temptations
- "My Heart Belongs to Daddy," by Cole Porter
- "Sunrise, Sunset," from *Fiddler on the Roof*
- "Thanks for the Memory," Bob Hope
- "Through the Years," Kenny Rogers
- "What a Wonderful World," Louis Armstrong
- "Wind Beneath My Wings," Bette Midler

Mother-Son Dance

- "I Get a Kick Out of You," Frank Sinatra
- "I Love You," by Cole Porter
- "Misty," Johnny Mathis
- "Moon River," Andy Williams
- "The Greatest Love of All," Whitney Houston
- "Thank You," Ricky Scaggs

- "You Are the Sunshine of My Life," Stevie Wonder
- "Tonight and Forever," Carly Simon

Cake Cutting

- "Love and Marriage," Frank Sinatra
- "Our Love Is Here to Stay," by George Gershwin

Bouquet Toss

- "Church Bells May Ring," The Willows
- Drumroll
- "Girls Just Want to Have Fun," Cyndi Lauper

Garter Toss

- "Legs," ZZ Top
- "Let's Hear It for the Boy," from *Footloose*
- "Luck Be a Lady," Frank Sinatra

Departure of Bride and Groom

- "Have I Told You Lately That I Love You," Rod Stewart, Van Morrison
- "I Got You Babe," Sonny and Cher
- "I'll Always Love You," Taylor Dane
- "Let's Stay Together," Al Green
- "The Way You Look Tonight," Frank Sinatra
- "Unforgettable," Nat King Cole

RECEPTION MUSIC CHECKLIST

Reception Activity	Time	General/Specific Music Ideas
Receiving line	_____	_____
Arrival of bride and groom	_____	_____
First dance	_____	_____
Father-daughter dance	_____	_____
Mother-son dance	_____	_____
Cake cutting	_____	_____
Bouquet toss	_____	_____
Garter toss	_____	_____
Departure of bride and groom	_____	_____
Last dance	_____	_____
Other _____	_____	_____
_____	_____	_____

BEYOND THE BAND: MORE RECEPTION ENTERTAINMENT IDEAS

Your wedding reception entertainment doesn't have to begin and end with music. Other options—to supplement the performance of your band/DJ or to be used as an alternative—include a comedian (review his/her material beforehand); a mime; a laser or light show; fireworks; skywriting above your reception site; or costumed musicians such as Renaissance-style minstrels, a Dixieland band, or bagpipers.

Finding and Hiring Entertainers

• Get recommendations from family and friends. Otherwise, check the yellow pages under "Entertainers."

• Check the advertisements in local newspapers. If the paper is reporting on a social event, skim the article to see if they mention any entertainers.

• Never hire entertainers without first calling

the Better Business Bureau and checking on whether complaints have been filed against them.

• Talk to the entertainer's booking agent (or the performer him/herself) to discuss your preferences, the mood of the party, the size of the audience, and the length of the performance.

• Preview recommended artists at another party.

• Draw up a contract specifying the indi- vidual performer(s) by name, the arrival time, length of act, scheduled breaks, and performance details such as songs, routines, and attire. Be sure both you and the other party sign.

• Find out what equipment is needed (sound system, spotlight, etc.). Will the performer provide it? Can your reception site accommodate it? (Speak to the banquet hall manager.)

AN AFFAIR TO REMEMBER: FOURTEEN WAYS TO MAKE YOUR RECEPTION UNIQUE

No two loves are alike—but a lot of wedding receptions are. Throw a party everyone will remember. Here are some distinctive touches:

1. Incorporate the foods of your romance into the menu. Did you meet over the tomato bins at the farmers' market? Then serve tomato bisque as a first course. Did you spend languid evenings at the beach shucking clams? Then serve some steamers at a traditional clam bake–style reception. Can't get that Peking duck you shared on a vacation together to San Francisco out of your mind? Serve it as a main course. Menu cards can list each course and its significance to your relationship.

2. Acknowledge family milestones. Toast your uncle Jim's eightieth birthday; announce the birth of a new niece or nephew; publicly acknowledge a guest's graduation or your parents' anniversary.

3. Include a memory card with your invitations, along with a request that each guest write down a special memory of you, your fiancé, or the two of you. Have guests return it with the response card. You can glue them into an album and place it near the guest book for everyone to look through.

4. Show a short video (no more than ten minutes) that follows both of you from childhood to courtship to the wedding. Incorporate videotapes, home movies, snapshots, and interviews with friends and relatives.

5. If your families serve particular foods at special occasions, include them in your menu. **Ask your caterer to work with your families' recipes.** Note the dish's originator on the menu card, and mention why it's significant to your family.

6. If your officiant will not be **reciting a prayer before the meal**, give the honor to a special relative—be sure to give him/her prior notice. Invite the person to stand at the head table during the invocation so other guests will be able to see and hear him/her.

7. Ask guests to bring a photo of themselves with one or both of you and put someone in charge of attaching them to a large board. It's a great conversation piece for your guests, a great keepsake for you.

8. Order special labels for the wine. You could design them yourselves and have a printer create them. This is especially nice if you're giving half bottles as favors.

9. Place a letter of introduction on each guest table that outlines who the tablemates are and what their relationship is to the bride and groom.

10. Recruit testimonials. Ask people from different aspects of your life—close family members; grade school, high school, and college chums; work buddies—to share a brief anecdote about their relationship with you.

11. After your first dance, **request the first dance from your parents' wedding reception.** Have your DJ or bandleader make the appropriate announcement.

12. Say it with cake. What you put on top of your wedding cake says a lot about you as a couple. If you're both into photography, you might highlight your cake with a double portrait as a cake topper. Nature's your thing? Crown your cake with a pair of ceramic lovebirds.

13. Ask your caterer to donate whatever food is left over to a local shelter or food agency that feeds the hungry.

14. For a Christmas wedding, ask guests to bring a tree ornament with them to the reception. Have a bare Christmas tree on hand and let guests decorate it. After the reception's over, donate the tree to a needy family.

RECEPTION DON'TS: FIVE DEADLY SINS

1. A long lag between the ceremony and reception. If it can be helped, don't leave guests hanging for hours between events. Try to have your reception follow an hour or less after the ceremony (take travel time into consideration). If this isn't feasible, set up a hospitality suite with drinks and snacks at the hotel where out-of-town guests are staying. Alternatively, a local relative or friend might host a postceremony, pre-reception gathering.

2. Devoting major reception time to formal photos. Your guests shouldn't have to wait an hour or more for you to arrive at your own party. Arrange with your photographer to have group pictures taken at the ceremony site before the wedding or immediately after.

3. Not having a receiving line. If you're having more than fifty guests, receive them. To cut back on the amount of time spent in line, limit the number of people who'll stand with you. The line need only include the two of you, your parents or just your mothers (siblings, attendants, grandparents, even the bride's father, are all optional). Greeting guests as they file out of the wedding site or into the entrance of your reception hall ensures that you won't miss anyone.

4. Suggestive garter removal. It's a wedding, not a burlesque show (besides, your family is watching). Opt for clever, not lewd.

5. Cake in the face. Who started this, anyway? Smooshing cake in each other's faces might seem funny—but it's also messy. After all the money you spent on your dress and the effort you went to to get your hair and makeup just so, do you really want them ruined by buttercream? Talk to your fiancé beforehand and let him know you'd prefer to be fed by fork—neatly.

TABLING IT: WHO SITS WHERE?

Having a formal reception with a seated dinner or even a buffet dinner? Then you need a formal seating plan.

Step one. Find out from your caterer or banquet hall manager how many tables will be available and the number of seats at each one.

Step two. Go over your response list, devise a chart with the appropriate number of tables and seats, and then start thinking about who should sit where. Guests with similar hobbies, jobs, and personalities will enjoy sitting together, as will single friends. To encourage mingling, try to create a mix. Instead of seating all your college friends together, for instance, seat a few at one table, a few at another. However, make sure you do seat spouses together, as well as single friends and their escorts. Sprinkle family members among the tables. Use the Reception Seating Chart on page 73 to arrange guest tables.

Step three. After you decide what table guests will be sitting at, write out a table card (with a table number) for each guest. Use first and last names (Mary Jones or Mrs. Jones—not Mrs. David Jones). Have the cards arranged in alphabetical order on a table near the entrance of your reception hall.

Step four. If you're having a very formal wedding, you might want to use place cards to designate who sits where at the table. Write the guest's name on the back and front of the card—

so everyone around the table will know who the other guests are.

Step five. Write out place cards for the head table. (Usually this is a long, rectangular table raised on a platform.) The bride and groom sit in the center, with the groom on the bride's left and the best man on her right. To the groom's left sits the maid of honor. Ushers and bridesmaids alternate seats. Sometimes spouses or dates of the attendants can sit at the head table—if there's room. Otherwise they sit at separate tables nearby.

Step six. Write out place cards for the parents' table. To facilitate conversation, seat each parent at opposite ends of the table, away from his/her spouse. (If parents are divorced, seat them at separate tables. The parent who raised you can sit with your groom's parents; your other parent can host a table of family and friends elsewhere.) Your clergymember and his/her spouse also get seats of honor at the parents' table.

TIPS ON TIPPING

Many wedding professionals—florists, photographers, bridal consultants, and caterers, among others—are tipped only for extra special service (generally 15 to 20 percent of the total bill). But before you tip, check your contract. Some gratuities are automatically included in the final catering bill; in other cases, the establishment may request wait staff and bartender tips in advance. You should also arrange tips for parking, coatroom, and powder-room attendants beforehand (guests should not have to pay for anything).

Any gratuities not paid before the wedding or

included in a final bill are given to wedding professionals in sealed envelopes by the reception host (often the father of the bride) or wedding consultant at the end of the reception. Delivery-truck drivers are tipped at the delivery site, limo drivers when they reach the reception site. Musicians or DJs receive an optional gratuity when the party is over. Here are more suggestions on whom to tip when—and how much. Remember, these are guidelines. You may tip more or less depending on local custom or feelings about the quality of service you received.

RECEPTION SEATING CHART

Use this space to draw reception tables and determine who sits where.

Whom to tip	How much	When and by whom
Caterer, club manager, hotel banquet manager, bridal consultant	Fee usually covers everything; tip 15–20%, for extra-special service only.	Reception hosts pay bill on receipt. Add any tip to payment.
Waiters/waitresses, bartenders, table captains	If not included in final bill, 15–20% of bill. Give to captain or maître d'hôtel to distribute to staff.	If included, reception host pays tip with final bill. If not, tips are paid at the reception's end.
Powder-room attendants, coatroom attendants	$1 per guest, or arrange a flat fee with the hotel or club management.	If flat fee, reception host pays with bill. If not, right after reception.
Florist, photographer, baker, musicians, limo driver	15–20% for driver. Others tipped only for extra-special service (15–20%).	Ceremony host tips driver at reception site. Add other tips to bill payments.
Civil ceremony officials (judges, justices of the peace, city clerks)	Some judges cannot accept money; ask. If they do accept money, tip whatever you feel comfortable with— $10 to $20 extra.	Groom gives fee to best man, who pays after the ceremony.
Clergymembers (minister, rabbi, priest)	Usually a donation ($25 and up, depending on ceremony size). Ask clergyperson for guidelines.	Groom gives fee to best man, who pays after the ceremony.
Altar servers, sextons, cantors, organists	Sometimes covered by church fee (or ask clergy what's customary).	Ceremony host pays church fee when billed; separate fees or tips are paid after the service.

Chapter 6:

YOUR INVITATIONS, ANNOUNCEMENTS, AND THANK-YOU CARDS

Don't get caught up in a paper chase. Here is letter-perfect advice about devising a guest list, choosing a stationer, wording your invitations, and more.

YOUR GUEST LIST

How Do We Arrive at a Number?

Consider these factors:

1. Space. Determine how many people your ceremony and reception sites can comfortably and safely hold. Invite too many, and you're likely to be cramped—and in violation of local fire codes. If you're planning an outdoor wedding, you need a tent or an alternate indoor site for all your guests in the event of rain.

2. Budget. How many people can you afford to serve at the reception? You and your families may have to decide what's important to you: a seated dinner and open bar for fewer guests, or the ability to invite everyone you want to a party that's less elaborate.

3. Mood. You may prefer a gathering of a few close friends to a big bash, or vice versa.

How Many Guests Does Each Family Get to Invite?

The fairest way is to decide how many people you'll invite, then split the number between his side and yours. Or divide the number in thirds,

allowing a third for the bride and groom's friends and a third for each of the families. If one of the families lives far from the wedding site, chances are they won't have as many friends and family coming to the wedding; think of ways to redivide the number of guest spots still open. More pointers: Look for duplicates on each set of lists. As you receive regrets (expect about 20 percent of guests to decline), you can send invitations to others. Although the bulk of your invitations should be mailed six weeks in advance, it's acceptable to mail last-minute ones up to two and a half weeks before the wedding.

Who Should Be Invited?

Deciding who does and who doesn't make the guest list is a major headache for couples planning a wedding. Your short list should include immediate relatives, close friends, and any friends close to both sets of parents. Don't forget to send invitations to your officiant and his/her spouse and the wedding party along with their spouses. It's not necessary to invite dates for single friends, but if you do, proper etiquette dictates that you send them separate invitations at their addresses rather than writing "and Guest" on an invitation. If there's room, you can also invite coworkers and business associates. Send wedding announcements to people whom you feel should know about the marriage but are not invited to the wedding. (Neither a wedding invitation nor an announcement requires the recipient to send a gift.)

Paring a List Down

Start by eliminating certain categories of people, such as business associates, coworkers, and acquaintances you have from professional organizations, social groups, your health club, etc. If you seem to have a lot of disappointed friends, consider planning a postwedding bash after you return from your honeymoon and settle down a bit.

To Invite Kids or Not?

Children can add joy—and sometimes mayhem—to a wedding. Whether or not you include children in your wedding celebration is up to you. But here are some pointers:

• **Make sure the church or synagogue in which you're holding your ceremony has a room** where children can be taken if they start to misbehave or cry.

• **Keep them occupied.** Hire a baby-sitter to keep an eye on the kids so their parents can enjoy the party. In a room adjoining the reception, you can also provide toys, coloring books, games, and a VCR with tapes they'll enjoy watching. Hiring a mime, clown, or magician is also a good idea.

• **Cater to their needs.** Have the caterer prepare food you know they'll enjoy eating—chicken fingers or cocktail franks, for example. Also, have your band leader or DJ play some songs they'll like to dance to.

If Kids Aren't Included

• **Make it clear on the invitation that children are not invited** by addressing the inner envelope only to the parents.

• **Have your family, friends, and attendants discreetly let guests know** that children are not invited.

• **Hire a baby-sitter to watch the kids of any of your out-of-town guests** who have traveled with their children. The baby-sitter and kids might best enjoy the time if it's spent in the child-friendly home of a relative or friend. Or, simply ask the baby-sitter to come to the hotel where your guests are staying.

CHOOSING A STATIONER

Now that you have the guest list, it's time to do the inviting. Follow these strategies for choosing a stationer:

• Ask friends, family, and recent brides for recommendations.

• Check out the company's status with the Better Business Bureau.

• Look at the sample books each stationer offers.

• Make sure the stationer fits your style—is she/he pushing you toward something traditional when you'd prefer something contemporary?

• Ask for estimates on prices (remember, a heavier invitation needs additional postage).

• When you've settled on a stationer, make sure you order your invitations six months before your wedding. You'll need that much time to have your order printed and delivered. Plus, you'll want a few weeks for addressing the envelopes, which should be dropped in the mail six to eight weeks before your wedding.

Before you close a deal with a stationer, ask the following questions.

Does Your Stationer Get Your Stamp of Approval? Thirteen Questions to Ask.

1. What styles of lettering and embossment are available?

2. Is there a variety of paper stock available?

3. Will you custom-design invitations?

4. What's the total cost including paper and printing?

5. How much extra will enclosures cost?

6. Will you design/print maps and directions? What will they cost?

7. Can you recommend someone to do calligraphy for the envelopes? What will it cost?

8. Can you offer advice on wording? Do you have a sample book?

9. Will you call me so that I can proofread the master invitation, envelope, and enclosures before the order is sent to the printer? If possible, will you fax me the materials?

10. When will the order be ready?

11. Can you print rush invitations? How much will a rush order cost?

12. If an error is made or I need more invitations, how quickly can you print them?

13. Will you send me the envelopes in advance so I can begin addressing them?

CHOOSING AN INVITATION

• Classic, traditional invitations ($5^1/_2'' \times 7^1/_2''$ embassy size with black engraving on heavy, ecru cotton paper) are popular—especially for first marriages.

• For informal or second marriages—or for couples who want to set themselves apart—invitations with unexpected artistic touches are becoming a trend. Gray, navy, red, gold, silver, French blue, and green inks are all being used, as are papers embedded with dried flowers. Other choices are hand-painted invitations and invitations with tulle, lace, or Florentine paper borders. The look is different, but still appropriate.

• More new trends include the use of papers from around the world (e.g., European and Australian marbleized papers, Japanese rice papers); cardboard cutouts of cherubs and hearts on the invitations; and natural ornamentation in the form of moss, twigs, and dried flowers.

• If you're planning a wedding with fifty or fewer guests, it's perfectly acceptable to handwrite your invitations.

Print Possibilities

Engraving is the traditional choice. The paper is pressed onto a specially treated steel or copper plate to "cut" the letters into the paper, resulting in print that's slightly raised from the page. But as printing quality gets better and better, engraving is gaining competition. **Thermography** is a printing process that fuses ink and powder to resemble engraving—at a lower cost. The letters are raised in front, but they can't be felt in the back. **Offset printing** is another affordable option. With the help of a rubber cylinder, it imprints letters onto paper, although the look is less formal than engraving or thermography.

To address your invitations, look into **calligraphy** (elegant or stylized handwriting or lettering).

Your stationer can put you in touch with a calligrapher. Some shops even offer **computerized calligraphy**, or you can check your local computer store for calligraphy software programs. Want something clean and simple on your envelopes but have terrible penmanship? Ask a **friend with great handwriting** to do the addressing. If she's not up for the job, have your stationer direct you to someone who can help.

As far as typeface goes, there are many options. Popular choices include **Royal Script**, **Palmer Script**, **Shaded Antique Roman**, **London Script**, **St. James**, **Flemish Script**, **Solid Antique Roman**, **Cathedral Text**, **Rook Script**, and **Statesman**. Work with your stationer on choosing one that fits your tastes.

Stationery on a Budget

You don't have to go broke getting it all down on paper. Here are some ways to cut costs:

• Stick with white or ivory paper. Colors are pretty—but costly.

• Opt for simplicity. Sheets with printed or embossed designs are more expensive than plain paper.

• Before you decide on a colored ink or photographs or illustrations, consider costs. Adding extras can get expensive.

• Think weight. Every enclosure card adds to the bulk of the invitation—which will then cost more to mail.

Before You Put It on Paper

• Know exactly **the date**, **time**, and **day of your wedding.**

• **Have the correct spellings** and the addresses of the ceremony and reception sites (only include the ceremony address if there are churches/synagogues in your town with similar names, or if many guests are unfamiliar with the area).

• Decide whether or not the **groom's parents will be listed** on the invitation.

• **Spell everything out in full.** Outside of Mr. and Mrs., and in some cases Dr. and Jr. (when space is tight), do not use abbreviations. Spell out names, numbers, states, and full church/synagogue names.

• Use the wording **"request the honour of your presence"** only if the ceremony is being held in a house of worship. Otherwise, use the wording **"request the pleasure of your company."**

• **Include your surname only if it is different** from that of your parents (you were previously married) or the sponsors of your wedding (family friends are hosting your celebration).

• If you, your groom, or one of your parents has a **professional title such as "Doctor,"** use it in the invitation. If space is tight, "Doctor" may be abbreviated. Here are some examples:

Doctor and Mrs. Howard White
request the honour of your presence
or
Mr. Howard White and Dr. Samantha White
or
. . . at the marriage of their daughter
Dr. Julia White
to
Mr. Robert Montgomery

• Consider whether you want to include **reception response cards**. Traditionally, they are not used with formal invitations—a personal reply is preferred. But using them will make it more convenient for your guests to respond (and for you to get an accurate head count). If you don't use a response card, include an RSVP note in the left-hand corner of your invitation. Or include with your invitations a card that is blank except for the words "The favor of a reply is requested" to encourage guests to respond.

WORD IT RIGHT

Here are sample wedding invitation wordings for every situation.

- **The bride's parents are hosts:**

Mr. and Mrs. Andrew Lyle Smith
request the honour of your presence
at the marriage of their daughter
Sarah Jane
to
John Reginald Jones
Saturday, the first of June
at four o'clock
First Congregational Church
Newtown, Massachusetts

- **Both the bride's and groom's parents are hosting:**

Mr. and Mrs. Andrew Lyle Smith
and
Mr. and Mrs Charles Jones
request the honour of your presence
at the marriage of their children
Sarah Jane
and
John Reginald
Saturday, the first of June
at four o'clock
First Congregational Church
Newtown, Massachusetts

- **The bride's parents have divorced:** The parent who raised you does the inviting. If that's your mother and she has not remarried, then she may use both her maiden and married names in the invitation (Mrs. Taylor Adams). If she wants to drop the Mrs., she can, replacing it with her first name (Lucille Taylor Adams). It's also appropriate for her to use her first name, middle name, and married surname, along with Mrs. For example:

Mrs. Lucille Katherine Adams
requests the honour of your presence
at the marriage of her daughter
Susan Louise . . .

- **Divorced parents jointly issue the invitation** (an acceptable gesture if your parents are still very friendly):

Lucille Katherine Adams
and
George Thomas Adams
request the honour of your company
at the marriage of their daughter
Susan Louise . . .

- **The bride's divorced or widowed mother is remarried and hosting the wedding:**

Mr. and Mrs. Ronald Miller
request the honour of your presence
at the marriage of Mrs. Miller's daughter

(if you're especially close to your stepfather, you can use the words "their daughter")

Susan Louise Adams . . .

- **The bride's divorced or widowed father hosts the wedding:**

Mr. George Thomas Adams
requests the honour of your presence
at the marriage of his daughter
Susan Louise . . .

- **The bride's divorced or widowed father has remarried and is issuing the invitation:**

Mr. and Mrs. George Thomas Adams
request the honour of your presence
at the marriage of Mr. Adams's daughter

(if you're very close to your stepmother, use the words "their daughter")

Susan Louise Adams

• **Divorced parents sending two separate invitations:** This is a good option if your divorced parents want to be officially recognized on the invitation but don't want their names to be written together. Have one parent do the inviting to the ceremony, the other to the reception, and mail both invitations together in one envelope. For example:

Ceremony Invitation

Lucille Katherine Adams
requests the honour of your presence
at the marriage of her daughter
Susan Louise
etc.

Reception Invitation

George Thomas Adams
requests the pleasure of your company
Saturday, the first of June
at five o'clock
Shady Brook Country Club

R.s.v.p.
Twenty-four Sycamore Lane
Oneonta, New York 56789

• **The bride's family issues the invitation as well as the divorced parents of the groom:**

Mr. and Mrs. Andrew Lyle Smith
request the honour of your presence
at the marriage of their daughter
Sarah Jane
to
John Reginald Jones
son of
Mrs. Paula Ann Jones
and
Mr. Charles Peter Jones . . .

• **The bride's divorced-and-not-remarried mother hosts the wedding with her live-in partner:**

Mrs. Barbara Lee Jackson
and
Mr. Douglas W. Clark
request the honour of your presence
at the marriage of Mrs. Jackson's daughter
Mary Alexandra . . .

• **The bride and groom host:**

The honour of your presence
is requested at the marriage of
Miss Diana Margaret Connolly
to
Mr. Christopher Mark Lewis
Saturday, the first of June
at two o'clock . . .

• **The bride's aunt, sister, brother, or other relative hosts:**

Mr. Daniel William Carson
requests the honour of your presence
at the marriage of his sister
Janet Elaine
to . . .

- **Friends of the bride or groom host:**

Mr. and Mrs. Brian Kelly
request the honour of your presence
at the marriage of
Miss/Ms. Leslie Jean Brown
to
Mr. Gregory Charles Page

More of the Write Stuff

- **Sample informal wording:**

John and Anne Smith
and George and Lois Rowe
invite you
to share in the joy
of the marriage
uniting our children
Nicole and Jason
Four p.m.
Unitarian Church
New Hope, California
or
Tom and Beth Grant
ask those dearest to us
to join us in worship and celebration
at the marriage of our daughter
Marcia Jill
to
Michael Jones
Saturday, July 5th
9:30 a.m.
First Presbyterian Church
Newell, Idaho

- **Sample reception card:**
Formal

Mr. and Mrs. Andrew Lyle Smith
request the pleasure of your company

Saturday, the first of June
at five o'clock
Shady Knoll Country Club
Seventy-nine Horseshoe Lane
Newtown, Massachusetts
R.s.v.p.
Sixty-three Rogers Street
Newtown, Massachusetts 12345

Simplified

Reception
immediately following the ceremony
Shady Knoll Country Club
Seventy-nine Horseshoe Lane
Newtown, Massachusetts

- **Combined ceremony/reception invitation**

Mr. and Mrs. Andrew Lyle Smith
request the honour of your presence
at the marriage of their daughter
Sarah Jane
to
John Reginald Jones
Saturday, the first of June
at four o'clock
First Congregational Church
Newtown, Massachusetts
and afterwards at
Shady Knoll Country Club
R.s.v.p.
Sixty-three Rogers Street
Newtown, Massachusetts 12345

- **Sample response card:**

The favour of a reply is requested
by the fourth of April
M_____
will _____ attend

INVITATION WORKSHEET

My invitation will read (see samples):

_____

_____

_____

_____

_____

_____

My reception card (if any) will read:

_____

_____

_____

_____

My response card (if any) will read:

_____

_____

_____

_____

_____

Cost per hundred $ _____

Number of invitations to order _____

Total invitation cost $ _____

How Many to Order?

Count on one invitation for every married couple and for couples who live together. Your officiant and his/her spouse should also receive an invitation, as should each of your attendants. Single people should be sent one invitation each. If you'd like to invite them with a date, ask them for the name and address of that person, and send each a separate invitation. Those over the age of eighteen are sent their own invitations, even if they live with their parents (for children under eighteen, send their parents one invitation but include the children's names on the inner envelope). Order a few extra invitations (to give to your parents and keep as mementos) as well as twenty-five to fifty extra envelopes, in case you make some addressing mistakes. Use the worksheet on page 84 for your guest list. Photocopy number of guests invited.

INVITATION PROOFREADING CHECKLIST

Proofreading date _____ Envelopes _____ Invitations _____

When the printer or stationer asks you to review your invitation wording and order, read it carefully, compare it to the one you wrote out in the Invitation Worksheet, and answer the following questions:

_____ Is the invitation worded the way you want it?

_____ Do the lines fall in the proper places ("to" on one line, the entire date on another)?

_____ Is everyone's name spelled correctly—your parents', your's, your groom's, his parents', if they are listed?

_____ Is there a u in the word "honour"?

_____ Do the day of the week and the date correspond? (Check a calendar.) Is the time written in words, not numbers? Is it correct?

_____ Are the names of the ceremony and reception sites spelled correctly? Are any addresses complete and correct?

_____ Are the commas in the right places? Apostrophes? Are there periods after all abbreviations?

_____ Is the paper the color you chose? The lettering style? What about any borders or designs?

_____ Is the return address on the outer envelope correct? Is the spelling?

Corrections, if any _____

_____

_____

Pickup or delivery date _____

GUEST/ANNOUNCEMENT WORKSHEET

Names _____ Phone _____ Fax _____

Children _____

Address _____

City _____ State _____ Zip _____

____ Wedding announcement

____ Wedding invitation

____ Reception invitation

Number attending _____

Gift descriptions

1. _____

2. _____

3. _____

Date thank-you sent

engagement _____

shower _____

wedding _____

Names _____ Phone _____ Fax _____

Children _____

Address _____

City _____ State _____ Zip _____

____ Wedding announcement

____ Wedding invitation

____ Reception invitation

Number attending _____

Gift descriptions

1. _____

2. _____

3. _____

Date thank-you sent

engagement _____

shower _____

wedding _____

BEYOND INVITATIONS: WHAT YOU'LL NEED FROM YOUR STATIONER

There's more to bridal stationery than just the wedding invitation. You might also want to send out wedding announcements or rehearsal-dinner invitations, or reserve certain pews for special guests at the ceremony (called between-the-ribbon cards or pew cards). You'll save time and money if you order all your stationery at the same time and from the same stationer as you order your wedding invitations.

The Bride Orders:

• **Engagement announcements**

• **Engagement party invitations** if her parents host a party

• **Wedding announcements.** These are sent to people who are not invited to the wedding but who will still want to know about your nuptials—business associates, faraway friends, etc. Paper, printing, and format are similar to invitations. They should be addressed and ready to mail immediately after the wedding.

• **Wedding invitations,** including any inserts or extras such as:

Reception cards

Reply or response cards. These invitation inserts save guests from having to write out their acceptance or regret notes. Guests fill in their names, check whether they're coming, and return them in the provided stamped and addressed envelope. Traditionally, they are *not* used with formal invitations; a personal, handwritten reply is preferred.

Direction cards/maps. They'll make it less likely people will get lost en route to your wedding or reception site and arrive late. Have them printed in the same style as your invitations. Besides inserting them into invitations, also have some available at your ceremony site.

Hotel accommodation cards

Rain cards. They inform guests attending an outdoor wedding where to go in case of inclement weather.

Transportation cards. They let guests know about any wedding-day transportation arrangements—such as specially arranged buses or vans that will take them from the hotel to the ceremony and reception and back.

Parking-arrangement cards to indicate parking locations.

Between-the-ribbon or pew cards

Table cards. Later, you'll fill them in with guests' names, so they know at which table they are sitting.

Place cards. Unless the wedding is very formal, these are generally used only at the bride's and the parents' tables. They tell guests exactly what seat to take.

• **Bridesmaids' luncheon invitations**

• **Wedding programs**

• **Monogrammed matchbooks, napkins, labels for individual bottles of wine, swizzle sticks, paper coasters etcetera,** if you choose to have them at your wedding

• **Guest book**

• **Thank-you cards**. The classic is folded gray, pearl, ecru, or white paper with blue or black ink. Order some of the notes printed with your maiden name or initials, to use for shower and other prewedding thank-yous; have others printed up with both your names (e.g., Mr. and Mrs. Samuel Geller or Mr. Samuel Geller and Ms. Amy White if the bride is keeping her name) or your joint initials to use for post-wedding thank-you.

The Groom Orders:

• **Rehearsal-dinner invitations**

• **Thank-you notes** (for bachelor-party gifts)

Bride and Groom Order Together:
- **At–home cards** (for your new address; insert them with your invitations)
- **Thank–you cards** (for thank-you notes written after the wedding)
- **Notepaper**

Attendants Order:
- **Bridal–shower invitations**
- **Bachelor–party invitations**

STATIONERY WORKSHEET

Estimate #1

Name _____

Phone _____

Fax _____

Item	Number	Cost
Invitations _____		
Announcements _____		
Thank-you notes _____		
Response cards _____		
At-home cards _____		
Napkins/ Matchbooks _____		
Programs _____		
Maps _____		
Rain/Travel cards _____		
Long-weekend wedding cards _____		
Other _____		

Total cost $ _____

Estimate #2

Name _____

Phone _____

Fax _____

Item	Number	Cost
Invitations _____		
Announcements _____		
Thank-you notes _____		
Response cards _____		
At-home cards _____		
Napkins/Matchbooks _____		

Programs _____

Maps _____

Rain/Travel cards _____

Long-weekend
  wedding cards _____

Other_____

Total cost $ _____

Estimate #3

Name _____

Phone _____

Fax _____

Item	Number	Cost
Invitations		
Announcements		
Thank-you notes		
Response cards		
At-home cards		
Napkins/ Matchbooks		
Programs		
Maps		
Rain/Travel cards		
Long-weekend wedding cards		
Other		

Total cost $ _____

Final choice—name, address, phone, fax _____

_____

Date Contract signed   Deposit paid/date   Balance due/date

_____

ADDRESSING ADDRESSED

• **Address invitations by hand.** If your handwriting is difficult to read, hire a calligrapher or secretarial service (ask your stationer or wedding consultant for referrals). Other options are a computer that prints in script and can handle envelopes, or a friend with neat penmanship. A definite no: typewriting.

• **Write out all names, street/avenue/road/drive, states, etc.** Nothing should be abbreviated except Mr., Mrs., Ms., Jr., Dr., and Esq., the last of which should be omitted if you're addressing an invitation to a husband and wife. Make sure you use full names (James instead of Jim, for example). On the inner envelopes, omit first names, using titles and last names only (see pages 88–89 for examples). Leave the envelope unsealed.

• **If several members of a family are to be invited**, avoid using the phrase "and Family." Address the outer envelope to the heads of the household. List children invited on the inner envelope. For example:

Outer envelope

Mr. and Mrs. Edward James Farrell
24 King Street
Little Rock, Arkansas 12345

Unsealed inner envelope

Mr. and Mrs. Farrell
Monica and Malcolm

• **When a female guest is divorced,** you have a variety of addressing options. If she still uses her married name, you can address the envelope using that name, for example: *Mrs. Anna Jordan.* Or use a combination of her married and maiden names: *Mrs. Baker Jordan.* If the guest is using her maiden name, use that on the envelope.

• **When a female guest is separated,** proper etiquette dictates that you still address the envelope using her married surname, for example: *Mrs. Kathleen Blake.*

• **A widow** is addressed with her late husband's name: *Mrs. Michael Russell.*

• **A single woman**—even a child—is addressed with the title "Miss" or "Ms."

• **A boy younger than thirteen** is addressed with the word "Master," for example: *Master Paul Reynolds.*

• **If a married female guest is a doctor but her husband isn't,** address the envelope as follows:

Outer envelope

Dr. Rachel Lancer
Mr. Jonathan Lancer

Inner envelope

Dr. Lancer and Mr. Lancer

• **Are both partners in the couple doctors?** Just use the plural.

Outer envelope

The Doctors Lancer

Inner envelope

The Doctors Lancer

• **If a married female guest uses a military title** but her husband doesn't, address the invitation as such:

Outer envelope

Captain Ellen Gold
Mr. Richard Gold

Inner envelope

Captain Gold and Mr. Gold

• **If a couple is married but using different surnames,** or if an **unmarried couple is living together,** address the invitation using both names, starting in alphabetical order. For example:

Outer envelope

Mr. Lawrence Dean
Ms. Patricia Wright

Inner envelope

Mr. Dean and Ms. Wright

Assembly How-Tos

• **If your invitation is on large paper that must be folded in half**—and most traditional ones are—slip it into the envelope with the folded side inserted into the envelope first, with the typeface toward the back of the envelope.

• **If the invitation isn't folded,** place it into the envelope so that the side with lettering will face the recipient when the inner envelope is opened.

• **Place inserts,** such as the reception card, on top of the engraved/printed side of the invitation.

• **Tissues placed by the stationer** to prevent smearing of the ink while it dries on engraving may be discarded or left in, as you prefer.

• **The unsealed inner envelope** is placed in the outer envelope so that the guest's name is visible when the outer envelope is opened.

Mastering the Mail System

• **Order envelopes early,** so you can begin addressing while waiting for printing or engraving to be completed. Have the envelopes printed (not embossed, which is hard for the postal service to read) with a return address.

• **Completely assemble one invitation** (include any inserts, such as a long-weekend wedding program, at-home cards, etc.) and bring it to the post office. Ask the clerk to weigh the invitation and determine its mailing cost. Look for stamps with hearts, doves, flowers, or the word "love."

• Ask the postal clerk to **hand cancel your invitations.** Some will do it, some won't—but it's worth asking. Hand canceling will help ensure that invitations aren't torn or damaged, or addresses smudged, by a machine, What's more, if you do have an embossed return address on an envelope, hand canceling will help guarantee that it won't be flattened and thus become unreadable.

• **Mail your invitations six weeks before your wedding.** Allow more time (eight weeks) if you're inviting a lot of out-of-town guests or your wedding will be held on a holiday or long weekend.

WHO'S COMING TO YOUR WEDDING?
SETTING UP AN RSVP COMMAND CENTRAL

Don't let the RSVPs leave you reeling. Here is a chart to keep it all straight. If you find you're receiving a lot of regrets, make up a wish list of other people you'd like to invite and send them invitations. Just make sure those guests receive your invitations at least two and a half weeks before the wedding—earlier if you can manage it. If you still haven't heard from some guests by the response date, you'll have to do some phoning (your family and attendants can help). It's important that your caterer have a final head count and that you have an accurate list of who's coming and who isn't, so you can arrange your reception seating plan.

RSVP CHART

Guest Name(s)	RSVP Received	No. Attending Reception

Guest Name(s)	RSVP Received	No. Attending Reception

Total Number Attending Reception _____

Chapter 7:

YOUR WEDDING FLOWERS

Wedding flowers have come a long way from the bunches of herbs brides carried under their veils during ancient Roman times, hoping to ward off evil spirits. Here are all the basics on blooms—from choosing bouquets to ordering boutonnieres to decorating your buffet tables.

CHOOSING A FLORIST: TWENTY-FOUR QUESTIONS TO ASK

Start looking for a florist early—ideally, twelve months before your wedding. Get recommendations from family, friends, and recent brides (call the Better Business Bureau to see if they have any unresolved complaints lodged against them), then make an appointment to see the florist. Check out the shop. Are the arrangements in the cases creative or ho-hum? Do the flowers look healthy? Does the florist do a brisk or slow business? Consider how receptive she or he is to your ideas. Does the florist you're interviewing insist that your bridal bouquet be white although you'd like it to be multicolored?

Once you settle on a florist, be sure to list all the details of your order, including flower types, deposit, cost, and cancellation policy, in a signed and countersigned contract. Before you do that, though, weigh all your options. Here are some questions to ask as you shop around:

1. Do you charge a consultation fee for the initial meeting?

2. How do bouquet shapes, sizes, and flowers vary in price?

3. Do you have a price and color list I can take home?

4. May I see photographs of, or actual flower arrangements made for other weddings?

5. Have you worked at my prospective wedding site?

6. Will you inspect ceremony and reception sites to get ideas for arrangements and how they should be placed?

7. Will you make a sample bridal bouquet and arrangement?

8. Are you willing to experiment with the arrangements and bouquets? How about with the variety of flowers used?

9. What sort of flowers—and how many—can I order and still stay within my budget?

10. If the flowers I ordered are unavailable that day, what's your policy on using substitute flowers? Will I be able to approve the substitutions before they are placed in bouquets and arrangements?

11. On my wedding day, what flowers will be in season (in-season blooms are the freshest and most cost-effective).

12. Are there any benefits to placing a large order? For example, will I receive a free bouquet to throw, rose petals for scattering after the ceremony, or birdseed holders?

13. Are there certain varieties of flowers I should avoid because they may go limp in the heat or wilt early in the day?

14. How will you ensure/guarantee that flowers will look their best on my wedding day (e.g., that blooms will open, look fresh, etc.)? Will you deliver the flowers freshly misted and specially wrapped to retain the moisture?

15. What time—and where—will the flowers be delivered?

16. Can the flowers be delivered to specific sites—say, boutonnieres for the groom and his ushers to the church, table arrangements to the reception site?

17. Who will be responsible for on-site setup that day? Who will be the backup person in case of emergency? Do they have a beeper number?

18. When will you arrive to set the flowers up? How long will it take? (Make sure there's adequate time between the floral setup and the start of your ceremony.)

19. Can you provide other decorations (e.g., aisle runners, potted plants, columns, etc.)?

20. Will you decorate the cake and cake table with flowers? How about other areas of the reception site—mantelpieces, staircases, etc.?

21. What are some of your professional tips for holding my flowers gracefully as I walk down the aisle?

22. If ceremony arrangements will be transported to the reception site, will you assist in moving them?

23. Do you preserve the bouquet? If not, can you give me a referral and/or advice on how to preserve my own?

24. What's the total cost of my order? Will you set up a payment schedule for me? Is there a set policy for payments?

FLOWER POWER

Finding the florist is one thing. Choosing your wedding flowers is another. Like your dress, they'll be a focal point, so go for visual impact. Here are flower facts to consider:

Choosing Your Bridal Bouquet

• **Choose a bouquet that goes with your dress and is in proportion to your body size.** A slim sheath looks best with a small bouquet; a dress with a lot of detail on the bodice or skirt is best served by a bouquet that's held to the side; petite brides may be overwhelmed by a large bouquet.

• **Think beyond the traditional bouquet—** a grouping of flowers affixed to a plastic holder. You might consider cut flowers tied with ribbon, a rounded bouquet of flowers called a nosegay, or a

Hand-Tied Bouquet

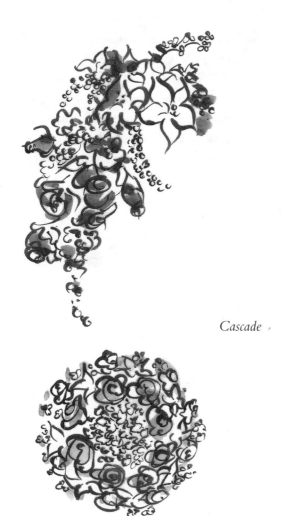

Cascade

Nosegay

Victorian tussie-mussie—a bouquet that's generally placed in a horn-shaped holder and has one prominent flower at its center while smaller flowers form the outside perimeter. More contemporary options are a flower boa placed over your shoulders; a cascade bouquet for the look of tumbling, flowing flowers; or a bouquet created by hand-sewing the petals of dozens of flowers together to create one or two full, voluptuous blooms.

• **Include in your bouquet an element that echoes a detail of your dress** (e.g., full-bloom roses to mirror floral lace or a bouquet tied with organza ribbon to match organza cuffs or a collar).

• **For a natural-looking bouquet,** vary the size, texture, and color of the flowers and greenery.

• **Choose in-season blooms.** Besides being more affordable, they'll also look the healthiest. If you're having a wedding in a particularly hot locale, talk to your florist about what blooms hold up best.

• **Incorporate seasonal elements into your bouquet.** Try adding dried berries and wheat for a fall wedding; garden tulips and daffodils for spring; herbs for summer nuptials; holly, pine cones, and bayberries for a winter ceremony.

• **All-white bouquets are classic,** and there are many white flowers—from creamy-white roses to stark-white freesia—to mix together for a textural look, **but there are other options.** Consider the blushing pastels of pale tulips and yellow daffodils for a spring wedding, the fresh, vibrant look of wildflowers for a summer wedding, the rich golden tones of bunched chrysanthemums for fall nuptials, and evergreen mixed with joyous holly berries for a winter/holiday wedding. Still prefer the look of white but want to shake it up? Consider adding accent color to the bouquet. Blue violets, irises, and other colored blooms can do the trick.

• **Choose blooms that have significance to you as a couple.** Perhaps he brought you red tulips on your first date. Maybe bluebells remind you of the summer hike when he proposed.

• **Blend silk or dried flowers with real ones**—they'll be a lasting keepsake. Also consider silk or dried flowers if you or your attendants have allergy problems.

• **Talk to your florist about creating a "throwaway" bouquet** for you to toss during the reception. Get the cost in writing.

Choosing the Attendants' Flowers

• **The honor attendant's bouquet is often different** in size and sometimes color from the bridesmaids' flowers.

• **Bridesmaids' bouquets are usually similar in shape to the bride's bouquet,** but smaller, and in harmony with the wedding colors.

• Traditionally, flower girls carry baskets of loose petals to strew in the aisle before the bride. However, brides and wedding guests have been known to slip on the petals, so many **flower girls today carry miniature bouquets or baskets of flowers down the aisle.**

• **If several children will be walking down the aisle together,** you might "connect" them by having them hold on to a boa of greenery.

• **The smaller the flower girl, the smaller the flowers she carries.** For a young girl, choose sweetheart roses instead of the full-size variety. There are miniature varieties of many flowers.

Choosing the Groom's and His Attendants' Flowers

• The **groom and ushers traditionally wear boutonnieres** in their left lapels.

• **The groom's boutonniere should be different from that of the other men in the wedding party.** Often he wears a flower found in your bouquet (it could be a stephanotis, lily of the valley, or freesia). You could literally pluck it from your bouquet (have your florist wire the flower for easy removal) and pin it to his lapel at the start of your ceremony. Other possibilities include a calla lily, phlox, bachelor's button, red rose, or gloriosa lily.

• Your groom might also want to choose **a flower with special significance.** A forget-me-not means true love; lily of the valley, happiness.

• **The best man wears a boutonniere similar**—but not identical—**to that of the groom.**

• **A white rose** is the customary choice for ushers and fathers.

Choosing Corsages for Mothers and Other Honored Guests

• **Traditionally, mothers and grand-mothers receive flowers in colors that complement their dresses** (find out these colors in advance so the florist has time to order flowers). The classic corsage is pinned to the dress just below the shoulder. Many women, however, prefer the look of flowers around their wrists or attached to gloves, purses, or waistbands. An added bonus is that delicate dress material isn't damaged. Before you order corsages, ask what style each person would prefer.

• **In place of corsages,** see if your mothers and grandmothers would like to carry a small bouquet or a single flower.

• **Honor other significant female guests,** ceremony readers or soloists, for example, **with a corsage.** If you weren't able to include your groom's sisters in the bridal party, giving them a corsage is a nice gesture, too.

CEREMONY FLOWERS

A wedding is a multisensory event. There's the music. There's the beautiful apparel. And of course, there are the flowers.

• **Consider the size of your ceremony site before you settle on floral arrange-**ments. Overly elaborate floral decorations can be distracting—not to mention dwarfing; small ones will get lost in a big place.

• **Flowers should direct attention to the bridal couple.** Have your florist place arrangements on either side of the altar (perhaps on columns or pedestals). Garlands—entwined with tulle and strings of pearls—can festoon entrances and exits. You might even have the florist create an arbor—say, of flowers, vines, and dogwood branches—to frame you and your groom at the altar. If you're including a chuppah in your ceremony, ask your florist to create one out of fresh flowers and greenery.

• **Choose arrangements that match the formality of your wedding.** Bunches of daisies or hydrangeas, for instance, are perfect for an alfresco summer wedding. Huge, lavish sprays match the mood of a large, formal church wedding.

• **Stemmed flowers aren't your only option when it comes to decorating your ceremony site.** Not-your-garden-variety choices: Wrought-iron candelabras with lit candles add a touch of drama (check out local fire ordinances beforehand). Pots of azalea bushes, cut forsythia branches placed in vases, and weeping cherry blossom limbs draping over a decorative pitcher look simple, yet stunning. Tiered pots of poinsettias; urns loaded with evergreen and holly, then dotted with bayberries; and planters with crimson, golden, or purple mums are other options.

• **Think green.** Containers of cascading English ivy and lush palms, ficus trees, full ferns, and other greenery can take the place of floral arrangements.

RECEPTION FLOWERS

Like the music that's played and the food that's savored, your reception flowers can set a mood. They can color-coordinate with the hues of your wedding. They can embellish a wedding theme. They can turn a stark, nondescript room into a stunning, can't-forget one. (After the reception, ask a friend to deliver the flowers to a nearby nursing home or hospital.) Here are petal pointers for your party:

• **For a uniform look,** reception flowers should echo your wedding colors and the flowers found in your bridal bouquet.

• **Floral arrangements are appropriate in any place where guests will concentrate their attention**—on guest and buffet tables, near the band, on mantels and staircases, near the entrance where the receiving line is positioned, and on the cake table.

• **Keep centerpieces low to encourage conversation.** They don't have to be identical, just complementary. If they are high, make sure they're placed on a pedestal, so they don't block guests' eye-level view.

• **Warm a large room with ficus trees, palms, and other greenery** that can be rented for the day.

• **Centerpieces need not be your standard grouping of flowers placed in a vase.** Consider distinctive touches. Cluster small bud vases in the middle of each reception table—when the wedding is over, guests take home a vase as a favor. You might do the same with groupings of herbs or tree saplings. Or how about topiary centerpieces? A terra cotta pot filled with hydrangeas, hyacinths, azaleas, or purple heather? Flowers placed in pitchers or watering cans—each somewhat different but still coordinated? Hurricane-lamp centerpieces with flowers or greenery decorating the base?

• **Consider decorating with flowers— and then some.** Twinkling lights, mirrors, and candles all lend a festive touch.

Creative Centerpieces

A centerpiece need not be floral, just decorative. Here are some unique ideas:

- **Piles of beautiful seashells** (especially appropriate for a wedding with a nautical theme)
- **Cornucopia** overflowing with fruits and vegetables (perfect for a fall wedding)
- **Spun-sugar sculptures**
- **Miniature tiered wedding cakes**
- **Jack-o'-lanterns** (for a Halloween wedding). Create distinctive faces.
- **Palm-frond centerpieces in terra cotta pots** (for a jungle or tropical theme)
- **Maypole-style citrus tree centerpieces**
- **Ethnically diverse centerpieces** that take their cue from foreign wedding customs and folklore. For example, place chunks of coconut in a glass dish along with a handwritten note explaining how in India, the coconut is passed over the newlyweds, then shattered on the ground to chase away evil demons. Research other customs at your local library.

THE LANGUAGE OF FLOWERS

Every flower tells a story. Here are what some common blooms mean:

Amaryllis: Splendid beauty
Bluebell: Faithfulness, constancy
Camellia: Perfect loveliness
Daffodil: Regard
Daisy: Innocence
Forget-me-not: True love
Gardenia: Joy
Honeysuckle: Affection
Ivy: Fidelity
Jasmine: Amiability

Holly: Foresight
Lily of the valley: Happiness
Myrtle: Love
Orange blossoms: Purity
Red chrysanthemum: I love you
Red rose: I love you
Red tulip: Love declared
Rosemary: Remembrance
Violet: Modesty
White lilac: First emotions of love
White lily: Purity
White rose: I am worthy of you
Yellow tulip: Hopeless love

FLORIST WORKSHEET

Estimate #1   *Ideas*   *Costs*

Name _____   Bridal bouquet_____

_____   _____ $ _____

Address _____   Bridesmaids' bouquets_____

Phone _____ Fax _____   _____ $ _____

                                 Mothers_____ $ _____

                                 Groom _____ $ _____

                                 Ushers_____ $ _____

                                 Fathers _____ $ _____

                                 Flower girl _____ $ _____

                                 Ring bearer _____ $ _____

                                 Other participants_____

                                 _____ $ _____

                                 Ceremony_____

                                 _____ $ _____

                                 Reception _____

                                 _____ $ _____

                                           TOTAL COST $ _____

Estimate #2   *Ideas*   *Costs*

Name _____   Bridal bouquet_____

_____   _____ $ _____

Address _____   Bridesmaids' bouquets_____

Phone _____ Fax _____   _____ $ _____

                                 Mothers_____ $ _____

                                 Groom _____ $ _____

                                 Ushers_____ $ _____

Fathers _____ $ _____

Flower girl _____ $ _____

Ring bearer _____ $ _____

Other participants _____

_____ $ _____

Ceremony _____

_____ $ _____

Reception _____

_____ $ _____

TOTAL COST $ _____

Estimate #3   *Ideas*   *Costs*

Name _____   Bridal bouquet _____

_____   _____ $ _____

Address _____   Bridesmaids' bouquets _____

Phone _____ Fax _____   _____ $ _____

Mothers _____ $ _____

Groom _____ $ _____

Ushers _____ $ _____

Fathers _____ $ _____

Flower girl _____ $ _____

Ring bearer _____ $ _____

Other participants _____

_____ $ _____

Ceremony _____

_____ $ _____

Reception _____

_____ $ _____

TOTAL COST $ _____

Final selection—name, address, telephone, fax _____

_____

_____

Contract signed   Deposit paid/date   Balance due/date

_____

PRESERVING YOUR BOUQUET

Wake up and smell the roses—even on your fiftieth anniversary.

1. Speak with your florist before the wedding about incorporating flowers that dry well—roses, hydrangeas, baby's breath, and others—into your bouquet.

2. Before you leave on your honeymoon, start the drying process. Hang your bouquet upside down and leave it in a dry, dark place (e.g., an attic) for about two weeks. Later, use the bouquet to decorate a wall or a shelf—but keep it out of harm's way. Dried flowers are extremely fragile. If your bouquet's wilted from a day of handling or it was tossed at your reception, ask your florist to make you a smaller version of the one you carried and dry that.

3. Create potpourri. Remove the petals from the stems while they're still fresh and place them in a single layer in a wide-brimmed bowl. Place the bowl in a dry place outside of direct sunlight for about two weeks. Later, add aromatic potpourri oil for fragrance.

4. Cut fresh flowers close to their base (cut big-headed flowers like roses or hydrangeas in half as well); place between the pages of a large book. Put more books on top for added weight. In two weeks, remove the flowers. Glue to the pages of your wedding album.

5. Not up for the job yourself? Talk to your florist. He/she may be able to preserve your bouquet for you, or recommend someone who can.

FLOWER CHECKLIST

DECORATIONS FOR THE CEREMONY SITE (church, hotel, etc.)

Where	Kinds of flowers	Color	No. of arrangements	Cost
Altar or canopy	_____	_____	_____	$ _____
	_____	_____	_____	$ _____
Pews	_____	_____	_____	$ _____
Aisles	_____	_____	_____	$ _____
Windows	_____	_____	_____	$ _____
Doors	_____	_____	_____	$ _____
Other	_____	_____	_____	$ _____
_____	_____	_____	_____	$ _____
_____	_____	_____	_____	$ _____
_____	_____	_____	_____	$ _____
			TOTAL COST	$ _____

Flowers for other decorations

What	Where	How many	Flowers, if any	Cost
Candles	_____	_____	_____	$ _____
Candleholders	_____	_____	_____	$ _____
Aisle runner	_____	_____	_____	$ _____
Other	_____	_____	_____	$ _____
_____	_____	_____	_____	$ _____
_____	_____	_____	_____	$ _____
_____	_____	_____	_____	$ _____
			TOTAL COST	$ _____

Delivery

Ceremony site _____

Address _____

Person to see _____

Phone _____   Fax _____

Date _____   Time _____

FLOWERS FOR THE BRIDE AND HER ATTENDANTS

Bride

Style of bouquet _____

Kind and colors of flowers _____

_____

_____

Ribbon color _____

Cost $ _____

Maid/Matron of honor

Style of bouquet _____

Kind and colors of flowers _____

_____

_____

Ribbon color _____

Cost $ _____

Bridesmaids

Style of bouquet(s) _____

Kind and colors of flowers _____

_____

_____

Ribbon color _____

Total cost of all $ _____

Flower girl

Style of bouquet/basket _____

Kind and colors of flowers _____

_____

_____

Ribbon color _____

Cost $ _____

Mother of the bride

Style of corsage _____

Kind and colors of flowers _____

_____

_____

Ribbon color _____

Cost $ _____

TOTAL COST $ _____

Delivery of flowers for the bride and her attendants

Place (home of bride, church, etc.) _____

Address _____

Person to see _____

Phone _____ Fax _____

Date _____ Time _____

FLOWERS FOR THE GROOM AND HIS ATTENDANTS

Groom

Kind and color of boutonniere _____

_____

Cost $ _____

Ushers

Kind and color of boutonnieres _____

_____

Total cost of all $ _____

Fathers

Kind and color of boutonnieres _____

_____

Cost of all $ _____

Ring bearer

Kind and color of boutonniere _____

_____

Cost $ _____

TOTAL COST $ _____

Delivery of flowers for the groom and his attendants

Place (church, hotel, home, etc.) _____

Address _____

Person to see _____

Phone _____   Fax _____

Date _____   Time _____

Mother of the groom

Style of corsage _____

Kind and colors of flowers _____

_____

_____

Ribbon color _____

Cost $ _____

Delivery

Place (church, hotel, home) _____

Address _____

Person to see _____

Phone _____   Fax _____

Date _____   Time _____

Flowers for others (grandparents, aunts, uncles, readers, etc.)

Styles _____

_____

Kinds and colors _____

_____

How many _____

_____

Cost of all $ _____

TOTAL COST $ _____

Delivery

Place(s) (church, hotel, home) _____

Person to see _____

Phone _____   Fax _____

Date _____   Time _____

TOTAL COST $ _____

TOTAL COST OF FLOWERS FOR WEDDING PARTY/OTHERS $ _____

DECORATIONS FOR THE RECEPTION

Where	Kinds of flowers	Color	No. of arrangements	Cost
Receiving line area	_____	_____	_____	$ _____
Buffet table	_____	_____	_____	$ _____
Bridal table	_____	_____	_____	$ _____
Parents' table	_____	_____	_____	$ _____
Guest tables	_____	_____	_____	$ _____
Top of cake	_____	_____	_____	$ _____
Cake table	_____	_____	_____	$ _____
Cake	_____	_____	_____	$ _____
Cake knife	_____	_____	_____	$ _____
Bandstand	_____	_____	_____	$ _____

Other _____ _____ _____ _____ $ _____

_____ _____ _____ _____ $ _____

_____ _____ _____ _____ $ _____

_____ _____ _____ _____ $ _____

TOTAL COST $ _____

Delivery

Reception site _____

Address _____

Person to see _____

Phone _____ Fax _____

Date _____ Time _____

PARTY FLOWERS (for bridesmaids' luncheon, rehearsal dinner, etc.)

Where	Kinds of flowers	Color	No. of arrangements	Cost
Buffet table	_____	_____	_____	$ _____
Bridal table	_____	_____	_____	$ _____
Guest tables	_____	_____	_____	$ _____
Other	_____	_____	_____	$ _____
_____	_____	_____	_____	$ _____
_____	_____	_____	_____	$ _____
_____	_____	_____	_____	$ _____

TOTAL COST $ _____

Delivery

Party site _____

Address _____

Person to see _____

Phone _____ Fax _____

Date _____ Time _____

TOTAL COST OF ALL WEDDING FLOWERS $ _____

Chapter 8:

YOUR WEDDING PHOTOGRAPHS AND VIDEO

Your marriage ceremony will be over in a few minutes, your reception in a few hours. But the photographs and video-tape of your wedding will be enjoyed by family members for generations. Don't entrust the job to just anybody. It's essential that the people who photograph and videotape your wedding be professionals whom you trust.

GETTING FOCUSED: HOW TO HIRE A PHOTOGRAPHER

Nobody wants their wedding-day shots to be blurry, cropped haphazardly, or missed altogether. Choosing a top-notch, professional photographer can help you avoid a negative experience. To make sure you have a good selection, start your search early. Top-drawer photographers are often booked nine months to a year ahead, especially in prime wedding months. It's best to hire yours soon after you confirm your site. Here are some tips.

When You're Checking Them Out

• Ask family, friends, your caterer, and your florist for **recommendations**.

• Check out the photographer's **reputation** with former clients—they'll know best whether the photographer's work is first-rate or not. Don't forget to also call the Better Business Bureau.

• Ask to see **sample books** from a variety of different photographers—not just a compendium of the studio's collective work. Next step: Ask to see a **proof book** of the photographer's shots

from *one* wedding (instead of his/her best shots from many different weddings, compiled in one book). You're looking for consistently good shots, from beginning to end.

• Meet with the photographer you're interested in. Try to get a sense of the person's **experience level, personality, and enthusiasm for wedding photography,** all of which will affect your photos. How intuitive is he/she?

• When you interview a prospective photographer, ask about his/her **style**. Does he/she prefer taking candids or posed shots? About what percentage of his/her work is posed, what percentage is unstaged? If you want more portraiture than candids, look for a photographer who takes about 75 percent posed shots to 25 percent non-posed ones—or vice versa. If the photographer's style isn't to your liking, move on.

• Question the photographer about his/her **equipment**. Is it state-of-the-art? High-speed films, telephoto and wide-angle lenses, and cameras operated via remote control are some items that help photographers capture wedding-day action without being intrusive. Equipment like this is especially helpful if you want your photos to have a journalistic quality.

• Ask about **backup plans.** What happens if a camera or the lighting equipment doesn't work (does the photographer carry other gear he/she can switch to?), the photographer gets sick, or inclement weather makes for bad lighting situations?

• Inquire about **cost.** What's the total price? Will you pay by the hour? If so, does this include transportation time and travel expenses? Is there a standard wedding package? Can photos be ordered individually, and for how much? Are original proofs part of the package? What styles of wedding albums are available?

When You're Ready to Book

• Ask if the photographer has **experience shooting weddings at your ceremony and reception sites.** The more familiar he/she is with the layout and lighting requirements, the better your pictures are apt to be. Also, having worked at a site before, the photographer will be aware of any photo restrictions (e.g., no-flash policies) that the site enforces.

• Make sure the photographer is **receptive to what *you* want,** be it lots of candids, black-and-white photos, etc. Avoid any miscommunication by giving your photographer a list of must-take shots.

• Ask how long the photographer will need to take posed shots. Work with the photographer to **devise a time-efficient schedule.** For example, instead of taking all the family and group shots immediately after the ceremony (which will cut into your reception time), have some posed photos taken before the ceremony. Formal portraits can also be done well in advance of the wedding.

• When will the **previews or proofs** be ready? How long may proofs be kept before the prints are ordered? Can that period be extended, and is a late fee charged?

• How long does the photographer keep **negatives**? (You may not be able to afford many prints right away but may want the option of ordering more in coming years.)

PHOTOGRAPHY WORKSHEET

Estimate #1

Name of studio _____

Name of photographer _____

Address _____

Phone _____   Fax _____

Recommended by _____

Comments about style/work _____

_____

Cost (per hour, by the package, etc.) $ _____

Estimate #2

Name of studio _____

Name of photographer _____

Address _____

Phone _____ Fax _____

Recommended by _____

Comments about style/work _____

_____

Cost (per hour, by the package, etc.) $ _____

Estimate #3

Name of studio _____

Name of photographer _____

Address _____

Phone _____ Fax _____

Recommended by _____

Comments about style/work _____

_____

Cost (per hour, by the package, etc.) $ _____

Final selection—name, address, phone, fax _____

_____

_____

_____

Date contract signed   Deposit paid/date   Balance due/date

_____

NEW TRENDS IN WEDDING PHOTOGRAPHY

Soft-focus portraits and double-exposure shots are standard and still used in wedding photography. What's cutting edge?

1. Photojournalism. Today, about 15 percent of wedding photographers consider themselves to be photojournalists—spontaneous photographers who don't stop the action but instead unobtrusively capture it at its peak. They will also take portraits of the bride.

2. Black-and-white photos. They have a classic look—and actually age better than color photos. Because black-and-white film gives pictures a serious note, it's ideal for emotional moments like your walk down the aisle. (One caveat: Because it may require switching cameras and different developing techniques, your photographer may charge you more for black-and-white photography.)

3. Remote-control cameras. Because they're often shooting from the back or the side (so as not to be disruptive), many photographers miss front-on shots of the bride's and groom's reactions during the ceremony. A way to remedy that is by placing a remote-control camera on a tripod behind the officiant.

4. Nontraditional wedding "albums." Some photographers will mat photos for you and place them in an artist-style portfolio rather than an album. They may also include a frame or an easel so you can display one or a variety of selected photos. Another new option is an album that has the look of a magazine layout. Action shots are mixed with reaction shots on facing pages—for example, a full-page shot of the bride walking down the aisle paired with four quarter-page shots of important onlookers, such as the groom, his parents, the bride's mother, and her maid of honor.

SAY CHEESE: GETTING THE BEST POSED AND CANDID SHOTS

Generally, there are two types of wedding photos—formal posed shots (of you and your groom, your entire family, and your attendants) and candid action shots (you walking down the aisle, exchanging rings, having your first dance, cutting the cake, kissing) that have the look and feel of classic, fly-on-the-wall photojournalism. Here are tips for getting the best of both.

Posed

• For **engagement photos,** ask your photographer about backgrounds. As a general rule, wear medium to dark tones for a dark background, light colors for a light background (avoid vibrant prints and plaids).

• A **formal bridal portrait** is usually taken one to three months before your wedding date; it's the picture you submit to newspapers when announcing your marriage. Because you'll dress just the way you will on your wedding day, many brides still choose to have their portrait taken alone (so as not to let their grooms see how they'll look). Your portrait may be taken at the bridal salon during your final fitting, or you can arrange to have it taken at the photographer's studio. If flowers will show, have your florist create a bouquet identical to the one you'll carry on your wedding day for the photo session. This may, however, be costly.

• Anywhere from a few days to a few weeks after your portrait session, the photographer will send you **previews or proofs.** At that time, you'll decide on the various sizes and quantities of prints you want to order. Don't forget to order enough for friends and relatives.

• To cut down on the time spent on **posed wedding-day shots** (which take you away from your guests and all the activity), ask your photographer to take whatever photos possible before the wedding (at your home before you leave for the ceremony, at the rehearsal, even at the rehearsal dinner). He or she can also save time by taking group shots. For example, instead of taking photos of you and your groom with the bridesmaids and then the ushers, you can request that all the attendants be posed together and one group photo be taken.

• Give your photographer **a list of desired shots** and who should be in them. Designate someone to identify those guests for the photographer.

• Even if you want mostly spontaneous shots, **don't forgo posed photos altogether.** Rely totally on candids, and your photos may miss some key people.

Candids

• If you want your pictures to have a **photojournalistic style,** you'll need to find a professional who specializes in that type of photography. A good starting point is calling newspapers and asking staff photographers if they know of wedding photographers who work in the photojournalistic style. Look closely at their books. Do the photos have a spontaneous feel to them? Do they have personality? Do you see people's feelings and reactions in the shots? Do you feel like you know the people, or is it like looking at strangers?

• **Be very clear with your photographer** about how many—and what sort of—candids you'd like. Do you want a shot of your mother's reaction as you walk down the aisle? Do you want a picture of you and your groom as the best man makes a toast? Of course, the action will dictate what pictures are taken, but give your photographer something to go on.

• Assign someone to **point out significant people** to your photographer so he or she will be sure to get their shots.

• Supply each reception table with **a single-use camera** (along with instructions on how to use them and where to leave them at the party's end). These shots can supplement your professional photos.

WEDDING PHOTOGRAPHY CHECKLIST

Whether you're opting for formal photos, candids, or a mixture of both, there are some must-have, can't-be-missed shots every bride wants. Check off on the list below which special moments you'd like to see in your wedding album—be it *your* maids scrambling for your bouquet or your father dabbing a tear from his eye. Then clip out the list and take it to your photographer, just to be sure he or she captures all those happy memories on film.

BEFORE THE CEREMONY
✓ The bride at breakfast
✓ The bride in her dress
___ The bride's mother adjusting her veil
___ The bride with her mother/stepmother
___ The bride with her father/stepfather
___ The bride with both parents, stepparents
___ The bride with her honor attendant
___ The bride with her bridesmaids
___ The bride touching up her hair, makeup
___ Everyone getting flowers
___ The bride leaving the house
___ The bride and her father getting into the car
___ The groom waiting alone
___ The groom with his best man
___ The groom with both parents, stepparents
___ The groomsmen getting boutonnieres
___ Other moments getting ready

___ _____

___ _____

AT THE CEREMONY
___ Guests outside the ceremony site
___ The bride and her father getting out of the car
___ The bride and her father going into the church
___ The ushers escorting guests
___ Children passing out programs
___ The groom's parents/stepparents being seated (or in the procession)

___ The bride's mother/stepmother in the procession (or being seated)
___ The soloist and musicians
___ The groom and his ushers at the altar
___ The bridesmaids walking down the aisle
___ The maid of honor walking down the aisle
___ The flower girl and ring bearer walking down the aisle
___ The bride and her father walking down the aisle
___ The giving-away ceremony
___ The groom meeting the bride
___ The altar or chuppah during the ceremony
___ The bride and groom exchanging vows
___ The ring ceremony
___ Lighting the Unity Candle
___ The first married kiss
___ The readers at the ceremony
___ The bride and groom coming up the aisle
___ The bride and groom on the church steps
___ The bride alone in the sanctuary
___ The signing of the marriage license
___ The bride and groom among guests, wedding party
___ Guests throwing rice, petals, birdseed, etc.
___ The bride and groom getting in the car
___ The bride and groom in the backseat of the car

_____ Other ceremony moments

_____ _____

_____ _____

POSED SHOTS BEFORE THE RECEPTION

✓ The bride and groom together

✓ The bride with her parents /stepparents

✓ The groom with his parents/stepparents

✓ The bride and groom with their honor attendants

_____ The bride and groom with children

✓ The bride with her attendants

✓ The groom with his attendants

✓ The bride, groom, and all the wedding party

✓ The bride, groom, and all the parents

✓ The bride and groom with their grandparents

✓ The bride and groom with each family (parents, stepparents, grandparents, siblings, their spouses, and children)

✓ Other post-ceremony moments

_____ _____

_____ _____

AT THE RECEPTION

_____ The bride and groom arriving

_____ The bride and groom getting out of the car

_____ The bride and groom going into the reception

_____ The receiving line (posed and unposed)

_____ The bride and groom in the receiving line

_____ The bride's mother/parents in the receiving line

_____ The groom's mother/parents in the receiving line

_____ The buffet table

_____ The bride and groom at their table

_____ The parents' table/head table

_____ The bride and groom dancing

_____ The bride dancing with her father

_____ The groom dancing with his mother

_____ The best man's toast

_____ Guests doing the hora and other ethnic dances

_____ The musicians

_____ The bride and groom talking to guests

_____ The signing of the guest book

_____ The cake table

_____ The bride and groom cutting the cake

_____ The bride and groom feeding each other cake

_____ The bride and groom toasting

_____ The throwing/catching of the bouquet

_____ The groom taking off the bride's garter

_____ The throwing/catching of the garter

_____ The wedding party decorating the car

_____ The bride changing into her going-away clothes

_____ The groom changing

_____ The bride and groom saying good-bye to their parents

_____ The bride and groom ready to leave the reception

_____ Guests throwing rice, petals, birdseed, etc.

_____ The bride and groom getting into the car

_____ Guests waving good-bye

_____ The rear of the car as it's being driven away

_____ Other reception moments

_____ _____

_____ _____

ROLL 'EM: HIRING A VIDEOGRAPHER

Your wedding photos can capture a lot—but they can't capture the sounds of your wedding day: the applause as you head down the aisle, the good wishes your guests offer you in the receiving line, the best man's toast. Video can do all that—and more. It preserves the action of your wedding, bringing it to life days, weeks, even years later. But your video will only be as good as the person who shoots it. Here are tips on finding a great videographer.

When You're Checking Them Out

• Determine if your ceremony or reception site has any **restrictions** against the use of cameras, lighting, tripods, etc.

• Give yourself enough time to **shop around.** You'll want to book your videographer about twelve months in advance—around the same time you book your other wedding professionals.

• Ask friends, family, your photographer, and recently married couples for **recommendations.** (Many photography studios also provide video-taping services.) Contact the Better Business Bureau to further check out the reputation of the videographer.

• Get **references**—and call them.

• If you want professional quality, then **go with a professional.** Sure, a friend could do it, but he or she is apt to miss some crucial elements (e.g., your friend-cum-videographer is schmoozing with guests while you're cutting the cake). Plus, a professional is more likely to have top-notch equipment, so images aren't blurry, or dark.

• Ask potential videographers what type of **experience** they have. How many weddings have they shot? Where?

• Get a sense of the videographer's **style.** If you want someone to quietly observe and unob-

trusively capture the day's events, then you don't want a loud, director-type videographer.

• View **sample tapes.** Does the work appear professional? Are images bright, not fuzzy? Is the lighting dim—or too glaring? Are there a variety of shots—close-ups, panning crowd shots, fade-aways? Is the sound audible? Don't hire anyone whose tape you haven't watched.

• Inquire about the videographer's **equipment.** If it's up-to-date, industrial-strength lights won't be needed.

• Ask about **backup plans.** Who'll videotape your wedding if the videographer you booked can't make it due to illness or emergency? What happens if a camera breaks down mid-ceremony?

• Get details about the sort of wedding **videos available.** Will the videographer shoot footage and then edit it so it flows smoothly? Will he/she input special effects, music, etc., and will this cost extra?

• Get **prices.** How many hours of service does the price quote cover? What sort of packages are available? Will you receive extra copies of the tapes, and for how much?

When You're Ready to Book

• Ask your videographer if he/she is willing to **visit your ceremony and reception sites** beforehand so as to determine where cameras will be set up, if special electrical outlets will be needed, etc.

• Inquire about whether or not **camera assistants** will also attend your wedding. Many videographers work with a backup, but the larger the crew, the more of a distraction they'll be.

• Ask that your videographer dress in **attire that's appropriate** for your wedding.

• Give your potential videographer **a list of important wedding events** you want covered. Does he/she seem willing to oblige?

• Make sure your videographer is willing to meet with your **still photographer.** They'll need to coordinate activities, figure out placement of cameras and lights, etc.

• If you think the video costs might put you over budget, ask if there are ways to make it more **affordable.** Can you eliminate some music and special effects?

LIGHTS, CAMERA, ACTION: CHOOSING A VIDEO PACKAGE

Here are some common wedding-video styles to consider:

Nostalgic. While some of your favorite songs play in the background, this type of video starts with vintage photos of you and your groom plucked from family albums, progressing to photos of the two of you during your dating days and engagement. Scenes from the ceremony and reception, as well as still photos from the honeymoon, complete the tape. Because of the heavy editing and special effects (interspersing of photos, etc.), costs can run high.

Documentary. This type of video uses scenes of the wedding day only. It may include shots of you and your groom getting ready beforehand, scenes of guests arriving, and panoramas of your ceremony and reception sites. Your groom can wear a cordless microphone to record your vows at the altar. During the reception, your videographer can conduct interviews and capture guests' insights on love and marriage, or childhood anecdotes about the two of you.

Straightforward. This is a cost-conscious option, since only one camera is used to shoot your wedding scenes. At the reception's end, the tape—unedited—is ready for your home viewing.

VIDEOGRAPHY WORKSHEET

Estimate #1

Name _____

Address _____

Phone _____ Fax _____

Recommended by _____

Comments about style/work _____

_____

_____

_____

Cost $ _____

Estimate #2

Name _____

Address _____

Phone _____ Fax _____

Recommended by _____

Comments about style/work _____

_____

_____

_____

Cost $ _____

Estimate #3   Comments about style/work _____

Name _____   _____

Address _____   _____

Phone _____ Fax _____   _____

Recommended by _____   Cost $ _____

Date contract signed   Deposit paid/date   Balance due/date

_____

Chapter 9:

YOUR WEDDING-DAY TRANSPORTATION

If ever there were a day you wanted to arrive on time and in style, your wedding day is it. Will it be in a hot-air balloon? Horse and buggy? Or a Model T? Whichever you choose, don't forget about making transportation arrangements for your family, bridal party, and any wedding guests needing a lift. If you don't hire professional drivers for your wedding party, assign friends with clean, comfortable cars to drive them. Friends can also help drive out-of-town guests without cars. Be sure to thank drivers by paying for a tank of gas and a car wash. Use the Driver's Checklist to help them know whom to pick up, when, and where. Here are more pointers.

GETTING IN GEAR: BOOKING LIMOUSINES

A limousine is a traditional—and elegant—choice. Ask friends, family, and newlyweds you know, as well as your other wedding professionals (caterer, photographer, consultant) for the names of reliable companies. You can also look in the yellow pages (but check references as well as the company's status with the Better Business Bureau). Depending on the size of your budget and wedding party, you may hire one or many. It's customary for one limousine to take you and your father to the ceremony site, while another transports your mother and attendants (if you have a large wedding party, you may need several). The groom and his parents or grandparents may also be picked up by limo. After the ceremony, you and your groom travel to the reception in the same car you and your father arrived in. You might even take it to the airport or a hotel after the reception.

But don't get taken for a ride. Here is how to protect yourself:

- **Don't wait until the last minute.** Book your limo at least six months before your wedding.
- **Do use a limo company close to your wedding site** to avoid add-on costs for the limo's traveling time and expenses.
- **Don't go with an inexperienced firm.** Ask how many weddings the limo company has taken part in. Get references. Call them.
- **Do ask if the company has wedding packages** available—it may save you some money.
- **Don't book a limo for more time than you need it.** If a limo service has a minimum rental time that's in excess of the time you need the car for, look elsewhere.
- **Do inquire about the cars**—the color choices, how many people they accommodate, their makes and models. Also ask about what's included in your price. Champagne? Soda? Snacks?
- **Do ask if gratuities are included** in the total price. If not, tip the driver at least 15 percent.
- **Do visit the limousine service and check out their fleet.** Ask to see the car(s) that will be used on your wedding day. Is it up to your standards? Does it have the features you want—a bar, a phone, a sunroof?

• **Don't take chances.** When you visit the limo company, ask to see their insurance papers and city licenses. Is everything up-to-date and in order?

• **Do ask that the driver dress in appropriate attire** for your wedding.

• **Don't be caught unprepared.** Ask the fee for overtime charges.

• **Do specify all the details**—including the exact car(s) you want, deposit fees, and cancellation policies, in a contract that's signed and countersigned.

LIMOUSINE WORKSHEET

Estimate #1

Name _____

Address _____

Phone _____ Fax _____

Recommended by _____

Comments (types of cars available, packages, etc.)

_____

_____

_____

Cost $ _____

Estimate #2

Name _____

Address _____

Phone _____ Fax _____

Recommended by _____

Comments (types of cars available, packages, etc.)

_____

_____

_____

Cost $ _____

Estimate #3

Name _____

Address _____

Phone _____ Fax _____

Recommended by _____

Comments (types of cars available, packages, etc.)

_____

_____

_____

Cost $ _____

Final selection—name, address, phone, fax _____

_____

_____

Contract signed   Deposit paid/date   Balance due/date

_____

DRIVER'S CHECKLIST

(Give a copy to each driver.)

Passengers

Name _____

Address _____

Phone _____ Fax _____

Name _____

Address _____

Phone _____ Fax _____

Name _____

Address _____

Phone _____ Fax _____

Name _____

Address _____

Phone _____ Fax _____

Name _____

Address _____

Phone _____ Fax _____

Address of gathering place _____

_____

Directions _____

_____

Arrival time _____

Ceremony site and address _____

_____

Directions _____

_____

Arrival time _____

Reception site and address _____

_____

Directions _____

_____

Arrival time _____

Special notes (e.g., luggage will be stored in the trunk, a passenger also needs a ride from the recep-

tion to her home) _____

_____

WEDDING-DAY TRANSPORTATION WORKSHEET

TO THE CEREMONY SITE

Name	Time and place of pickup	Who will drive

Bride _____

Father _____

Mother _____

Maid/Matron of honor _____

Bridesmaids _____

Groom _____

Best man _____

Ushers _____

Groom's parents _____

Grandparents _____

Other guests _____

_____

_____

TO THE RECEPTION SITE

Name	Time and place of pickup	Who will drive
Bride and groom		
Bride's attendants		
Groom's attendants		
Bride's parents		
Groom's parents		
Grandparents		
Other guests		

FROM RECEPTION SITE TO HOTEL, HOME, ETC.

Name	Time of pickup	Destination	Who will drive
Bride and groom			
Bride's attendants			
Groom's attendants			
Bride's parents			
Groom's parents			
Grandparents			
Other guests			

Other Wheels and Deals

Limos aren't the only way to get from here to there. You could rent a classic or vintage car (a 1919 Model T, a chrome-heavy '57 Chevy, a Corvette or Mustang etcetera.). To find rental companies, look in the yellow pages under "Auto Renting and Leasing" or "Limousine Services" and ask about their vintage models. Or check out the antique-car rental advertisements in city and regional magazines. Other sources to help steer you in the right direction are your wedding consultant, the local chamber of commerce, or a historical society.

Want something a little more offbeat than your standard four-wheel automobile? You have options. How about making a grand entrance and exit in a helicopter, fire engine, boat or gondola, private plane, bicycle, or horse-drawn sleigh? Again the yellow pages can help, as can your wedding consultant and local chamber of commerce.

Getaway Get-ups for Your Car

Traditionally, male attendants sneak out of the reception to festoon the getaway car with "Just Married" decorations (if your attendants have made any hints about doing this, make sure they know exactly which car is yours beforehand). The custom of tying tin cans to the back of the getaway car and honking the horn is symbolic of the belief that the noise would ward off evil spirits. Here are other decorating ideas:

• Many party stores sell **ready-made "Just Married" kits.** Or do it yourself by affixing **balloons, signs, and crepe paper** to the car.

• **Use washable white shoe polish** to write on the car (to make sure it comes off easily, dab a small amount on an unobtrusive part of the car and wash it off).

• A classy choice is to have a florist decorate the car with **garlands of flowers,** using floral tapes and clips that won't harm the paint.

• **Do consider safety.** Don't obstruct the driver's view in front or back. Avoid glue, cellophane tape, shaving cream, or rubber cement, which may damage the car's finish.

Chapter 10:

YOUR WEDDING ATTIRE

Here is a head-to-toe guide to get you—and the rest of the wedding party—down the aisle in style.

IN SEARCH OF YOUR WEDDING DRESS

Shopping for your wedding gown is a singular experience. It can be exhilarating, emotional, and—believe it or not—easy. This expert advice will get you started.

Finding the Right Salon

• **Start shopping eight months to a year before your wedding.** That's not such a big lead time, considering that it takes three to four months for a dress to arrive after it's been ordered, plus time for alterations.

• **Visit reputable bridal salons**—but call before you go, to see if you need an appointment. Word of mouth is a good starting point. Also note the salons frequently mentioned in dress ads—they are authorized dealers of those manufacturers, which helps ensure on-time dress delivery.

• **Look for service.** A professional, trusted bridal salon will have workers who know everything about every dress and can tell you what styles will look best on you. It will also have expert seamstresses (on-site or as independent contractors) who will fit your dress perfectly.

Finding the Right Style

• **Look at bridal magazines** to see what styles appeal to you. Mark the pages and bring the magazines along when you shop.

• Ask yourself this question: **How do I picture myself walking down the aisle?** Will you have a formal church wedding? An intimate garden ceremony? Tell your bridal-salon salesperson as many facts about the wedding as possible—the style, its site, time of day, etc. The more information she has, the more she can help you find an appropriate dress.

• **Experiment.** Try different silhouettes—a straight sheath, a ball-gown skirt—and necklines to find the styles that look best on you. Keep an open mind—this is, after all, the shopping trip of a lifetime, so have fun. Maybe you never thought of wearing something off-the-shoulder until you saw how great it looked on you. If you've always dreamed of wearing your mother's dress, try it on and see what alterations need to be made. You might even consider shopping in a vintage store for an antique gown.

• **Be up-front about how much you can**

spend. There are gorgeous dresses in every price range—and you'll save yourself a lot of time and torment if you narrow your search to those that you can afford.

• **Dress details can be changed**—sleeves shortened, beading added—**but for a price.**

Finding the Perfect Fit

• **Most bridal salons carry sample dresses in sizes 8 to 12.** If you're not one of those sizes, your dress will have to be pinned and/or unzipped, so you can get a sense of how it will look.

• Once you've decided on a gown, **your measurements will be taken** and the salon will order your dress in the size closest to yours using the manufacturer's sizing chart.

• **Wedding gowns usually run small.** Don't be alarmed if you're normally a size 10 and the salon orders you a size 14.

• Just about every dress needs **alterations.** Ask for a price estimate when you order your dress (usually $150 to $300).

• Typically, you'll have **two fittings.**

Choosing a Headpiece

• Think about your **wedding-day hairstyle.**

Your bridal salon consultant will show you headpieces that complement it—as well as your dress.

• You may **choose your headpiece** when you first select your dress, before your first fitting, or at your first fitting.

• Once you've decided on the headpiece, your bridal salon consultant will help you **choose an appropriate veil length and style.**

Accessories

• Choose your **shoes** before or at the first fitting; heel height affects the length of your dress. A one-and-a-half-to-two-inch heel is comfortable for dancing.

• Bring your **lingerie** (while salons usually have bras and slips on hand for you to wear while you try on dresses, bring the exact underpinnings you'll use with your dress to your first fitting; they'll help determine how your dress is fit). If you've decided on gloves, jewelry, etc., bring those to the fitting as well.

When You Order

• Make sure the name of the manufacturer, the dress-style number, size, color, price, alteration fees, payment schedule, and delivery date are all included in a **signed, countersigned contract**—or marked on your receipt.

FIFTEEN QUESTIONS TO ASK WHEN SHOPPING FOR A WEDDING DRESS

1. Does the store have a good reputation with other brides I've talked to? With wedding consultants? Are there any consumer complaints registered with the local Better Business Bureau?

2. Do I feel comfortable with the salespeople and the atmosphere of the store? Do I *want* to shop here?

3. If I'm unsure of what I want in a dress, is the salesperson willing to work with me to find something in my price range that matches my taste and the formality of my wedding?

4. Is the salesperson paying attention to my comments and reactions to different dresses? Is she encouraging me to voice my opinion?

5. Is the salesperson being honest about how I look in each gown, not just saying what she thinks I want to hear?

6. Can I book all follow-up appointments with the same salesperson?

7. Will the store order a sample I saw in a bridal magazine if they don't have a sample in-house?

8. Does the store custom-design gowns? Update heirloom gowns? If I want a different neckline or sleeves on a gown, can it be ordered that way? Can it be altered? What will it cost?

9. Is the store able to sell me a headpiece too? Can it customize a headpiece or create one for me?

10. What are the alteration fees—and when are they due? Can I get these fees in writing? Does the salesperson have any cleaning tips for the fabric?

11. How much money am I required to put down as the initial deposit?

12. Can I place a rush order if necessary? How much will it cost?

13. Will the store deliver the dress to my home, or must I pick it up? When? Can I borrow the dress for my bridal portrait, return it to the store for safe storage, then pick it up right before my wedding day?

14. What other services and products does the store sell/provide (jewelry, bridesmaids' dresses, referrals to florists)?

15. If I order my bridesmaids' dresses through the same store, what is the procedure if my bridesmaids are out-of-towners and cannot come to the store for fittings?

WEDDING FASHIONS: WHAT STYLE IS APPROPRIATE FOR YOUR WEDDING?

Wedding fashions differ for very formal, formal, semiformal, and informal celebrations. The time of day and location are also a factor. While styles do change from year to year, the following guidelines will help you, your groom, your mothers, and the wedding party dress appropriately—and beautifully.

Bride

Very formal, evening. A floor-length gown of satin, lace, or peau de soie, with a cathedral train. Long, floor-length veil and headpiece with lace, beading, silk flowers, or fur. While the veil and the train are traditionally the same length, a new trend is to have them be of contrasting proportions—say an elbow-length veil with a sweep train. Opera-length gloves. Shoes to match. Bouquet or flower-trimmed prayer book.

Very formal, daytime. Traditional dress with a cathedral or extended chapel-length train of a nonglittery fabric, like lace, organza, silk satin or silk shantung, with embroidery of ribbons or pearls. The veil's length typically matches the length of the gown. The bodice is covered up and sleeves are generally long. Matching shoes and gloves are optional. The bouquet is elaborate.

Formal evening. Traditional floor-length dress with chapel, sweep, or detachable train. Veil length typically matches dress length. Same accessories as for a very formal wedding, but with a simpler bouquet.

Formal daytime. Traditional, floor-length dress of a nonglittery fabric like lace or organza with silk flowers. Chapel, sweep, or detachable train (dress may also be shorter, with a detachable train). The veil's length should complement the gown. A hat is also appropriate. Matching shoes, perhaps gloves. Less elaborate bouquet than at a formal evening wedding.

Semiformal. If evening, floor-length or short dress in chiffon, knit, or lace. White is not mandatory—consider neutrals and pastels as well. Train is optional. If daytime, short or long dress, usually without a train, in white or a pastel. Chapel or ballet veil with a long dress with chapel-length train; elbow- or shorter length veil, hat, headband, or flowers in hair with shorter dress. Shoes to match. Small bouquet or flower-trimmed prayer book.

Informal. An elegant knee-length suit or dress (in any color except black). Accessories should include a nosegay, wristlet, or corsage.

Mothers

Very formal, evening. Long evening or dinner dresses in shades that blend with, rather than match, bridesmaids' dresses. Complementary shoes, gloves, flowers.

Formal evening. Long or short dinner dresses or suits. Both mothers should dress in similar styles—e.g., both long or short dresses, etc. Gloves optional. Complementary flowers.

Formal daytime. Elegant knee-length dresses or suits (sans beading or glitter, which is too flashy for day). Hats optional, unless expected in a house of worship. Gloves optional. Complementary flowers.

Semiformal. If evening, stylish evening dresses or dinner suits; if daytime, elegant suits (not business suits, though) or dresses. Complementary accessories and flowers.

Informal. Elegant knee-length dresses or suits. Complementary accessories and flowers.

Groom and Men of the Wedding Party

Very formal, daytime/before six P.M. Gray or black cutaway coat, gray striped trousers, gray waistcoat, formal white shirt with wing collar. Striped ascot. Gray gloves optional.

Very formal, evening/after six P.M. White tie: black tailcoat, satin-trimmed trousers, white piqué waistcoat, stiff-front shirt with wing collar, French cuffs. Studs, white piqué bow tie. Top hats and white gloves optional.

Formal evening. Black tie: Black or charcoal gray dinner jacket with matching trousers, white pleated-front shirt with turned-down or wing-tip collar and French cuffs, a black vest or cummerbund. Black bow tie. White or ivory dinner jackets are a formal warm-weather option.

Formal daytime. Traditional: Black or gray stroller, striped trousers, gray waistcoat. White shirt with turned-down collar, striped tie. Gray gloves optional. Contemporary: Formal suit in light colors (or navy) for summer; darker shades for fall. Dress shirt, bow or necktie, and vest.

Semiformal. Traditional: If evening, dinner jackets, dress shirts, bow ties. If daytime, suits with plain white or striped shirts, neckties. Contemporary: For a summer wedding, white linen jackets with black or gray trousers.

Informal. Suits or blazers with trousers.

Bridesmaids

Very formal, evening. Floor-length dresses (for a daytime wedding, dresses are less evening-wearish). Complementary gloves, shoes, flowers, jewelry. Hair ornaments such as headbands or flowers.

Formal evening. Floor-length or shorter dresses. Gloves optional. Complementary hair ornaments, shoes, bouquets, jewelry.

Formal daytime. Floor-length or shorter dresses. Matching headpieces (flower wreaths, hats, etc.). Complementary flowers and shoes. Gloves optional.

Semiformal. Long or knee-length evening-wear dresses or suits (less elaborate if in the day). Gloves, hats, flowers for hair optional. Complementary shoes and jewelry. Small bouquets or wristlets.

Informal. Dresses or suits. Small bouquets, wristlets, corsages.

Definite Don'ts

• **Don't wear a glitzy, evening look**—say, a sexy sheath or halter gown—for a daytime wedding.

• **Don't dress your entire bridal party in** solid black or solid white (the latter is acceptable only if you're having a "snowball wedding," in which women of the wedding party dress in identical shades of white). Vary the palette with a vibrant sash or brightly colored gloves or shoes. A richly hued bouquet can also do the trick.

• **Don't have the groom dress exactly like all the other men in the wedding party.** Something—a slightly different bow tie, cummerbund, or vest—should distinguish him.

• **Don't ask the men in your wedding—including the groom—to wear tuxedos unless** your wedding will be formal *and* held in the late afternoon or evening (with the reception beginning after six P.M.).

BRIDAL SHOP TALK

Decisions, decisions. Satin or organza? Chapel train or ballet length? A fresh floral wreath or lacy Juliet cap? Once you speak the wedding-fashion language, shopping for the right look will be easy. Take this glossary with you on bridal salon visits.

Sheath, Detachable Train, Wedding Band Collar

Ball gown, Sweetheart neckline, Basque Waist

Silhouettes

Ballgown: Nipped, natural waist with a voluminous skirt.

Basque: Natural waist with a dropped V-shaped front.

Princess Line, Scoop-neck, off-the-shoulder

Bustier: Strapless with a sculpted bustline.

Empire: A small, scooped bodice with a high waist that falls just under the bustline and a slender or A-line skirt.

Princess/A-line: Skims the outline of the body. Has vertical seams flowing from the arms down to the hem of the flared skirt (there are no seams on the waist).

Sheath: Narrow, body-hugging style shaped at the waist.

Lengths and Trains

Floor length: Hem skims the floor.

High-low length: Hem falls slightly below the knee or midway between the knee and ankle in front, ankle- to train-length in back.

Knee length: Just covering the knees.

Midcalf/Ballet length: Hem swirls to the ankles. May also just reach midcalf.

Cathedral train: Tumbles $6\frac{1}{2}$ to $7\frac{1}{2}$ feet from waist.

Chapel train: The most popular kind of train—trails about $3\frac{1}{2}$ to $4\frac{1}{2}$ feet from waist.

Detachable train: Train that attaches with hooks and loops and can be removed. May be of any length.

Extended cathedral train/Monarch train: Flows 12 feet from waist.

Semicathedral train: Falls $4\frac{1}{2}$ to $5\frac{1}{2}$ feet from waist.

Sweep train: The shortest train, barely sweeping the floor.

Fabrics

Brocade: A heavy, jacquard-woven material with an interwoven, raised design.

Charmeuse: An even-textured, lightweight, satiny fabric that's glossy.

Chiffon: A sheer, delicate fabric with simple weaving. It's often silk or rayon, with a soft or stiff finish.

Crepe: A lightweight silk or rayon fabric with a subtle matte texture.

Embroidery: Threads or ribbon are sewn into the fabric in a decorative pattern.

Eyelet: Open-weave embroidery used for decoration.

Moiré: Silk taffeta material that's patterned with ripples. When light shines on the fabric, it glistens like water.

Empire waist, A-line, Bateau neckline

Organza: Sheer, crisply textured, almost translucent fabric.

Silk-faced satin: A glossy silk fabric with a lustrous sheen that has a matte finish on the back.

Silk shantung: A silk with a rough, nubby texture. Can be man-made.

Stretch tulle/stretch illusion: Same as tulle, with a bit of elastic for give.

Taffeta: A smooth, crisp, glossy fabric that has body.

Tulle: Tiny-meshed net of silk, cotton, or synthetics.

Laces

Alençon: A delicate, yet durable needlepoint lace, originating in Alençon, France. The lace designs are on sheer net.

Chantilly: Graceful floral sprays on a fine lace background, outlined with silk threads. Often has rounded, scalloped edges. This is the most delicate and lightweight of laces; from Chantilly, France.

Duchesse: A bobbin lace that often has raised flower patterns.

Guipure: A heavy lace with large designs placed over a thick net.

Schiffli: A machine-made, light floral embroidery.

Venise: A heavy lace with raised floral designs; first made in Venice.

Necklines

Boat or bateau: This neckline gently follows the curve of the collarbone. It's high in front and back, opening wide at the sides, ending in the shoulder seams.

High: A close-to-the-neck collar.

Jewel: A collarless, rounded neckline that hugs the base of the throat, just above the collarbone.

Off-the-shoulder: A graceful neckline that hovers above the bustline; sleeves start below the shoulders.

Portrait collar: A fold of fabric creates a collar and frames the face. Usually worn off-the-shoulder.

Queen Anne: Rises high at the nape (back) of the neck, then sculpts low to outline a bare yoke.

Square: Shaped like half of a square.

Sweetheart: Shaped like the top half of a heart.

Wedding band: Same as a high neckline.

Sleeves

Cap: Very short, fitted sleeves that cover shoulders and very tops of upper arms.

Fitted: Slim-fitting sleeves that taper in size as they reach the wrist.

Juliet: Sleeves puff slightly at shoulder, then gradually taper to the wrist.

Puff: Gathered into a gentle puff near the shoulders.

Three-quarter: Sleeves covering three-quarters of the arm—ending on the forearm, below the elbow and above the wrist.

T-shirt: Semifitted short sleeves cover the upper arm, much like a T-shirt.

Headpieces

Bow: Lace, ribbon, or fabric, sometimes trimmed with flowers and/or streamers, and often worn at the back of the head.

Floral wreath: A ring of fresh, silk, dried, or porcelain flowers. Rests atop the head or midforehead. May be adorned with ribbon, streamers, or tulle.

Garden hat: A wide-brimmed, face-framing

hat of straw, lace, satin, or other stiff material. May be decorated with ribbon, silk flowers, etc.

Headband: A wide, ornamental strip of fabric-covered flexible plastic that sits across the head from ear to ear. May be embellished with pearls, flowers, and other decorations.

Juliet cap: A small, rounded cap that fits snugly on the back of the head. It's often covered with lace or satin and decorated with pearls or semiprecious stones.

Pillbox: A small, flat-topped, round or oval hat worn on top of the head.

Profile comb: A comb decorated with flowers, lace, pearl sprays, etc. Sits on one side of head, or in back.

Tiara: Crownlike headpiece made of semiprecious metal and adorned with rhinestones, pearls, other gems. Sits high on top of the head.

Veils

Once worn to hide the bride from evil spirits, today a veil is a symbol of youth and purity.

Ballet or waltz length: Falls to the ankles.

Birdcage: Falls just below the chin and is gently shirred at the sides. Usually attached to hats.

Blusher: A loose veil worn forward over the face or back over the headpiece (after the ceremony). Often attached to a longer three-tiered veil or hat.

Cathedral length: Cascades 3⅓ yards from the headpiece.

Chapel length: Falls 2⅓ yards from the headpiece.

Fingertip: Veiling that gracefully touches the fingers.

Floor length: Brushes the floor.

Mantilla: A fine-laced veil, usually secured to an elegant comb; gently frames the face.

Pillbox

Bow

Juliet Cap

Mantilla

Tiara

Garden Hat

Ribbon-edged: Short layers of tulle are banded in icy pastels or white of grosgrain, satin, or velvet ribbon.

Shoulder length: Multilayers that brush the shoulders, usually worn with an informal, ankle-length dress or a style with too-pretty-to-hide details in back.

Tiered: Multilayered veils affixed together, which vary in length. (Most veils—which are traditionally the same length as the train—are made of a nylon material called illusion. These veils have small gathers of veiling at the crown of the headpiece, which create a waterfall effect. Floral wreaths often have flowing silk or satin ribbons called streamers, tied into sentimental love knots.)

WHICH DRESS FOR YOUR FIGURE?

The right dress details and silhouette will flatter your best features. Here are tips on finding the dress that looks best with your figure type:

Petite (five feet four inches and under). Look for a fitted waist, elongated lines, and delicate accents. Shop for dresses with neat seams or lace appliqués that run up and down lengthwise. Consider empire, princess, A-line, or sheath gowns with small collars and cuffs and trim at the neckline, to draw the eye up. Sleeves should be in proportion to arms (delicate puff sleeves). Avoid belts, sashes, or voluminous skirts that cut your body in half.

Tall (over five feet nine inches). Look for dresses with trim that wraps all around (a shirred bodice). Large collars, big cuffs, and raglan sleeves will also be in proportion to your body. Flared, tiered, or ball-gown skirts go well with long legs.

Small bust. A pleated bodice or one with lace appliqués, a bow front, and/or straps adds dimension. A halter or off-the-shoulder style, for example, accents the neck and shoulders, drawing attention away from the bust. High necklines and empire waist shapes are also good choices.

Big bust. Stick to V- and U-shaped necklines or high necklines with a keyhole yoke. Avoid cinched waists, empire styles that come up high under the bust, and fabrics that cling.

Hourglass. Ball gowns flatter the curves of an hourglass shape—a well-endowed bust and hips with a narrow waist. The V lines of a basque waist highlight the cinch of a narrow waist; a rounded, not-too-low, V neckline and vertical lace appliqués slim the bust.

Full figure. Consider a princess silhouette featuring vertical panels and no waist seam, or the straight, sleek lines of a chemise. Avoid body-hugging styles, such as sheaths. To minimize hips, a basque or dropped V waist works well. Look, too, for neckline details (sweetheart, jewel, or open necklines are the most flattering) such as beading or lace embroidery, which can bring the eye up toward your face, long or three-quarter sleeves to conceal arms, and a full skirt.

Slim. Choose fabrics that have texture and sheen, nap, or horizontal ribbing (some examples: velvet, satin, brocade). Other details that add pounds: Long puff sleeves, a cropped jacket, a sash in a color different from the rest of the dress, a wide sculpted collar.

Thick waist. Aim for the slimming effect of a lifted waistline, such as an empire style and an A-line skirt. Avoid tight waists, cummerbunds, and shaped midriffs in contrasting colors.

Wide hips. Choose an A-line or gently flared half-circle of a skirt. Balance your upper half with your lower one by choosing a broad collar or portrait neckline and a puff sleeve.

PRESERVING YOUR GOWN

Forget the plastic bag and padded hanger. To look great years down the line, your dress needs *serious* tender loving care.

1. Get to a dry cleaner as soon after your wedding as possible—and definitely do it within a month of your nuptials. The longer you wait, the likelier it is that stains will bond to the material.

2. When choosing a cleaner, ask how the dress will be handled. The gown should be turned inside out to protect beading and embroidery and, if possible, should be cleaned individually, not in combination with other gowns. Stains should be hand treated. Ask your cleaner about an anti-sugar-stain treatment, which removes sugar stains (like champagne) that are not dissolved by regular dry-cleaning fluid.

3. Request that the headpiece be packaged separately. The glue, rubber, and metal parts found in many headpieces can brown your dress. For the same reason, have bust and shoulder pads removed.

4. Choose a packing method that uses acid-free tissue paper and an acid-free box (acid burns fibers). If the box has a window, make sure it's acetate, which is acid-free, instead of plastic, which is not. A windowed box is often encased in another windowless box to prevent yellowing.

5. Ask to see the dress before it's packed. This is more likely if the dry cleaner does on-site preservation. Many, however, send the gowns out, receiving them back already packed. If it doesn't violate the terms of any preservation guarantee, put on gloves, unseal the box, inspect the dress, and then reseal it.

6. Store the dress in an area with a relatively even temperature and low humidity. Do not store it in a basement or an attic.

7. If you want to do it yourself, remove bust and shoulder pads and wrap (don't hang) your dry-cleaned dress in a clean, all-cotton sheet or piece of freshly washed muslin.

TOPPING IT ALL OFF: YOUR HEADPIECE

The headpiece is the crowning touch of your total bridal look. Purchase it when you first select your dress or at the time of your first fitting. Here are tips for buying one that flatters.

Consider your hairstyle. What comes first, the headpiece or the hairstyle? Ideally, the hairstyle. It's the most important factor in deciding what headpiece you'll wear. A blunt cut looks elegant with a simple headpiece, while a French twist works well with almost any style. If you like smooth, pulled-back hair, choose a small, exquisitely ornamented headpiece. Accent a chignon with a profile comb or pillbox. For short hair, try a Juliet cap or floral wreath. A lace mantilla or tiara will complement any hair length.

Choose a headpiece to go with your gown. Try them on together. If your gown is rich in detail, opt for an elaborate or richly detailed headpiece; with an understated dress, a simple headpiece is best. Your headpiece should be the same color as your gown and made of the same fabric or lace with, perhaps, matching beads, sequins, and crystals. Or opt for a jeweled tiara.

Don't forget to consider the style, site, and time of your wedding. For instance, a garden hat is most appropriate for an outdoor summer wedding held in the daytime.

Traditionally, veil length should be in keeping with the length of your gown. But a contemporary look popular today is pairing a shorter veil with a longer dress—or vice versa.

Consider wearing a fingertip veil with a chapel-length gown or a chapel-length veil with a gown that barely sweeps the floor. Just be sure that the veil complements the proportions of the dress. If your dress has back details that you don't want to hide, choose a veil that you can remove at the reception, or select a floral wreath or hat.

Fit the headpiece to your figure and face. The wide brim of a garden hat can flatter a long face. A round face looks elegant framed with a pillbox hat or high tiara. To de-emphasize a short, full figure, stay away from billowy veils. Instead, try a wreath.

Make sure it's comfortable. Can you turn your head? Bend over?

Reception hints: Ask your headpiece designer or bridal salon to attach the veil to the headpiece with snaps or hooks and loops, so it can be removed after the ceremony. Or switch to a smaller hair ornament for the reception—a satin bow, fresh or silk flowers. Be sure your hairstyle will work well with both your ceremony veil and reception ornament.

Heading Off Trouble: Headpiece Dos and Don'ts

Hats

• While hats are appropriate at most weddings—except very formal affairs—they do look best at an informal, outdoor wedding that takes place in the daytime.

• Avoid being photographed from above—the light bouncing off the hat's brim will create shadows on your face.

• Choose a hat with an upturned brim in a soft material. Guests—and the groom—shouldn't have to bend under it to kiss you.

• Try a lightweight material, like straw, for summer. Fur, satin, velvet, or felt looks great in winter.

• Choose a hat in the same shade of white or ivory as your wedding dress, or in a complementary color, such as pale blue, lavender, peach.

• If you're looking for a hat at a millinery shop (or somewhere other than where you bought your dress), bring your gown (or a picture of it) with you, to match everything precisely.

• Be hairstyle conscious. Hats work best with low chignons, loose and flowing styles, or sleek, short cuts.

Flowers

• Choose small, hardy flowers (roses, stephanotises, narcissus, orchids) for your hair, rather than large ones. They won't overwhelm your face or feel heavy. Plus, they're easy to affix.

• Avoid bulb flowers, such as daffodils, which tend to wilt quickly.

• Add a few greens—ivy, smilax, or ferns.

• Have your florist attach silk flowers to the ends of a fresh-flower hair wreath—they won't get damaged from the handling.

• If you're adding flowers to a comb, barrette, or headband *and* you're wearing a veil, attach the veiling to the headpiece first, position it on your head, and then add flowers.

• Have your florist individually wire and tape flowers, then anchor them onto the headpiece—they'll last longer that way.

• Make sure you're not allergic to the flowers beforehand—and that you like the scent.

Comb, Headband, Tiara

• Secure the headpiece with hairpins or combs (it'll be even more secure if you can have loops and combs sewn inside the headpiece).

• Tease hair slightly to create a better foundation for the pins.

• Before the wedding day, practice walking and dancing in the headpiece.

Headpiece Happenings: New Trends

• **Tiaras** encrusted with pearls and crystals or rhinestones. Colored gems—such as amber coupled with sapphire and cooled by amethyst—are also popular. Don't be afraid of metallics like gold or silver, either. Both work as a neutral when paired with white.

• **Colorful floral headpieces**—a blooming trend. A band of yellow silk daisies, for example (to which you attach tulle), can contrast beautifully with an all-white silhouette.

• **Chic rhinestone clips** with a cloud of veiling.

• **Pearl-encrusted combs and barrettes** mixed with ice-blue crystals.

• **Caps of fresh flowers,** with veiling attached to the bottom.

• Silk-flower **cloches.**

• Pearl-encrusted **bows.**

• **Faux-fur pillboxes** with tiered veiling.

• Filigree **bun rings.**

• Vintage fifties plastic daisy **bun crowns.**

• **Porcelain** headpieces.

• Bows of **baby carnations.**

• Fresh flower **headbands.**

SOLE MATES: CHOOSING YOUR SHOES

It used to be that basic white pumps were your only bridal-shoe option. Not anymore. In beautiful fabrics such as peau de soie, faille, damask, and brocade, bridal shoes are more in step with fashion than ever before. Far from plain, today's styles burst with subtle, stylish accents: ribbon, tiny rosette decorations, retro rhinestone buckles, lace accents, and pearl piping. Even dyeing techniques have improved, making color matching easier for you and your attendants. Some new style features to note: shoes with sexy straps, touches of reembroidered lace, a rounded toe, and a wider, more supportive two-inch heel—all the better to dance with. To help you get a leg up on selecting your wedding-day shoes, here are some shoe-shopping tips:

• **Start looking for shoes as soon as you've selected a gown;** this leaves time for comparison shopping and custom work.

• **Coordinate shoes with the style of your dress.** A sweeping train goes well with pumps; with a contemporary short dress, consider sleek, strappy slingbacks.

• **Don't neglect comfort.** You'll be standing, walking, and dancing for several hours.

• **Consider heel height.** A medium-height heel (one to two inches) offers elegance and support. Ballet-style slippers are lovely if you don't want to add height. Marrying outdoors? High or spiked heels might sink into the grass.

• **Shop for shoes in the afternoon,** when feet are likely to be largest (feet swell during the day).

• **Wear shoes around the house to break them in** a bit before the wedding. Scuff the bottoms to prevent slipping.

• **Take shoes to each dress fitting** to determine proper hem length.

FINISHING TOUCHES: LINGERIE AND ACCESSORIES

Wedding lingerie serves a dual purpose: It makes you look good *and* feel good. The right underpinnings can cinch your waist, lift your bust, and sculpt your curves. They can anchor your dress so everything stays where it should, all the while lending it shape and smoothness. And far from being a suit of armor, today's lingerie can be wedding-night appropriate, with lacy cutouts, satiny textures, and sexy good looks. Here is the lowdown on what you'll need to go underneath it all:

Slip or petticoat. This can usually be purchased at the same place you buy your wedding gown. The right petticoat can improve the shape and movement of your wedding dress. Petticoats—usually made of tulle or stiff netting, with high or low waists—come in various degrees of fullness. Choose a very layered petticoat for lots of fullness, a not-so-layered one for a less full skirt. Hoops work best with the fullest of skirts. A slim sheath needs a body-clinging liner with a side slit. If you choose a petticoat that shows underneath your dress, look for one decorated with lace or ribbons.

Bra. The proper bra can define and emphasize your bust or minimize it, if desired. There are a variety of styles available—demi-cup, underwire, push-up, cleavage-enhancing, etc. Have a salesperson help you obtain the proper fit. Note: Be sure no straps show. An off-the-shoulder dress needs a strapless bra; a sheer-back dress requires a low-back bra (or a bra built into the gown). Also, choose a bra that works with the fabric of your dress (don't choose a lacy bra for a clingy fabric—the pattern will show through). Bring your bra (or several, to see which one looks best) to your first dress fitting. Be sure your choice is comfortable—you'll be wearing it for hours.

Body-shaping lingerie. Depending on your gown and your figure, you might want to check out the new body-sculpting lingerie available today. Choose from those that nip your waist, lift your butt, or flatten your tummy.

Hosiery. All whites and ivories are not created equal. Take a close look at the color of your gown. Does it have a soft pink or peach hue? Then sheer pale pink or peach hose will look wonderful. A dress with gray tones? Try a silvery stocking. Look for interesting textures: Fishnet, lacy, or floral patterns, ankle or side embroidery.

Another option is satiny, glimmering fabric. For an ultrasexy look, forgo pantyhose altogether and choose thigh-high stockings with a lacy top. Whatever you choose, buy a spare pair, in case you get a run on your wedding day. And watch for figure-flattering hose to help define and tone the waist and legs.

Gloves. Gloves should reflect the formality and season of your wedding. Longest are most formal, but some skin should always show between the sleeve and the glove. That means opera-length gloves, reaching over the elbow, are paired only with sleeveless or strapless gowns. Short gloves are paired with any length sleeve (except those that cover the wrist). Choose lightweight fabric such as cotton with Lycra for warm weather, kid leather when it's cooler. Gloves can echo a design element of your gown—ruffles, pearls, beading, ribbons, rhinestones, or lace cuffs. When you order your gown, ask for extra beads and lace from your dress so you can customize your gloves.

Handbags. A wedding-day bag should be small and coordinate with your gown. Today there's everything from soft drawstrings to more constructed shapes in silk and satin. Choose one with decorative accents, such as bows or flowers, and perhaps in a soft color: pale pink, muted blue.

Jewelry. Pearls—from freshwater to baroque—are a classic. A gown with a sweetheart or portrait neckline looks stunning with a pearl choker. A simple bodice can be dressed up with a long strand of pearls, perhaps with a gold or diamond pendant. Equally timeless are diamonds—in the form of stud earrings, a bracelet, or a simple locket. When choosing earrings, keep in mind your hairstyle, headpiece, and face shape. An ornate veil looks best with simple, button, or stud earrings. Want to incorporate some heirloom jewelry into your wedding-day look? Pin your grandmother's brooch inside your petticoat.

Bibles and books. Some brides choose to carry a family Bible or prayer book, which can be covered with embroidered brocade or petit point, or decorated with ribbons and flowers. Tuck a rose or bookmark between the pages of your favorite passage. You might also carry a Victorian posy book of pressed flowers, or a leather-bound volume of treasured poems.

Garters. This is a place to have fun. Consider a garter appliquéd or embroidered with hearts, flowers, four-leaf clovers, or holiday motifs (pumpkins, flags, Christmas trees). Or personalize one by sewing on a piece of lace from your mother's wedding gown, a new blue ribbon, and a jewel borrowed from a friend. You'll fulfill the tradition of wearing something old, something new, something borrowed, something blue in one fell swoop. Place it on your left leg (it's closest to your heart), just above or below the knee.

BRIDESMAIDS' DRESSES

Your attendants' dresses should complement your wedding gown in style and degree of formality. The style of the dress is up to you, but most brides get some input from their attendants. Pick three or four dresses you like, and then let your attendants make the final selection. Keep their budgets, tastes, and figures in mind, and try to choose a dress that can be worn again (yes, they do exist).

Most often the bridesmaids wear identical dresses, while the honor attendant wears a dress differing slightly in color or style, but your attendants—especially if they're of diverse ages, skin colors, or body shapes—may appreciate a little variation. Some options: Choose dresses in the same color and fabric, but with varied styling, to complement different figures (an A-line to balance the proportions of a tall bridesmaid, a sheath to elongate a short one). Or select complementary—but not identical—shades of the same dress to flatter different skin colors (magenta, cherry, and raspberry can all look beautiful together). Can a bridal party look unified if some bridesmaids wear prints, others wear solids? Absolutely—as long as the dresses are in identical fabrics and styles. Or give your bridesmaids free rein to choose whatever dress they want, with the stipulation that they all stay in one color family. Coordinating—not matching—is the name of the game here. Whichever option you choose, stay with the same manufacturer to achieve a unified look.

Bridesmaids' dresses can be ordered from a bridal salon. Customarily, bridesmaids pay for their own attire, but it's fine for the bride to make a gift of some or all of the outfits if there are money problems that would keep friends and close family from participating.

When bridesmaids live out of town, the smartest option is to choose a dress from a national manufacturer that's available in your attendant's hometown bridal shop—she can check out the dress there. If you'd like to order all the dresses from one shop, however, have your attendant fill out a measurement form (for bust, hips, waist, height; it's usually available from the bridal shop) and mail it back to you. Have your out-of-town attendant(s) arrive a few days before the wedding, so any alterations can be made. Or have the store mail out the dress so she can use her own seamstress for alterations.

As for accessories, discuss with your attendants what you'd like them to wear. Specify the style and color of their shoes (they should color coordinate with the dresses and all be of the same heel height), hosiery, gloves, and jewelry (keep it understated). If you know of stores that carry exactly what you want, tell your bridesmaids where to head. If any special undergarments are needed—a strapless bra, a slip with a slit—let your bridesmaids know in advance.

Junior bridesmaids should wear more youthful

versions of the bridesmaids' dresses—for example, a gown with a higher neckline and lower-heeled shoes—or a more sophisticated version of the flower girl's dress. Flower girls wear long or short dresses that reflect the wedding's style and perhaps even echo some of the details of your dress—puff sleeves, pearl piping, etc. White dresses—a popular choice—can be sashed to match the bridesmaids' dresses. Flowers or ribbons in the hair are perfect accompaniments.

Mothers of the bride and groom wear dresses that reflect the formality of the wedding (long gowns for a formal evening wedding, tea length for the afternoon). Traditionally, the bride's mother selects her dress first, then describes it to the groom's mother, who finds one in a harmonizing style, length, and color (the dresses should never be identical). The mothers' dresses should also complement—but not match exactly—the color of the bridesmaids' dresses. Have your mothers avoid an all-black ensemble or one that's all white (it's a color reserved for the bride—unless you're having a snowball wedding, in which case the entire female wedding party dresses in white).

BRIDAL ATTIRE CHECKLIST

Wedding gown purchased at _J&B Bridals_

Address _____

Contact person _Jackie_

Phone _____ Fax _____

Description of dress _____

_____

Date ordered _____ Cost _____

Delivery date _____

Fitting dates: First fitting _____ Second fitting _____

Date dress will be ready _____

Deposit paid/date _____ Balance due/date _____

Headpiece/veil purchased at _____

Address _____

Contact person _____

Phone _____ Fax _____

Description of headpiece/veil _____

_____

Date ordered _____   Cost _____

Date headpiece/veil will be ready _____

Deposit paid/date _____   Balance due/date _____

Shoes purchased at _____

Address _____

Contact person _____

Phone _____   Fax _____

Description of shoes _____

_____

Date ordered _____   Cost _____

Additional costs for dyeing, etc. _____

Date shoes will be ready _____

Deposit paid/date _____   Balance due/date _____

OTHER ACCESSORIES

Item	Date purchased and where	Contact name	Other facts (alterations, added costs)
Petticoat/slip			
Bra			
Underwear			
Hosiery			
Gloves			
Earrings			
Necklace			
Bracelet			
Garter			
Other			

Maid/Matron of honor's dress purchased at _____

Address _____

Contact person _____

Phone _____ Fax _____

Description of dress _____

_____

Date ordered _____ Cost _____

Date dress will be ready _____

Fitting date(s) _____

Deposit paid/date _____ Balance due/date _____

Bridesmaid's dress purchased at _____

Address _____

Contact person _____

Phone _____ Fax _____

Description of dress _____

_____

Date ordered _____ Cost _____

Date dress will be ready _____

Fitting date(s) _____

Deposit paid/date _____ Balance due/date _____

Bridesmaid's dress purchased at _____

Address _____

Contact person _____

Phone _____ Fax _____

Description of dress _____

_____

Date ordered _____ Cost _____

Date dress will be ready _____

Fitting date(s) _____

Deposit paid/date _____   Balance due/date _____

Bridesmaid's dress purchased at _____

Address _____

Contact person _____

Phone _____   Fax _____

Description of dress _____

_____

Date ordered _____   Cost _____

Date dress will be ready _____

Fitting date(s) _____

Deposit paid/date _____   Balance due/date _____

Bridesmaid's dress purchased at _____

Address _____

Contact person _____

Phone _____   Fax _____

Description of dress _____

_____

Date ordered _____   Cost _____

Date dress will be ready _____

Fitting date(s) _____

Deposit paid/date _____   Balance due/date _____

Attendants' headpieces purchased at _____

Address _____

Contact person _____

Phone _____   Fax _____

Headpiece description _____

_____

Date ordered _____ Cost _____

Date headpieces will be ready _____

Deposit paid/date _____ Balance due/date _____

Attendants' shoes purchased at _____

Address _____

Contact person _____

Phone _____ Fax _____

Shoe description _____

_____

Date ordered _____ Cost _____

Additional costs for dyeing, etc. _____

Date shoes will be ready _____

Deposit paid/date _____ Balance due/date _____

ACCESSORIES FOR ATTENDANTS

Item	Date purchased and where	Contact name	Other facts (alterations, added costs)
Petticoat/slip			
Bra			
Hosiery			
Gloves			
Earrings			
Necklace			
Bracelet			
Other			

Junior bridesmaid's dress purchased at _____

Address _____

Contact person _____

Phone _____ Fax _____

Description of dress _____

Date ordered _____ Cost _____

Date dress will be ready _____

Additional information (fittings, if any; additional costs for alterations) _____

_____

Deposit paid/date _____ Balance due/date _____

Flower girl's dress purchased at _____

Address _____

Contact person _____

Phone _____ Fax _____

Description of dress _____

Date ordered _____ Cost _____

Date dress will be ready _____

Additional information (fittings, if any; additional costs for alterations) _____

_____

Deposit paid/date _____ Balance due/date _____

Hair decoration (description, place purchased, contact name) _____

_____

Shoes (description, place purchased, contact name) _____

_____

Other accessories _____

_____

THE MAN OF THE HOUR: CHOOSING MEN'S FORMALWEAR

You're not the only one who wants to turn some heads on your wedding day. Your groom does, too. What should he wear? That depends on the time and formality of your wedding. (See Wedding Fashions chart.) For some ideas, read this section and discuss his fashion preferences.

Note one thing: Wedding formalwear doesn't automatically mean black-tie, particularly if the reception begins before six P.M. A groom can look dashing any time of the day or night if he knows what's appropriate for when. The professionals at a formalwear shop can guide him in the right direction. Your groom might ask about single-breasted versus double-breasted jackets; shawl, peaked, and notch collars; bow ties versus ascots versus neckties; and whether to wear a vest or a cummerbund. He should also consider cuff links, studs, pocket squares, and suspenders (but *not* if he's also wearing a cummerbund). And with plenty of patterns to choose from—vests with floral embroidery or jacquards, pin-dot bow ties, acummerbunds in tiny weaves—your groom can let his personality shine through. These accessories can distinguish him and his best man from the rest of the bridal party (they may wear a paisley vest and bow tie, while the rest of the bridal party wears a solid color). The groom may differentiate himself from the best man by choosing to wear a cummerbund without the standard vest, wearing gemstone studs, and of course, wearing a distinctive boutonniere.

Fathers of the bride and groom usually wear formal attire that matches the groom's and his attendants'. The bride's father traditionally escorts the bride down the aisle, which makes him a member of the wedding party. The groom's father may also walk down the aisle, and will certainly be seated in a position of honor.

Ring bearers might wear cotton or wool Eton suits with short pants and knee socks. For very formal weddings, pantaloons in silk or velvet might be topped with a silk blouse. An older boy usually wears a scaled-down version of the men's formalwear.

In most cases, grooms and attendants rent their formalwear. Here are some tips.

Selection

• **A men's formalwear store** is usually the best place to rent wedding attire. These shops have **large selections** and can do **quick alterations.**

• Looking for a particular suit, perhaps one spotted in a bridal magazine or on the Internet (some formalwear manufacturers are now on-line)? **If the store doesn't have it in stock, it can probably be ordered.** Note that accessories such as a vest or cummerbund, suspenders, shirt, studs, cuff links, ties, even shoes (which should be a black tuxedo pump, suede or quilted slipper shoe, or a soft, matte-finish slip-on or lace-up—never your regular nine-to-five business shoe), may or may not be included in the package price. Ask.

• Your groom and his attendants should be **measured for formalwear three months before your wedding.** Out-of-towners can visit their own local formalwear shop, then send their measurements to the groom (to ensure that everyone gets exactly the same ensemble, it's best to order everything from one store). Ask the out-of-town men of the wedding party to arrive a few days before your big day to allow time for alterations.

Size

• Chances are the formalwear will need alterations—make sure the store has **a tailor on the premises or has an affiliation with one nearby.**

• **What to look for as far as fit is concerned?** Shirts should hug the neck. Pants should reach the shoes. Waistbands are usually adjustable. Jackets should fit snugly around the shoulders (no arm bulges), with some room at the waist. Vents in the back or on the sides should lie smooth. Jacket sleeves should end at the wrist bone and show from one-quarter to one-half inch of shirt cuff.

Picking Up the Suit

• In general, suits can be **picked up two to three days in advance of the wedding.**

• **Do a quality check:** Make sure there are no stains, fabric snags, or cigarette burns. Jackets should have the same number of buttons on each sleeve. Everything should be tried on.

• **A tailor can perform minor alterations.** Some stores have an **industrial hemmer,** which can adjust a pant leg in minutes.

Returning the Suit

• The **best man usually returns the groom's and the ushers' suits** the first working day after the wedding. It should be done promptly to avoid late charges.

• Food and beverage stains can usually be dry cleaned, but you will be expected to pay extra fees for **clothes with more serious damage.**

GROOM'S GLOSSARY

Formalwear language seems like a foreign one—until you know how to translate. Here's a dictionary.

Ascot. A neck scarf worn around the neck and wrapped under the chin; secured with a stickpin or tie tack and winged collars.

Boutonniere. Flowers, which coordinate with the bride's bouquet, worn on the left lapel by men in wedding party, including fathers.

Bow tie. Made of a formal fabric and worn with tuxedos or dinner jackets. As the name implies, looks like a bow.

Cummerbund. A pleated sash worn to cover the waistband (a cummerbund is worn

Very Formal Evening (After 6 P.M.) (White Tie and Tails)

Formal Evening Tuxedo (After 6 P.M.) (Black tie)

Formal Daytime Stroller (with Four-In-Hand Tie)

Very Formal Daytime Cutaway (Morning Coat)

instead of a vest or suspenders—it's not worn in combination). Pleats are worn facing up. May coordinate with the bow tie.

Cutaway (or morning coat). The daytime equivalent of a coat with tails. It's black or gray, with a single button at the waist and one broad tail in back. It's worn with striped trousers, a winged-collar shirt, and an ascot.

Dinner jacket. A white, ivory, or novelty-patterned jacket cut like a tuxedo jacket. Worn with formal black trousers (with a satin side stripe), it's a debonair alternative to the tuxedo, appropriate during warmer months.

Double breasted. Two rows of buttons run vertically down the jacket to close it.

French cuffs. Roll-back shirt cuffs fastened with cuff links.

Four-in-hand tie. A knotted tie similar to a business tie, but in a more formal fabric.

Laydown collar. A turned-down collar, similar to business-shirt collar, but in a formal fabric.

Notched lapel. A lapel with a triangular cut pointing inward.

Peaked lapel. A lapel with a cut pointing upward.

Pocket square. A small, visible pocket hand-

kerchief of linen, silk, or another dressy fabric to match or complement tie and cummerbund.

Shawl. The lapel is uninterrupted by cuts; instead, it is rounded.

Single breasted. One strip of buttons runs vertically down the jacket to close it.

Stroller (or walking coat). Black or gray coat cut slightly longer than a jacket and worn when the wedding reception will be starting before six P.M. It's paired with striped trousers, a laydown-collar shirt, and a four-in-hand tie.

Studs and cuff links. Worn in place of buttons on a formal shirt. They can be gold or silver-toned mother-of-pearl, or made of precious metals, and can be of various designs.

Suspenders. Also called braces. Worn instead of a cummerbund or vest.

Tails/full dress. A jacket that is short in front, with two tails unfolding in the back. It's worn with a white shirt and vest.

Tuxedo/black tie. Worn for formal weddings when the reception starts after six P.M. The black or gray jacket may be single or double breasted, with shawl, peak, or notch lapels in satin or grosgrain. It is worn with matching formal trousers, bow tie, and vest or cummerbund.

Vest/waistcoat. Worn to cover the trouser waistband. May match or contrast the fabric of the jacket. Worn in place of a cummerbund or suspenders.

White tie. The most formal menswear style, consisting of a black coat with tails, matching trousers, a tie and vest in white piqué, and a winged-collar shirt with a stiff, white piqué front.

Winged collar. The most formal dress shirt, consisting of a stand-up band collar with folded-down tips. The front panels of a winged-collar shirt may be pleated.

GROOM'S, USHERS', AND FATHERS' WEDDING CLOTHES CHECKLIST

Men's formalwear store _____

Address _____

Contact person _____

Phone _____ Fax _____

Description of all formalwear, including vests, cuff links, etc. _____

_____

_____

Date ordered_____ Fitting date _____

Date ready_____ Time _____

Date must be returned by _____

Who will return _____

GROOM

Item	Size	Cost
Trousers		
Shirt		
Coat/jacket		
Vest/cummerbund/suspenders		
Neckwear		
Other accessories (studs, pocket squares, etc.)		

TOTAL COST$ _____

BEST MAN

Item	Size	Cost
Trousers _____		
Shirt _____		
Coat/jacket _____		
Vest/cummerbund/suspenders _____		
Neckwear _____		
Other accessories (studs, pocket squares, etc.) _____		

TOTAL COST$ _____

USHER

Item	Size	Cost
Trousers _____		
Shirt _____		
Coat/jacket _____		
Vest/cummerbund/suspenders _____		
Neckwear _____		
Other accessories (studs, pocket squares, etc.) _____		

TOTAL COST$ _____

USHER

Item	Size	Cost
Trousers _____		
Shirt _____		
Coat/jacket _____		
Vest/cummerbund/suspenders _____		
Neckwear _____		
Other accessories (studs, pocket squares, etc.) _____		

TOTAL COST$ _____

USHER

Item	Size	Cost
Trousers		
Shirt		
Coat/jacket		
Vest/cummerbund/suspenders		
Neckwear		
Other accessories (studs, pocket squares, etc.)		

TOTAL COST$ _____

BRIDE'S FATHER

Item	Size	Cost
Trousers		
Shirt		
Coat/jacket		
Vest/cummerbund/suspenders		
Neckwear		
Other accessories (studs, pocket squares, etc.)		

TOTAL COST$ _____

GROOM'S FATHER

Item	Size	Cost
Trousers		
Shirt		
Coat/jacket		
Vest/cummerbund/suspenders		
Neckwear		
Other accessories (studs, pocket squares, etc.)		

TOTAL COST$ _____

TOTAL COST OF GROOM'S, USHERS' AND FATHERS' CLOTHES $ _____

Chapter 11:

BRIDAL BEAUTY

FINDING YOUR WEDDING-DAY LOOK

Last-minute jitters, nonstop kisses, and the occasional tear would put any woman's looks to the test. Now consider that someone is capturing it all on film. Keeping yourself pulled together, from your vows to the getaway, calls for the right makeup, the right hairstyle, and a few professional tricks. Here are some beauty basics.

Hair

1. When you start planning your wedding, start planning what your hairstyle will be. You'll need time to grow out a style or get hair in tip-top condition. Time also gives you freedom to experiment with color, coifs, cuts.

2. Go for a hair consultation (usually free) as soon as possible after you choose your dress and headpiece (your hairstyle should complement the dress, not overpower it). Ask friends to recommend stylists they like. Tell your stylist what the dress looks like, what sort of hairstyles you like, how you want your headpiece to sit on your head (bring it if possible), how much time you want to put into doing your hair on your wedding day—or whether you'll be hiring someone to do it for you.

3. Have your stylist photograph you in each hairstyle. Bring the photos home and ask for some objective opinions.

4. Test a new color at least six weeks before your wedding (you can get a touch-up two weeks before). Try a new haircut or perm at least six months before your wedding so if you don't like it, it has time to grow out.

5. If you're thinking about coloring your hair, get familiar with the options. Consult with your colorist to determine the best color technique for your hair.

6. Keep hair in great condition by treating it gently. Use products made specifically for your hair type.

7. When you condition—which you should do after every shampoo—concentrate the conditioner where it's needed most (usually from midway down on hair shaft to the ends).

8. If hair is ultrabrittle, consider cutting it. Short, healthy hair looks better than a long, damaged mane.

9. Keep blow-drying to a minimum (especially if your hair is color-treated, as the heat will strip hair of color). When you do blow-dry, use a low setting, and stop before hair is bone-dry. Try new pre-blow-drying treatments.

10. Don't think of damage as irreversible. Color can be corrected; hair can be conditioned.

11. If you've opted to color your hair, keep it in great condition by using a shampoo and conditioner made for color-treated hair.

12. A wedding-day don't: Don't deep condition hair on your wedding day—it will make hair feel too heavy.

Skin

1. Well before your wedding date (at least six months before) see a dermatologist about any existing skin problems. If you're planning a honeymoon in a hot destination, ask about skin care for the tropics. It's also a good idea to make other doctors' appointments—the dentist for a cleaning, the gynecologist and internist for checkups.

2. In the morning and at night, clean skin with a gentle soap or cleanser that's tailored to your skin type (dry, oily, combination). Next, use toner to tighten pores, a moisturizer to keep skin supple.

3. Keep your skin protected. Wear makeup, a moisturizer, or sunscreen that contains an SPF of at least 15.

4. Stress is inevitable—and your skin is bound to show it. Try to eat right, exercise, get plenty of sleep, and drink lots of water.

5. If you want to get a facial before your wedding, do it four to six weeks before the big day. This will give your skin time to clear up from any redness or breakouts. Ideally, get your first facial at least a year before your wedding, then follow up with facials every two months.

6. Exfoliate and moisturize—from head to toe—regularly. If your dress will expose your back, consider heading to the salon for a back facial.

7. The night before your wedding, get plenty of sleep. And stay away from alcohol (it can cause puffiness) and too much caffeine.

Nails

1. You can bet everyone will want to see the ring. Make sure your nails are looking great. Start going for regular manicures about two months before the wedding to get nails strong and healthy. Definitely get a manicure right before your wedding day.

2. Polish colors go in and out of style. Always appropriate are the pale, translucent shades of blush, rose and peach.

3. At the salon, look for a state license, non-communal nail files, disinfected instruments, and individually wrapped hand towels.

4. A paraffin (warm wax) treatment is the ultimate skin softener for hands and feet.

5. Get ready for a toe-baring honeymoon with a pedicure and reflexology treatment.

Makeup

1. Schedule a makeup lesson to get a pro's tips on how to enhance your look. Do this about three months before your wedding, so you have plenty of time to practice and perfect the look. If you like the makeup artist's work, you might consider hiring him or her to do your wedding-day makeup, for a professional look.

2. Wedding-day makeup should look natural. Keep colors neutral—browns and grays—and always blend well.

3. Don't apply makeup more than two and a half hours before you leave for the ceremony, to keep it looking fresh.

4. Create a canvas for your face. Smooth on a foundation that matches your skin tone as closely as possible (a damp cosmetic sponge can make for easier application). Blend on concealer (which should be one shade lighter than skin tone) only where you need it, usually under the eyes or to cover blemishes. Follow with powder to set makeup.

5. Unless your skin is very oily, choose products that have a dewy rather than matte finish. They'll add a glow to your skin—and still last all day.

6. Choose one feature to highlight—such as your lips or your eyes. Keep everything else subtle.

7. Definitely opt for waterproof mascara. Few brides can make it down the aisle without shedding a tear or two.

8. Don't line under eyes—it's bound to smudge. On upper lids, use brown or black eye shadow applied with a very thin brush instead of liner. You'll get a soft, flattering, indefinite line.

9. Groom brows by tweezing or waxing any strays (a professional at a salon can do the job for you). One caveat: Make sure you remove hairs at least a day before (preferably a few days before) your wedding, to allow for any redness to subside. The same applies to removing hair from the legs, arms, bikini line, and face.

10. For a defined look that's not too heavy, brush groomed brows with an appropriate eye shadow shade, such as honey brown.

11. Prepare an even surface for eye shadow. Blend foundation or concealer on lids, then dust with powder. Lightly dust on a pale, muted shadow from lashes to brow bone. Apply a deeper shade to eye crease. Aim for a glazing of the eyelid, not a dramatic swath of color.

12. Prep lips with a light dusting of powder. Then outline with a nude lip pencil—you'll get definition without an obvious line.

13. Use a brush to apply a muted lip color in the pink, coral, or brown families. Stay away from glossy products (they have minimal staying power) and very matte ones (they make lips look dry). The best finish is semimatte.

14. Use blush in the natural, tawny tone that your cheeks turn whenever you've been exercising. Apply with a fluffy brush; dust it lightly over the apples of your cheeks, extending lightly out to the temples.

15. Whenever you apply makeup, go lightly. A hint of color is enough. And be sure to blend thoroughly so there are no visible lines where color begins and ends.

16. Buy the necessary cosmetics and sunscreen for your honeymoon—your skin will have different needs in different climates.

PICTURE IT: MAKEUP FOR THE CAMERA

Color Photos

1. Wear makeup in soft, earthy, neutral shades, such as browns, corals, and gray. They'll look the most natural (color film tends to make bold shades look garish).

2. Avoid frosted shadows, which reflect light.

3. Apply powder—as often as you need to.

4. Use makeup sparingly. You want your wedding-day makeup to look polished—not poured on.

Black-and-White Photos

1. Use a minimal amount of blush—to avoid blotchiness.

2. Define upper lashes with mascara, lids with liner or shadow, brows with brow color.

3. Use matte shades on eyes (frosted will make them look puffy).

4. Opt for red lipstick to make lips stand out (but don't go *too* red; it will photograph black).

5. Blend makeup carefully and thoroughly so there are no lines of demarcation.

6. Buy a roll of black-and-white film, do your makeup, and have a friend take some photos of you wearing a white shirt. Review and adjust your look accordingly.

WEDDING-DAY BEAUTY TO-DO LIST

1. Treat yourself to some soothing aromatherapy. Add scented oils to warm bath water and soak in the tub.

2. Moisturize all over. Use a clear deodorant to avoid antiperspirant marks on your gown.

3. Relax. Lie down for thirty minutes or so. Even if you don't sleep, you'll feel refreshed.

4. Snack on a light meal. Then brush your teeth.

5. Mist on fragrance.

6. Style your hair—or have a professional do it for you.

7. Secure headpiece to hair.

8. Apply makeup. Use the techniques you've practiced, or have your makeup artist create the look you've agreed upon. Now is not the time for experimenting.

9. Step into your wedding dress (petticoat should be placed inside the dress), then into your shoes. Adjust headpiece. Add jewelry.

10. Take one final look. If you need to, touch up makeup, smooth your hair, etc.

BEAUTY 911: QUICK FIXES FOR WEDDING-DAY BEAUTY EMERGENCIES

Puffy Eyes

• Place a cloth soaked in cool, chamomile tea on eyes. Leave the compress on for ten minutes, freshening it every one to two minutes.

• Also try grated raw potatoes wrapped in gauze and placed over eyes (the potato enzymes work to reduce puffiness).

• Think ahead and purchase a skin care product for puffy eyes.

• Despite the great temptation, do not apply ice to eyes—it can cause capillaries to break.

Broken Nail

• Re-adhere the nail with a liquid nail adhesive applied with an orange stick (in a pinch, clear tape will do).

• Smooth the surface with a nail buffer.

• Dot polish in the shade that you're wearing over the adhesive, then repaint the entire nail.

• File the nail to smooth out the edges, but be careful not to scratch the polish (try filing underneath the nail).

Blemish

• Don't squeeze the pimple or try to dry it out—you'll just create more redness or hard-to-conceal flakiness.

• Try camouflaging. With your fingertip, dab on a mint-green concealer or blemish cream over the pimple (it will blend with your skin tone to mask the redness). With a fresh cosmetic sponge, smooth foundation over and around the blemish. Dust on translucent powder.

Frizzy Hair

• Combat humidity with styling products. Comb a texturizing lotion through wet hair (don't brush while blow-drying—it will remove the product).

• When hair is almost dry, add body by applying volumizing spray to roots.

• As a finishing touch, spritz hair with hairspray underneath the hair and on your hairbrush to give the style hold without making hair look heavy.

BEAUTY IN THE BAG: THIRTEEN BEAUTY ESSENTIALS TO CARRY WITH YOU ON YOUR WEDDING DAY

1. Translucent compact powder to reduce shine
2. Lipstick and lip brush
3. Eyebrow brush
4. Concealer
5. Blotting tissues
6. Regular tissues
7. Cotton swabs, to fix mascara or shadow that's smudged
8. Brush or comb
9. Hairpins
10. Eye drops
11. Breath spray
12. Purse-size fragrance spray
13. Hairspray

Chapter 12:

FIGURING YOUR WEDDING BUDGET

The expense of the wedding is the number one issue engaged couples fight about. And who can blame them? Hosting a traditional wedding can be an expensive proposition, and spending wisely takes effort and research. How much will your wedding cost? That depends on when and where you have it, how many people you invite, your geographic location, and more. Discuss with your fiancé and families how much money you have to put toward your wedding, then shop around for the best value for your dollar. You may be able to scrimp on the things that are less important to you and splurge on those that are really a priority. If you have a computer and want more help managing your wedding budget, consult a financial software program.

WEDDING BUDGET CHART

	Estimated Costs	Actual Costs	Deposit Paid	Balance Due	Who Pays*
Stationery	300				
Invitations					
Announcements	n/A				
Notepaper/Thank-you notes					
Reception napkins	n/A				
Cake boxes	n/A				
Other (at-home cards Stamps	100				
maps, programs, matches)					
Total					
Ceremony					
Site rental fee					
Officiant fee	I				
Other fees (sexton, cantor)					
Musicians (organist, soloist)					
Total					
Wedding consultant/party planner	n/A				
Total					

*bride's family, groom's family, couple

	Estimated Costs	Actual Costs	Deposit Paid	Balance Due	Who Pays*
Reception					
Rental for hall, club, hotel					
Food					
Liquor					
Bartenders					
Equipment (tent, linens, etc.)					
Wedding cake					
Music					
Gratuities					
Total					
Flowers					
For wedding	500				
Ceremony site decoration					
Bride's bouquet					
Attendants' flowers					
Corsages for mothers					
Boutonnieres					
For reception					
Buffet decorations					
Table centerpieces					
Cake table					
Other (bandstand, receiving line)					
Total					
Photography					
Formal engagement portrait					
Formal wedding portrait					
Candids at wedding					
Album					
Proofs					
Videotape	N/A				
Single-use cameras and developing					
Other (extra prints, albums, or tapes)					
Total					

*bride's family, groom's family, couple

	Estimated Costs	Actual Costs	Deposit Paid	Balance Due	Who Pays*
Bride's outfit					
Dress	1000	6			
Headpiece	100				
Accessories (slip, shoes, hosiery)	300				
Trousseau or honeymoon clothes					
Total					
Groom's attire					
Formalwear	200				
Honeymoon clothes					
Total					
Gifts					
Attendants	100				
Groom (optional)	100				
Bride (optional)	100				
Rings	1000				
Friends who hosted parties, helped					
Parents	100				
Total					
Transportation					
Limousines	NA				
Chauffeur tip	n/A				
Parking	n/A				
Gas for friends who drive	n/A				
Car wash for friends who drive	n/A				
Total	0				
Extras					
Favors					
Hotel accommodations (guests, attendants)					
Other					
Total					
Honeymoon					
Total	7000				

*bride's family, groom's family, couple

	Estimated Costs	Actual Costs	Deposit Paid	Balance Due	Who Pays*
Parties					
Engagement (if families hosting)	N/A				
Bridesmaids'					
Bachelor's (if groom hosting)					
Rehearsal dinner					
Weekend-wedding parties (if couple, families hosting)	N/A				
Total					
TOTAL WEDDING COSTS	$ _____				

*bride's family, groom's family, couple

WEDDING EXPENSES: WHO PAYS FOR WHAT

Today, there are no hard-and-fast rules about who foots which bill. You and your groom may choose to pay for the entire wedding yourselves, allow your parents to pay for it, or divvy up the cost among you and your fiancé, your parents, and his parents. If you want to follow tradition, however, use the following guidelines:

• **Stationery.** Virtually all paper needs—from the wedding invitations to the announcements, wedding programs, and thank-you notes—are paid for by the bride and her family. The groom and his family foot the bill for *his* thank-you notes and any personalized stationery he orders.

• **Parties.** Starting with the first engagement party, which the bride's family traditionally hosts, the bride and her family pay for an array of wedding-related parties, including the bridesmaids' luncheon, the reception, and any pre- or post-wedding parties for out-of-town guests who travel in for the wedding. If the groom's family decides to host an engagement party, they take on those costs, as well as the expenses for the rehearsal dinner.

• **Clothes.** The bride and her family pay for the complete bridal ensemble, from undergarments to shoes to the veil to the bridal trousseau. They also absorb the cost of the bride's mother's outfit and the bride's father's formalwear. The groom's family pays for his formalwear, as well as the mother-of-the-groom's outfit and the groom's father's formalwear.

• **Flowers.** Excluding her own bouquet, corsages for the mothers, and boutonnieres for the men, which are traditionally paid for by the groom and his family, the bride and her family pay all flower costs. That includes the cost of floral arrangements for the church/synagogue, table centerpieces, attendants' bouquets, flower girl baskets, pew markers, cake flowers, and whatever else may be needed.

• **Photos.** The bride and her family pay for it all—from the engagement photos to the wedding pictures, to the wedding video.

• **Ceremony.** The bride and her family take on the expenses for renting the church/synagogue/house of worship, hiring musicians, and securing the aisle runner, marquee, or chuppah.

The groom and his family pay the officiant's fee and the cost of getting the marriage license.

• **Transportation.** Limo fees for the bridal party are traditionally paid for by the bride's family. His side pays for transportation to the airport or hotel after the wedding.

• **Rings.** She pays for his wedding ring, he pays for hers.

• **Reception.** The cost of the wedding reception, including food, drinks, music, other entertainment, and decorations, traditionally falls to the bride and her family.

• **Honeymoon.** The groom and his family take care of it all.

• **Gifts.** The bride's gift to the groom and the presents for her attendants are paid for by the bride and her family. His side picks up the tab for the groom's gift to the bride, as well as gifts to the ushers.

Traditionally, What You Won't Have to Pay For

• Your own bridal shower or bachelorette party. Likewise, grooms are usually treated to the bachelor party.

• It's customary for the bridesmaids to pay for their own attire, the ushers their own formalwear. However, if you pick out a dress you know many of your bridesmaids can't afford, you may offer to supplement their cost.

• Travel expenses for the bridal party are the responsibility of the bridal party. But to cut down on cost, you may offer to put them up at the home of a friend or relative—or even pay for their hotel rooms, budget allowing.

Some Contemporary Cost-Sharing Options

Costs can be divided up however you see fit. Some possibilities include:

• **Parties.** Reverse roles: Let the bride's family pay for the rehearsal dinner, and the groom's family can pick up the tab for an out-of-towners' barbecue or a post-wedding-day brunch; both families contribute to the reception.

• **Flowers.** The bride's family may take on the costs of all the ceremony flowers, as well as the expenses for her bouquet, the mothers' corsages, and the men's boutonnieres. The groom's family may decide to pay for all reception flowers.

• **Photos.** The costs could be split—one family paying for the wedding photographs, the other covering the cost of the videographer.

• **Ceremony.** Maybe your groom and his family would like to pay for the chuppah or aisle runner.

• **Transportation.** The groom's family may wish to pay the limousine costs for the bridal party.

• **Rings.** As a welcoming gesture, perhaps his family can present you with an heirloom wedding ring—one worn by his grandmother or great-grandmother, for instance. You might want to do the same with a ring passed through your family.

• **Reception.** There are plenty of cost-sharing options here: Maybe you could pay for the band, and he could pay for the cocktail hour. You pay for the food; he pays for the liquor, etc.

CUTTING COSTS: A DREAM WEDDING ON A BUDGET

Even a small, simple wedding can be expensive. But if you're savvy—and resourceful—you can still get the wedding you want without breaking the bank. Consider these money-saving strategies that your guests will never notice—but your wallet certainly will.

Sites

• **Schedule your wedding for a Friday or Sunday,** rather than a Saturday, the most popular day for weddings. Many reception sites will have greater availability, offer lower rates, and be willing to work within your budget.

• **Think creatively when choosing your site.** Some off-beat places, such as university halls, publicly owned buildings, a business-district restaurant on a weekend, may be more affordable.

• **Shop around for the best prices on rental equipment** and borrow from friends whenever possible.

Reception

• **Limit the number of guests.** Be ruthless. Think twice before inviting all your coworkers and friends you've lost touch with.

• **Book your reception as far in advance as possible**—more than a year ahead if feasible. You may be able to negotiate a better price.

• **Consider an off-peak wedding month** (November through April) and **an off-peak time of day** (morning versus evening) to have your ceremony and reception.

• **Have the reception in the same spot where you get married.** You'll have only one rental fee and can move ceremony flowers to the reception area more easily.

• **Pick a fully furnished reception site,** rather than one where you have to rent chairs, tables, dishes, etc.

• **Limit the reception to three hours** instead of the usual four.

Food

• **Compare prices.** Chicken is generally less expensive than beef or veal; broccoli is more reasonable than asparagus.

• **Serve an expensive food,** such as filet mignon, **as an hors d'oeuvre.**

• **Serve foods that are in season.**

• **Cut down on service personnel** (who are paid by the hour) by having stationary appetizers (wheels of cheese, platter of crudités, olives, breads) rather than passed hors d'oeuvres.

• Chew on this: Forgo the seated dinner and **consider having an easier-on-the-wallet reception featuring hors d'oeuvres, a pasta bar, and cake.**

• **Go ethnic.** A menu featuring Chinese or Mexican foods is generally less expensive than continental fare.

• **Think theme.** Depending on what you serve, a Cape Cod clambake or a Texas chilifest might be less costly than a traditional filet mignon dinner reception.

• **Eliminate the appetizer course if hors d'oeuvres will be served first.** Wedding cake can suffice for dessert.

• **Prioritize.** Would you prefer a lavish buffet and fewer guests, or a giant (less expensive) cocktail reception?

• **Ask friends and family known for their culinary ability to lend a hand** for an informal wedding.

• **Consider a wedding breakfast or brunch** to save on food costs and labor. Serve pastries, muffins, fruits, omelettes. Offer Bloody Marys and mimosas to cut down on liquor expenses.

• Rather than a dinner, **have a post-dinner reception** (8:30 or 9:00 P.M.) with hors d'oeuvres, cake, champagne.

• **Have an afternoon English tea reception.** Serve a sampling of teas, small finger sandwiches, scones, and jams.

• **Order a small, beautifully decorated wedding cake for display.** Behind the scenes, have the staff cut a sheet cake iced with the same frosting to serve to your guests.

• **Call local culinary and cooking schools;** they may have chefs and instructors who will work at your at-home wedding for lower wages than those from big-time restaurants and catering establishments.

Liquor

• **Cut back.** Liquor is a major expense for most couples. Instead of offering an array of spirits, serve only wine, beer, and champagne—most guests will find that sufficient.

• **Work with the caterer to get the best price you can on liquor.** You may be advised to buy cases yourself (unopened cartons and bottles may be returnable).

• **Serve traditional wedding punch**—a blend of alcohol, juices, and garnishes. You'll need less liquor and won't have to use the most expensive brands.

• **Offer hors d'oeuvres during the cocktail hour.** This will help cut down on alcohol consumption.

• **Close the bar an hour before the reception's end.** Serve juices, chilled teas, soft drinks, etc.

• **Consider serving carafes of wine**—they're less expensive than pouring bottles.

Photography

• **Compare hourly fee prices versus package prices.**

• Hire a professional photographer to take only formal portraits and ceremony shots; **encourage guests to take candids at the reception with single-use cameras set on each table.** Some manufacturers make these cameras expressly for wedding-day photo ops, packaging the camera in a pretty, wedding-appropriate box (check out the supply offered at your local camera store).

• **Call an art school's photography department** and examine the portfolios of students. They can supplement pictures taken by a professional.

• **Make sure the extra prints for relatives and friends are included in your package** or can be purchased later at reasonable prices.

• **Find out how long the photographer will keep the negatives.** You may prefer to buy additional prints in the future, after other wedding-related bills are paid.

Videography

• **Forgo special effects.** Opt for the simplest and least expensive video: a straightforward view of the wedding filmed by one videographer.

• **Compare hourly rates with package deals.**

Flowers

• **Carry in-season or locally grown blooms**—they're less costly than exotic, out-of-season ones. Ask your floral designer for suggestions.

• **Form bouquets with large flowers**—calla lilies, cattleya orchids, etc. You'll need fewer flowers for a lush look.

• **Have attendants carry one or two dramatic flowers** (sunflowers, French tulips).

• **Choose a bouquet of just one type of flower and greenery** (gardenias and ivy). It's elegant—and less expensive.

• **Accessorize nosegays or tussie-mussies with tulle or ribbon.** They'll appear larger.

• **Carry a family prayer book** and trim it with a simple floral spray.

• **Trim chuppahs and trellises with cost-conscious greenery.**

• **Rent potted plants** for the altar arrangement.

• **Share ceremony flowers (and costs) with another couple** marrying in your church or synagogue that same day.

• **Decorate the reception site with flowers from the ceremony.**

• **Plan your wedding during a holiday season** when the church, synagogue, or reception site may already be wonderfully decorated.

• **Use potted plants,** which are less expensive than flowers, **for centerpieces.**

• **Let bridesmaids' bouquets do double duty,** acting as centerpieces for the head table or as framing for the wedding cake.

• **Hold your wedding at a place with its own natural beauty**—a garden, park or beach.

Music

• **Hire musicians from your church or synagogue.** They may charge less than outside musicians.

• **Check into other church-affiliated musicians for reception music.** Their fees may be less than those of a commercial band.

• **Hire student musicians** from a local university or music school to supplement the work of professionals. Perhaps a string quartet made up of students could play during your cocktail hour.

• **Compare the cost of a DJ with that of a band.**

• **Ask a musically talented friend or relative to create tapes** of dancing and dining music for your at-home wedding.

• **Consider hiring three or four musicians** instead of a larger group (six or eight). They may charge you less, and you'll also save on any tips, meals, beverages, etc.

• **Ask if any of the musicians play other instruments.** You could hire someone from the band, for instance, to play the piano during your cocktail hour.

Bride's Attire

• To find the widest range of styles—and prices—**shop early for your dress.** Nine months before the wedding is ideal.

• **Avoid costly rush charges.** If alterations need to be done, do them early.

• **Ask the sales consultant about discontinued styles and sample dresses**—they may offer extra savings. Fabrics such as silk shantung, satin, organza, and taffeta are multiseasonal.

• **Check vintage clothing stores for heirloom wedding dresses.** They can be less expensive—but understand that alterations, and any repairs, will cost you.

• **Think about wearing an informal wedding dress,** which many manufacturers now make (check your bridal salon). Because of their simplicity, they're often less expensive.

• **Ask the sales consultant if the dress you've selected can be ordered in a less expensive fabric** (polyester shantung instead of silk shantung). Can the dress be made without expensive beading? Without lace at the hem?

• **Don't try to rework the dress,** changing a neckline, omitting sleeves, etc. All those alterations will cost money—and lots of it. Before buying, get an alterations price quote; the extra cost could put the dress out of your price range.

• **Be creative.** Bridal accessories—garters, ring pillows, purses—can be made, or embellished, at home.

Groom's Attire

• **Shop with plenty of time to spare**—at least eight weeks prior to the wedding. Ushers should be fitted by then as well. You don't want to incur costly rush alteration fees.

• **Have the best man return all rental tuxedos on time** to avoid late charges. Keep in mind that you will be charged a fee for any tuxedo that is damaged.

Invitations

• **Examine your options.** If you can't afford engraving, consider thermography. Like engraving, letters are raised in the front, but—unlike engraving—they cannot be felt in the back. Or buy prepackaged cards or notepaper and handwrite invitations with a gold calligraphy pen.

• **Ask the stationer if a package price is available** if you buy all your stationery (invitations, map cards, pew cards, thank-you notes, etc.) from him/her at the same time.

• **Order invitations that require only one regular stamp to mail.**

Favors

• **Group together vases of flowers or plants as centerpieces;** later, guests can separate them and take them home as favors. Or think creatively. Use bowls of goldfish, or small pots of herbs as centerpieces-cum-favors.

• **Favors don't have to be costly.** Consider seed packets and tree saplings. They'll help save the environment—and save you a little money.

Transportation

• **Use limousines for the minimum number of hours.** Avoid being charged waiting times by hiring one limo to go from home to the ceremony to the reception, another for the reception's end.

• **Hire just two limos**—one each for the bride and groom's families. Ask attendants to drive their own cars.

• **Ask about different kinds of cars.** A luxury stretch limo and a corporate stretch limo might be similar—except for price and a few incidental details. The luxury limo could have a VCR and TV, two items you're unlikely to be using on your wedding day.

• **Borrow or rent an antique or classic car** from a friend or relative.

Honeymoon

• **Get a referral to a knowledgeable travel agent who can get you the best deals.** Tell him/her about any alumni or professional organizations you belong to, which may entitle you to lower rates.

• **Ask if your travel agency has a honeymoon registry,** so guests can contribute to your honeymoon as a wedding gift to you.

• **Book a package,** which can save you money by including airfare, hotel, some food, and sight-seeing in one lump sum (but read the fine print before you sign on).

• **Plan in advance to take advantage of promotional airfares,** lower rates on rental cars, cruise berths, etc.

• **Save on airfare by flying Monday through Thursday.** Sometimes a Saturday-night stayover also entitles you to a lower fare.

• **Travel off-season for lower airfares and hotel rates** (which may mean postponing your honeymoon). For example, the Caribbean is less expensive from May to December; Bermuda in April; the Greek Isles in May or October. One caveat: While the prices might be lower off-season, the weather isn't always optimal.

• **Ask about specials at hotels before you book.** For example, booking the weekend package may entitle you to a free Sunday brunch.

• **Announce you're honeymooners** and chances are you'll get a free room upgrade, champagne, and other complimentary bonuses.

• **Limit the use of the hotel-room phone, minibar, room service, etc.** The costs will add up quickly.

• **Don't forget toiletries—toothpaste, sunscreen, film.** These items can cost you almost double in the sundries shop at a resort.

• **Check to see whether fees for snorkeling equipment, sailing, and tennis are included** in hotel/resort rates.

Rings

• **Consider matching sets** (an engagement ring and band), which may cost less than two rings purchased separately.

• **If you're interested in a diamond band, save money by buying one with stones stretching just halfway around,** instead of fully around the ring. And remember—a diamond doesn't have to be big to be brilliant.

• **Have an heirloom diamond ring reset in a contemporary setting.**

Chapter 13:

CONTRACT CONSIDERATIONS

This is one of the most important days of your life—don't leave things to chance. Insist on signed and countersigned contracts with all your wedding service professionals.

THE ANATOMY OF A CONTRACT

You're meeting with a florist your best friend recommended. She's listened to you describe the type of centerpieces you want, and she's agreed to make them exactly to your specifications. She seems professional and reliable and came personally recommended, so why bring up a contract?

Because as competent and dependable as your florist may appear, she can still make mistakes. What happens if she forgets that you wanted daisies in your centerpieces, or she transposes some numbers and writes down the wrong date and/or time for your wedding?

Don't risk it. Get all the details in writing, then sign the contract and have the florist sign it. A signed contract and countersigned will help ensure that you get the services you've asked for and that if there *is* a mistake, things will be set right—or your final bill will be adjusted as compensation.

Many wedding service personnel have standard contracts already prepared for you to sign. A photographer's regular contract, for instance, may have exactly how many hours of wedding-day service he/she provides, how many pictures he/she will take, etc. If you want anything out of the ordinary (say, black-and-white photos), write it

into the contract. Make sure both you and the photographer sign it. If a service provider doesn't have a contract, write down the specifics of what he/she will provide during your meeting. Include the date and time of his/her service, plus all costs. You and your service provider should each sign the agreement.

Make sure you have contracts or letters of agreement from the following:

- **Stationer**
- **Caterer**
- **Rental hall**
- **Florist**
- **Musicians**
- **Photographer**
- **Videographer**
- **Wedding dress shop**
- **Men's formalwear shop**
- **Limousine company**
- **Baker**
- **Bridal consultant**
- **Rental companies (for chairs, tables, etc.)**
- **Any other people providing a service for your wedding**, such as parking attendants.

Contract Considerations

• **Write out all the details.** For example, with floral arrangements describe the shape, size, color, number, types of flowers, and cost. Don't rely on oral assurances.

• **Read it over.** Don't be pressured into signing immediately. If there is something you don't like or understand, ask questions. You should have time to take the contract home and have someone else look it over as well.

• **Make sure the merchant signs the contract.** Some unscrupulous businesses get the bride and groom to sign, then avoid signing themselves.

• **Put down as little money as possible.** The less the deposit, the less you lose should you run into problems. In most cases, you shouldn't be asked to put down more than 50 percent of the total price before services are rendered.

• **Beware of large cancellation fees.** Last-minute cancellation fees are understandable, but you should not have to pay the bulk of the cost if you cancel months in advance, when a caterer can rebook a room, for example, and recover any lost income.

• **Be wary of any service provider who won't sign a contract,** saying you don't need one or his word is good enough. It may be true—and then again, it may be talk. If a particular service provider says he/she does not have a contract, draw up a letter of agreement specifying all the details. You and the service provider should sign it.

• **Before you pay out all wedding deposits, consider buying** an insurance policy that protects some of your wedding investments. Coverages and costs vary. Choose the wedding postponement/cancellation coverage on the policy offered by one company, for example, and

you'll be covered up to your policy limit (minus a deductible) for nonrefundable expenses incurred when the wedding has to be canceled or put off for certain reasons beyond your control (e.g., you, your groom, or someone essential to the wedding party is sick or injured; an earthquake destroys your reception site). What's not covered: change of heart.

Contract Terms, Defined

A contract is meaningless unless you understand it. Here is how to interpret the terms:

1. Balance due. The amount remaining to be paid after the deposit. Never pay in full before services are rendered.

2. Cancellation fees. Fees you must pay if you cancel your reception. The closer to your wedding date you cancel, the higher the fees.

3. Deposit. The amount you pay to reserve the services.

4. Gratuities. Some wedding professionals should be tipped, such as the chauffeur of your limo. Additionally, your caterer may charge you gratuities based on the total cost of food and liquor, for example, 20 percent of the food and liquor costs.

5. Liquor costs. Your caterer's drink charges. You may be charged per person/per hour ($X per person, per hour), by the drink, by the bottle, or a flat fee ($X,000 for a four-hour reception with open bar). Factors such as name brands and vintage wines influence costs. Ask your caterer about all the options.

6. Overtime costs. Expenses incurred if your reception, for example, runs past the time stated in your contract. The cost will depend on several factors—additional wages for waiters and bartenders, additional food and drink, etc.

WEDDING CONSUMER TRAPS: DON'T FALL PREY

Unfortunately, the worst does occasionally happen. The dress you ordered never comes in, the flowers arrive wilted, the wedding photographs are too dark. Here is how to protect yourself:

Engagement/Wedding Rings

• **Know the jeweler.** Even then, call the Better Business Bureau to see if there have been any complaints filed against the company.

• **Make the final sale contingent on an appraisal from an independent appraiser—** *not* one the jewelry store you're buying the ring from recommends. Tell the appraiser you want a genuine appraisal, as opposed to one for insurance purposes, which may be inflated.

• **Be wary of claims of discounts, sales, etc.** They may be a way to get you to buy an inferior stone quickly.

• **Look at the diamond under natural light.** Avoid jewelry stores with blue-tinted lights overhead. All diamonds, especially less valuable yellow ones, look good under blue light.

Wedding Attire

• **Pay as small a deposit as possible.**

• **Include a cancellation provision in your contract** (the store's contract may not have one), specifying that the deposit will be refunded if the clothing does not arrive on the desired date or in good condition.

• **Choose a delivery date that is several weeks before you actually need the wedding gown and bridesmaids' dresses.** (Men's clothing may only be available a few days before the wedding, since it's often rented.)

• **If your wedding attire is not provided on time and as ordered, try to renegotiate payment** with the company. If they won't coop-erate, consider taking them to small claims court to recover any money already paid.

Music

• **Be sure your contract lists the date and site of the reception,** the time the band should arrive, the number of hours the band will play, cost (including overtime rates), style of music to be played (swing, rock, jazz, a combination of all three?), specific songs, and the appropriate attire for the musicians.

• **If there are certain musicians whom you want to appear personally at your wedding** (a particular bandleader or vocalist, say), **specify their names in the contract.** Stipulate that you want them at the event in person.

• **Specify the number of musicians you are hiring and what instruments they play** (one drummer, two saxophone players, etc.).

Catering Halls

• **Pay special attention to the cancellation clause in the contract.** While you may think you would never cancel your wedding, you may well change your reception plans—find another site, move the date, change the time. You should only have to pay a small amount if you cancel months ahead of time. The caterer should be able to rebook the site and recoup his/her loss.

• **Ask about gratuities, overtime fees, coat-check fees, parking attendant fees, and any other "extra" expenses.** Specify the exact costs in writing.

• **Specify a date to give the caterer a final guest count.** Try to arrange to pay for the actual number of guests who attend, rather than for a rough estimate made several months in advance.

Photography

• Some studios employ several different photographers. **Specify the photographer you want in writing.**

• **Put a clause in your contract stating that you owe no money and that all deposits will be refunded if the photographs don't turn out.**

Flowers

• **Make sure your contract specifies what your florist will do if unusual, out-of-season flowers that you want are unavailable.** Choose several substitutes and write them into the contract.

• **Make the contract as detailed as possible with regard to the number, shape, size, and color of arrangements and bouquets.** Also include the exact type of flowers to be used. Include a clause stating that you will adjust the balance of the payment due if flowers are not fresh or if the arrangements are flimsy and wilted, etc.

Getting Even: What to Do When You've Been Had

Your service provider has reneged on part of his/her contract. Don't get mad, get even:

• **Renegotiate your final bill.** Write a letter to the president/owner of the company and explain why you're unhappy. Ask that your deposit be refunded—or renegotiate the balance due.

• **Consider taking your case to small claims court.**

• **File a complaint against the company with your area's Better Business Bureau.** They may be able to negotiate an agreement with your service provider. Also contact your state's department of consumer affairs.

• **Think about hiring a lawyer to recover your deposit money.**

Chapter 14:

PARTIES

From the first engagement party to the bachelor's bash, here's what to expect.

ENGAGEMENT PARTIES

An engagement is a cause for celebration. People will want to fete you—sometimes more than once.

Traditionally, the bride's parents host the first engagement party. Subsequent engagement parties can be hosted by friends, the groom's parents, relatives, even the bride and groom themselves. Here are some things to keep in mind:

• An engagement party can take any form. It can be a seated dinner party for twenty or a barbecue for eighty.

• An engagement party is not a bridal shower; your guests may or may not be bearing gifts. However, if you want to make sure that the gifts you do receive at an engagement party are likely to be ones you want, register at a department or specialty store shortly after you announce your engagement.

• Invite only those guests whom you'll invite to the wedding.

• Guests may be invited orally or via formal or informal written invitations.

• Give thanks where thanks is due. Show your appreciation to the hosts of the party by writing a thank-you note and giving them a small present (a potted plant, crystal candy dish, etc.).

SHOWER GUIDE

Traditionally, the bridal shower was an all-female tea or luncheon at which guests "showered" the bride with presents to help her set up her new home. Legend has it that the shower umbrella, a fixture at many bridal showers, shelters the bride and groom from harm. Nowadays, bridal showers take many forms. They can be co-ed, have certain themes, be an informal barbecue, or be a more formal seated brunch.

As a bride, your role in shower planning is minimal, except to provide the names and addresses of guests and the location of your bridal registry. Usually, your honor attendant, bridesmaids, and/or close friends host the shower. Encourage mothers, sisters, and aunts not to host a shower—it implies your family is asking for gifts. If you're remarrying, there's no reason why you shouldn't be given a shower. Figuring that you probably already own many basic items, however, guests may want to shower you with gifts that appeal to a special interest or hobby. Here are some more shower-planning tips.

The Guest List

• **Only those guests being invited to the wedding should be invited to the shower.** One exception: office showers, which are typically thrown by coworkers and colleagues, who may or may not be invited to the wedding.

• **At a traditional all-female shower,** female relatives (mothers, sisters, grandmothers) and close family friends on both the bride's and groom's sides are invited. If the shower is co-ed, invite men who also are close to the couple.

• **If more than one shower will be thrown in your honor,** have your attendants or whoever is hosting the shower tell repeat guests that they need give a gift only once.

• **Invitations should be mailed at least three weeks in advance** of the shower date.

• **Invitations might list your home-decorating colors and the place of your bridal registry** to inspire gift selections.

When and Where

• **Showers may be given from two months up to two weeks before the ceremony.** In some cases—such as when the bride or important members of her family live out-of-town—they can be held a few days before the wedding, when people have gathered for the wedding celebration.

• **Schedule showers well after the last engagement party.** You don't want to wear guests out with back-to-back parties.

• **If there's absolutely no time before the wedding,** a shower can be given after the couple returns from their honeymoon.

• **Showers can be held in a multitude of places**—a restaurant, hotel, club, or private home.

• **Keep in mind the work and social schedules of principal guests.** If the shower is a surprise for the bride, check with her groom or her family to see if she's available that day.

What Happens at the Party

• **Guests arrive before the bride.** Gifts are set up on a table.

• **Someone—usually the maid of honor or a bridesmaid—writes down who gave each gift as it is opened.** Another may collect ribbons and tie them together, to **make the bouquet that is sometimes used at the rehearsal** in place of a real bouquet.

• This is a party, after all. Most of the shower time will be spent **eating and chatting with guests**—and, of course, **opening gifts.**

• **Thank the hosts with a small gift**—note cards, or flowers—whatever you think they might enjoy.

Twelve Cool Shower Themes

1. Romance. Ask guests to bring gifts that inspire a never-ending honeymoon: satin sheets, massage oils, scented candles. Fill vases with roses and serve the foods of love—oysters, caviar, strawberries and cream, champagne, and a heart-shaped cake. Wrap Hershey's Kisses in tulle and tie them with red ribbon to give as favors.

2. Pick a country. Take the bride on a trip around the world. Each guest brings a gift associated with a particular country. Decorate the walls with maps and serve international foods. Dish out fetticini as she unwraps a pasta machine. Hand out chopsticks and plates of stir-fried chicken and vegetables as you give her a wok. With each gift and food course, make your way around the globe.

3. Comfort zone. Help her feel relaxed and pampered. Some suggestions are a certificate for a day of beauty, a foot massage, or yoga videos. Hire a masseuse to give everyone a ten-minute back rub. Serve up spa fare—fresh fruit, grilled vegetables, interesting snacks. Play soothing classical music.

4. The big picture. Everyone brings a photo of the bride and/or groom with a caption. Display the photos on a board for everyone to view and for the couple to keep. They'll treasure the sentiment, and guests will enjoy learning more about the couple. Some presents to shoot for are a damask-covered photo album, frames for wedding pictures, camera equipment, a VCR. Use small picture frames as place cards and favors.

5. Home office. Print invitations on Rolodex cards for a home-office shower. Circulate a leather-bound address book and ask guests to add their names. Other gift ideas are a telephone, answering machine, desk lamp, stationery, and computer accessories. Personalize pens and pencils with "Kim's Shower" and the date; give a set to each guest.

6. The clueless gourmet. Cuisine's the theme. Guests bring a recipe along with some of the equipment needed to prepare it. For example, give a cookie recipe along with a baking set, or instructions for making frozen drinks with a blender. Once the bride opens the gifts, put the recipe in a box she'll keep.

7. Fitness. Host the shower at a health club or decorate with a sports theme. Set up a juice bar and a buffet of raw vegetables, salads, and fruits. Some gift ideas are nonstick skillets (for low-fat cooking), a bathroom scale, hand-held weights, and a bicycle built for two.

8. Happy hour. Plan a co-ed party and give the couple gifts for a well-stocked bar. Guests bring their favorite wine or beer. Put some good vintages in a rack for the couple; set up a tasting table with the rest. Some gift options are glasses, a decanter, coasters, a blender, and an ice bucket.

9. The honeymoon. Draw inspiration from the couple's honeymoon spot: If they're planning a Hawaiian honeymoon, host a luau. Are they running off to Rome? Have a toga party! Ask guests to bring gifts of luggage, guidebooks, a travel alarm clock, etc.

10. Perfect Timing. Assign each guest an hour of the day and ask them to bring a timely gift: a coffeemaker for seven A.M,, a teapot for four P.M. A great group gift: a beautiful wall clock.

11. That's entertainment. Gift ideas include a VCR and popular movies, a CD player, a chess set, and sports or theater tickets. Serve hot dogs, pizza, popcorn, Milk Duds.

12. Holiday. Every guest is assigned a holiday and brings a present to help the couple celebrate it. Some gift ideas are tree ornaments (for Christmas), champagne flutes (for New Year's), heart-shaped cookie cutters (for Valentine's Day), and garden tools (for Arbor Day).

Shower Games

Get guests mingling with a few well-thought-out shower activities. One standard is pin-the-boutonniere-on-the-groom (blindfolded guests try to place a paper flower on a blown-up picture of the groom; the person who comes closest to his left lapel wins). Another is bridal bloopers, in which a guest writes down the bride's statements, such as "How did you know exactly what I wanted?" or "This is incredible," as she opens her wedding gifts. She then reads them back as "What Suzanne will say on her wedding night." Other perfect icebreakers:

1. Guests introduce themselves and give the couple their best advice for a happy marriage.

2. Have a "roast." Tell humorous stories or anecdotes about the couple.

3. Play a "famous couples" trivia game.

4. Test guests' knowledge of the two of you as a couple by playing Bridal Jeopardy. The hostess can think of things relating to the bride and groom, then recite them to guests in the form of a statement. À la *Jeopardy*, guests must answer using a question (Answer: A San Francisco trolley car. Question: Where did Jack propose to Patty?).

5. Wedding charades. Like regular charades, guests act out particular expressions while other guests guess their meaning. One hitch: The phrases are all wedding related.

Showering Together: Tips for Holding a Co-ed Shower

• **Pick a theme that works well for both men and women,** such as an entertainment, bar, or fitness shower. A handy-couple shower—in which guests bring the couple tools, garden utensils, gift certificates to home centers, and home-improvement books—is another option.

• **Move the party outdoors.** Make it a barbecue or picnic. Play a game of touch football, softball, or volleyball. Consider holding a doubles tennis tournament.

• **Skip the petits fours and tea sandwiches.** Serve up real crowd pleasers: chili, pizza, pasta.

• **Don't plan out every minute of the event.** Let guests mingle, chat, and listen to music. Think of it more as a cocktail party than a traditional shower.

SHOWER CHART

Theme (if any) _____

Hostess _____

Date _____   Time _____

Place _____

Guest	Address	Gift	Date Thank-you sent
_____	_____	_____	_____
_____	_____	_____	_____
_____	_____	_____	_____
_____	_____	_____	_____
_____	_____	_____	_____
_____	_____	_____	_____
_____	_____	_____	_____
_____	_____	_____	_____
_____	_____	_____	_____

SHOWER CHART

Theme (if any) _____

Hostess _____

Date _____ Time _____

Place _____

Guest	Address	Gift	Date Thank-you sent
_____	_____	_____	_____
_____	_____	_____	_____
_____	_____	_____	_____
_____	_____	_____	_____
_____	_____	_____	_____
_____	_____	_____	_____
_____	_____	_____	_____
_____	_____	_____	_____
_____	_____	_____	_____
_____	_____	_____	_____

SHOWER CHART

Theme (if any) _____

Hostess _____

Date _____ Time _____

Place _____

Guest	Address	Gift	Date Thank-you sent
_____	_____	_____	_____
_____	_____	_____	_____
_____	_____	_____	_____
_____	_____	_____	_____
_____	_____	_____	_____
_____	_____	_____	_____
_____	_____	_____	_____
_____	_____	_____	_____
_____	_____	_____	_____
_____	_____	_____	_____
_____	_____	_____	_____
_____	_____	_____	_____
_____	_____	_____	_____

BRIDESMAIDS' PARTIES

They've been your right-hand women. Now it's time to thank the members of your wedding party with a gathering of their own. If your attendants will be coming from out of town, the most convenient time for a gathering may be the wedding morning or afternoon. However, many brides choose to have the get-together a few days or a few weeks before, when things are more relaxed. Just about any style of party is acceptable: an afternoon tea, dessert and champagne party, elegant dinner party, or informal luncheon. It's a time for the bride to reminisce with close friends.

At the party, the bride gives her attendants their thank-you gifts and goes over the wedding-day schedule. A bridesmaids' party tradition is to bake a ring or thimble inside a pink cake. The woman who finds the ring or thimble in her piece will be the next to marry.

BRIDESMAIDS' PARTY CHECKLIST

Location _____

Address _____

Contact person _____

Phone _____ Fax _____

Date and time of party _____

Date invitations were sent _____

Guests

Name	Address	Response
_____	_____	_____
_____	_____	_____
_____	_____	_____
_____	_____	_____
_____	_____	_____
_____	_____	_____
_____	_____	_____
_____	_____	_____
_____	_____	_____
_____	_____	_____
_____	_____	_____
_____	_____	_____

Menu and beverages _____

_____

_____

Additional activities/notes (rental items, companies, costs, contact names, etc.) _____

_____

THE BACHELORETTE PARTY

All you need is one bride-to-be and a bunch of her female friends. Focus the party—usually hosted by the bride's attendants and her other close female friends—around any activity the bride enjoys (scantily clad beefcakes are completely optional). Some ideas:

1. Book a spa afternoon. Have manicures, pedicures, and massages with your friends. You'll unwind, they'll bond. Inquire about group packages.

2. Plan a weekend away at a beach house, ski chalet, etc.

3. Get active. Take a day trip to the mountains or other scenic locale to bike, hike, roller blade. Or just stay close to home and plan a tennis or bowling tournament.

4. Spend the day getting your hair and makeup professionally done, then paint the town red.

5. Have an all-girl sleep-over. Rent videos your boyfriends complain are too sappy, eat your fill of Twinkies and Sno-Balls, and, of course, dish some dirt.

6. Shop till you drop.

7. Wear your best dress and **go out for a fancy six-course meal.**

8. Rent a limousine and visit your favorite haunts—pubs, dance clubs.

THE BACHELOR PARTY

The old, stereotypical bachelor party conjures up images of barely dressed women jumping out of cakes, followed by lots of heavy drinking, poker playing, and an X-rated video or two. Those parties still exist, but they're not as prevalent. Sure, there will probably be drinks and cigars. But today bachelor parties have more to do with camaraderie than carousing. They can focus around a camping trip, fishing outing, or sporting event.

They can be held in a hotel suite, club, or private home. It's the groom's chance to get together with his friends and enjoy some time alone with them.

The bachelor party is generally hosted by the best man or a close male friend or relative of the groom. It should be held within a few weeks of the wedding, but never the night before.

OTHER PREWEDDING PARTIES

• **The wedding work party.** Invite friends over to help you with wedding tasks, such as addressing invitations, lettering place cards, or figuring out the reception seating. Make it easy on yourself: Serve pizza, a buffet dinner, or take-out.

• **Tasting parties.** Friends help you choose the hors d'oeuvres, cake, wine, punch, or champagne you'll serve at your reception. Have caterers and bakers make you samples; buy several brands of champagne or try out different punch recipes. Provide blindfolds and rating cards and put everyone to work.

• **Audition parties.** Play tapes of bands, DJs, and other performers and ask friends to rate them.

CHECKLIST FOR ADDITIONAL PREWEDDING PARTIES

Type of party _____

Location _____

Address _____

Contact person _____

Phone _____ Fax _____

Date and Time _____

Date invitations (if any) were sent _____

Guests

Name   Address   Response

_____

_____

_____

_____

_____

_____

_____

_____

_____

_____

_____

_____

Menu and beverages _____

_____

_____

Activities/notes _____

_____

_____

CHECKLIST FOR ADDITIONAL PREWEDDING PARTIES

Type of party _____

Location _____

Address _____

Contact person _____

Phone _____ Fax _____

Date and Time _____

Date invitations (if any) were sent _____

Guests

Name	Address	Response

Menu and beverages _____

_____

_____

Activities/notes _____

_____

_____

THE REHEARSAL DINNER

Generally held a day or so before the wedding, a rehearsal dinner (or party) is one last chance to bring everyone together before the big day. The groom's parents customarily host, but in some cases, friends or relatives of the bride, or even the couple themselves, extend the invitation. If the groom's family lives far away, the bride and her family can help organize the event by giving the groom's parents a list of recommended restaurants; his family can then make the necessary arrangements over the phone.

Everyone who attends the wedding rehearsal should attend the dinner—that includes the attendants and their spouses, ceremony readers and their spouses, your officiant and his/her spouse, and parents of any children in the wedding. Out-of-town guests who arrive before the wedding are also often included, as well as other close friends and relatives. Hosts trying to keep down costs, however, might limit the party to wedding participants only.

A rehearsal dinner can range from an elaborate formal banquet to a poolside picnic to a dessert buffet. A seated dinner, however, is still the most popular choice. It is more understated than the wedding, with fewer guests, a simpler menu, and less lavish decorations. Although the invitations may be telephoned, written ones are preferred—with all the wedding-related parties during the wedding countdown period, your guests are apt to get confused.

Once everyone has assembled, get things off to a warm start. Introduce family and friends to one another. Use a formal seating plan to put together people whom you think would get along well. Break the ice by passing around a picture album filled with photos of the two of you from babyhood onward. Give your attendants their gifts if you haven't already, along with your heartfelt thanks. Your parents or grandparents may even want to use the occasion to reaffirm their own wedding vows.

And don't forget to salute your love and your families with a toast or two. First, there is the customary toast to the couple by the best man. The groom then follows with a toast to his bride and his new in-laws. The bride then may respond with a toast to her about-to-be-husband and his family. From there, other attendants and guests (such as the maid of honor) can propose toasts that include anecdotes about the bride and groom. Encourage brevity—rambling toasts are less than riveting.

REHEARSAL DINNER CHECKLIST

Location _____

Address _____

Contact person _Mallorie & Ben_____

Phone _____ Fax _____

Date and time of dinner _____

Date invitations were sent _____

Guests

Name   Address   Response

_____

_____

_____

_____

_____

_____

_____

_____

_____

_____

_____

Menu and beverages Pot-luck dinner _____

_____

_____

Additional notes (rental items, companies, costs, contact names, etc.) _____

_____

_____

Chapter 15:

YOUR WEDDING GIFTS

Fine bone china. Gleaming crystal. Pale peach sheets of the softest cotton. A silky peignoir you can't wait to try on. Opening your gifts is one of the most exhilarating parts of the wedding experience. Traditionally, only those guests who accept your wedding invitation will send presents, but other people who know either you, your groom, or your families may want to send them also. Guests can send gifts anytime before the wedding (proper etiquette dictates that they deliver or mail a gift, rather than bring it to the reception) and up to a year afterward.

REGISTERING RIGHT: SIXTEEN EASY STEPS

1. Virtually all major department stores have gift registries—as well as many specialty stores, such as home centers. Look in unexpected places as well: stores that sell books, music, liquor, electronics, housewares, and computers. (If you have a favorite store, inquire with the manager about whether or not they have a registry—or if one can be set up for you.) Some catalogs also have registries (a convenient option if your guests live all over the country). The newest registries are those offered by travel agencies (so guests can contribute to your honeymoon) and mortgage companies (guests can give money toward a down payment on your future home). Registry options are also available on the Internet.

2. Register early—ideally, before any wedding-related events are thrown in your honor.

3. Visit several stores to see what's available. Then make an appointment with the bridal director at the store(s) you choose. Make it for an off-peak time, when the store won't be so crowded and the help so harried, and don't try to do it all in one day—you're bound to get overwhelmed.

4. If you register at several stores, don't duplicate your list (choose one store for linens, another for housewares, etc.). National chain stores or those with a computerized registry will make gift-giving more convenient for out-of-towners. (Guests can punch in your name or your groom's and get a copy of your registry pronto—or they can call the store and ask that a printout be mailed or faxed to them.)

5. Before you decide on what items to register for, think about your lifestyle. Will you be doing a lot of at-home entertaining for friends? Do you love to cook? Collectively, do you already own three phones—but not one answering machine?

6. Ask how long the registry will remain active. It could be from three months to two years. Your registry can be a great gift resource—for birthdays, anniversaries, etc.—even after the wedding.

7. Register for gifts in a variety of prices—from sterling silver serving pieces to silver-plated slotted spoons—to accommodate the price range of every guest.

8. Don't limit yourself to registering for just the traditional housewares or luxury

items, such as china, crystal, and linens. In addition, you might register for camping or home-office equipment, furniture, window treatments, stereos, security systems, etc.

9. When choosing china, glasses, and flatware, think about harmony in design. Pieces don't have to match exactly, but they should have something in common—complementary colors, hints of a similar motif or pattern, etc. A salad or dessert plate that's different from your dinner plate, yet still harmonious, can create a beautiful accent.

10. Get specific. Jot on the registry form everything about the item that there's room for—pattern name, model number, manufacturer, etc. Guests will be able to recognize the exact coffee-maker you want among the dozens of others on the shelves.

11. Be diplomatic. When guests ask what you'd like for a wedding gift, tell them where you're registered, but not the specifics about what's on the list.

12. Give the registry a shipping address to use (yours, your parents'—whoever you think will be home to accept gifts that are shipped or mailed). If gifts are being mailed to your new address, give the registry department an exact date when gifts can be shipped. Because registry personnel will sometimes notify you when things go on sale or are discontinued, it's a good idea always to alert them to changes in your address or phone.

13. Don't include your registry information on your wedding invitations (although it may be included on those for your shower). If asked, your family or attendants can pass the word to guests about where you're registered.

14. Open gifts as they arrive—and keep a list of who sent what.

15. Periodically—and especially after your bridal shower or an engagement party—**call the stores where you are registered and ask for a computer printout of your registry.** Make sure it's up-to-date, listing the correct number of items already received, those still desired, etc. If it

doesn't, call the store's bridal director and give her the right number. It's possible that some guests could have bought a gift listed on your registry from another store.

16. Send thank-you notes promptly. Try to thank each guest as soon as you receive the gift so they don't pile up. You might tackle ten per day. Every guest must be thanked within a year of the wedding, at the latest.

Gifts of Money

Gifts of money are customary in some cultures and are always appreciated. If you prefer monetary gifts, let your family or close friends discreetly spread the word. Never write your gift preference on your wedding invitations. Choose a trustworthy friend or relative to hold on to checks and cash that you receive at the wedding. You and your groom can endorse the checks after the wedding and give them to him or her for depositing while you're on your honeymoon. If you'd rather guests donate money to your favorite charity, you can have friends and family discreetly pass the word prior to the wedding.

What Should You Do with Damaged Gifts?

Step number one: Determine from the wrappings, the enclosure card, or labels where the gift was purchased, then call the store's customer service department. If the gift is from a store where you're registered, you might also call the registry office to see if they can intervene. Explain the problem—the store will most likely replace the gift for you (there's no need to tell the giver about the damage). If you can't tell where the gift was bought, check the package to see if there is a post office insurance stamp. If so, contact the giver so they can be reimbursed by the post office. They will probably send you a replacement gift. Call the giver and explain what happened.

Exchanging Etiquette

Not every gift you receive will be one you like—or necessarily want. But before you exchange it, think carefully. Each is from someone close to you, who will look for it when visiting your home. Would you rather make room for the gift—even in a less-than-prominent place—than risk some hurt feelings? On the other hand, if the giver is unlikely to find out about the exchange, it may be more practical to take it back and get something you really want. If you do decide to return the gift, remember that it's considered impolite to ask a giver where he or she made the purchase. Unless you can determine where it came from (examine the box or wrappings as well as the item itself for any clues), you may be out of luck.

Gifts at the Reception

Because of the potential for theft and damage, guests should send wedding presents rather than bring them to the reception. Nonetheless, some guests will arrive at your reception bearing gifts. Assign your maid of honor or a good friend to collect the gifts, secure the giftcards to the packages, and make sure they are safely stored (try a locked closet or an attended coat-check area at a hotel, club, or restaurant); she can later transport them to your home after the reception or keep them until you get back from your honeymoon.

TABLEWARE GUIDE

If you're like a lot of brides, a large portion of what's on your registry will be items for your table. Set it with style. Here are terms to know:

Decorative accessories. Many tableware manufacturers also make decorative giftware that enhances the beauty of any table. Items include vases, candlesticks, figurines, ornamental bowls (a bowl not necessarily used for food but displayed for its attractiveness or style), artwork, and even lamps.

Dinnerware. Commonly referred to as china. It includes place settings as well as serving pieces. It may be made of porcelain, fine china, bone china, stoneware, or earthenware. It's offered in open stock, place settings or sets, and is available in individual place settings or serving items.

Flatware. Informally known as silverware. It includes place settings and serving utensils. Flatware may be sterling silver, silver plate, or stainless steel, and might be accented with gold.

Glassware. Made of either crystal or glass. Includes both stemware and barware, such as glasses for wine, water, champagne, cocktails, brandy, juice, beer, and soft drinks.

Hollowware. Refers to pieces and vessels that have height and depth and are used for serving food or beverages. Hollowware can be made of many materials, such as silver, crystal, porcelain, or wood. Included are items such as water pitchers, sugar bowls and creamers, serving bowls, vegetable dishes, and gravy/sauce boats.

Linens. Choices for tablecloths, napkins, and place mats include fabric prints or solids, textured wovens or straw, or lace.

Table Talk: Selecting Your Tableware

• You and your fiancé will want to decide what type of **entertaining** you're likely to do as a married couple. Do you prefer casual, informal dinner parties with lots of friends? Then consider selecting some generously oversize serving pieces and rustic or woven checkered table linens. Are formal, seated dinner parties more your thing? Then definitely select some white linens and sparkling crystal. If you'll be entertaining in both styles, register for both casual and more formal items.

• **Think creatively about tableware elements.** Pair dinnerware with flatware, crystal, and accessories in contrasting patterns. A traditional rule is mix two patterned and one plain, one patterned and two plain. For example, pair dinnerware patterned with bright flowers with ornate flatware and sleek, smooth glassware. Or select a dinnerware pattern of fine white china banded with blue, simple flatware, and cut crystal glassware.

• Tableware can also be coordinated through **design motifs,** such as beading or braiding, that are repeated throughout the dinnerware, flatware, and crystal. Also think about mixing and matching pieces. Adding an accent salad/dessert plate with a design that coordinates with—but

does not match—your dinnerware adds visual impact.

• Consider adding a **holiday pattern**—say, one with a Thanksgiving, Christmas, or Hanukkah design—to give your table a festive look.

• **Collect extra pieces for variety and personality.** Stores and galleries offer unique designs in tableware items, such as colorful service/buffet plates to go under dinner plates, craftware serving pieces, unique demitasse cups, crescent salad dishes, compote bowls, colored glassware, and an assorted table linen wardrobe (choose informal and formal styles).

• Choose **two sets of tableware items**— one casual for everyday, one formal for more special occasions or for just making everyday occasions more special. Ones that mix and match offer the most versatility.

REGISTRY CHECKLIST

This checklist is the perfect helpmate for selecting wedding and shower gifts. Use it to note any patterns or manufacturers you're interested in and the number of items you'd like. Later, when you two visit the store's wedding gift registry, bring this list along as a worksheet to easily record your preferences. If there are items your store offers that are not on this list, simply record them under "other." As gifts arrive, mark the items received and keep the checklist up-to-date.

Dinnerware

PATTERN   MANUFACTURER

FORMAL PATTERN _____
CASUAL PATTERN _____

	FORMAL/QTY.	CASUAL/QTY.
☐ Dinner plate	_____	_____
☐ Dessert/salad plate	_____	_____
☐ Accent plate	_____	_____
☐ Bread/butter plate	_____	_____
☐ Tea cup and saucer	_____	_____
☐ Coffee cup and saucer	_____	_____
☐ Demitasse and saucer	_____	_____
☐ Mug	_____	_____
☐ Soup/cereal bowl	_____	_____
☐ Rim soup	_____	_____
☐ Cream soup/saucer	_____	_____
☐ Fruit bowl	_____	_____
☐ Salad bowl	_____	_____
☐ Service/buffet plate	_____	_____
☐ Serving bowl	_____	_____

☐ Platter _____ _____
☐ Gravy/sauce boat _____ _____
☐ Teapot _____ _____
☐ Coffeepot _____ _____
☐ Cream-and-sugar set _____ _____
☐ Other _____ _____

☐ Cake knife _____ _____
☐ Sugar spoon/tongs _____ _____
☐ Lemon fork _____ _____
☐ Carving set _____ _____
☐ Salad servers _____ _____
☐ Pasta server _____ _____
☐ Silver chest _____ _____

Flatware

	PATTERN	MANUFACTURER
FORMAL PATTERN	_____	
CASUAL PATTERN	_____	

	FORMAL/QTY.	CASUAL/QTY.
☐ Dinner fork	_____	_____
☐ Dessert/salad fork	_____	_____
☐ Dinner knife	_____	_____
☐ Soup spoon	_____	_____
☐ Tea/dessert spoon	_____	_____
☐ Cream soup spoon	_____	_____
☐ Iced beverage spoon	_____	_____
☐ Demitasse spoon	_____	_____
☐ Fish fork	_____	_____
☐ Fish knife	_____	_____
☐ Steak knife	_____	_____
☐ Butter/pastry knife	_____	_____
☐ Butter spreader	_____	_____
☐ Serving spoon	_____	_____
☐ Pierced spoon	_____	_____
☐ Serving fork	_____	_____
☐ Cold meat fork	_____	_____
☐ Tomato server	_____	_____
☐ Gravy/sauce ladles	_____	_____
☐ Pie server	_____	_____

Glassware

	PATTERN	MANUFACTURER
FORMAL PATTERN	_____	
CASUAL PATTERN	_____	

	FORMAL/QTY.	CASUAL/QTY.
☐ Water goblet	_____	_____
☐ Red wine	_____	_____
☐ White wine	_____	_____
☐ All-purpose stem	_____	_____
☐ Champagne flute	_____	_____
☐ Iced beverage	_____	_____
☐ Cocktail	_____	_____
☐ Double old-fashioned	_____	_____
☐ Highball	_____	_____
☐ Pilsner	_____	_____
☐ Brandy	_____	_____
☐ Sherry	_____	_____
☐ Cordial	_____	_____
☐ Fruit juice	_____	_____
☐ Finger bowl	_____	_____
☐ Other	_____	_____

Serving Pieces/Hollowware

	PATTERN	MANUFACTURER
☐ Serving bowl	_____	_____
☐ Serving platter	_____	_____
☐ Covered casserole	_____	_____
☐ Quiche dish	_____	_____
☐ Chafing dish	_____	_____

- ☐ Soup tureen _____ _____
- ☐ Well-and-tree carving platter _____ _____
- ☐ Gravy/sauce boat _____ _____
- ☐ Bread tray _____ _____
- ☐ Serving tray _____ _____
- ☐ Teapot _____ _____
- ☐ Coffeepot _____ _____
- ☐ Cream-and-sugar set _____ _____
- ☐ Cake plate _____ _____
- ☐ Dessert set _____ _____
- ☐ Compote _____ _____
- ☐ Salt-and-pepper set _____ _____
- ☐ Trivet _____ _____
- ☐ Cheese board _____ _____
- ☐ Napkin rings _____ _____
- ☐ Salad bowl _____ _____
- ☐ Candy/nut dish _____ _____
- ☐ Other _____ _____

Barware/Entertainment

	PATTERN	MANUFACTURER
☐ Ice bucket	_____	_____
☐ Wine cooler	_____	_____
☐ Decanter	_____	_____
☐ Cocktail shaker	_____	_____
☐ Pitcher	_____	_____
☐ Punch bowl set	_____	_____
☐ Corkscrew	_____	_____
☐ Bottle opener	_____	_____
☐ Jigger/bar tools	_____	_____
☐ Wine rack	_____	_____
☐ Coaster	_____	_____
☐ Other	_____	_____

Kitchenware/Bakeware

	MANUFACTURER	MODEL
☐ Toaster	_____	_____
☐ Toaster oven	_____	_____

- ☐ Coffeemaker _____ _____
- ☐ Espresso/cappuccino maker _____ _____
- ☐ Coffee grinder _____ _____
- ☐ Food processor _____ _____
- ☐ Blender _____ _____
- ☐ Stand mixer _____ _____
- ☐ Hand mixer _____ _____
- ☐ Deep fryer _____ _____
- ☐ Slow cooker _____ _____
- ☐ Pressure cooker _____ _____
- ☐ Waffle iron _____ _____
- ☐ Stock pot _____ _____
- ☐ Electric skillet _____ _____
- ☐ Indoor grill _____ _____
- ☐ Steamer _____ _____
- ☐ Wok/utensils _____ _____
- ☐ Electric knife _____ _____
- ☐ Can opener _____ _____
- ☐ Salt and pepper mills _____ _____
- ☐ Kitchen shears _____ _____
- ☐ Cookware set or individual pieces _____ _____
- ☐ Plastic storage containers _____ _____
- ☐ Ice trays _____ _____
- ☐ Vegetable and dish scrubbers _____ _____
- ☐ Dish towels _____ _____
- ☐ Pot holders _____ _____
- ☐ Dish drainer _____ _____
- ☐ Paper-towel rack _____ _____
- ☐ Apron _____ _____
- ☐ Drawer organizer for cutlery _____ _____
- ☐ Microwave oven _____ _____
- ☐ Microwave cookware _____ _____
- ☐ Round casserole: 2 qt. _____ _____
- ☐ Rectangular baking dish: 2 qt. _____ _____

☐ Rolling pin _____ _____

☐ Pastry brush _____ _____

☐ Pastry blender _____ _____

☐ Flour sifter _____ _____

☐ Wire whisk _____ _____

☐ Measuring cups, spoons _____ _____

☐ Muffin tin _____ _____

☐ Springform (with removable bottom) pan _____ _____

☐ Tube pan _____ _____

☐ Soufflé dish _____ _____

☐ Quiche plate _____ _____

☐ Two cake pans: 9-in. round _____ _____

☐ Biscuit and cookie cutters _____ _____

☐ Pastry bag and attachments _____ _____

☐ Cookie sheets _____ _____

☐ Two loaf pans _____ _____

☐ Pie plate _____ _____

☐ Set of mixing bowls _____ _____

☐ Wooden spoons _____ _____

☐ Grater _____ _____

☐ Colander _____ _____

☐ Metal tongs _____ _____

☐ Bottle opener _____ _____

☐ Vegetable peeler _____ _____

☐ Garlic press _____ _____

☐ Salad spinner _____ _____

☐ Bulb baster _____ _____

☐ Trussing needle, lacing pins _____ _____

☐ Barbecue skewers _____ _____

☐ Rubber bowl scrapers _____ _____

☐ Spice rack _____ _____

☐ Storage canisters _____ _____

☐ Turntable for cupboard shelf _____ _____

☐ Serving trays _____ _____

☐ Reamer (citrus juicer) _____ _____

☐ Juicer _____ _____

☐ Juice extractor _____ _____

☐ Bread maker _____ _____

☐ Pasta maker _____ _____

☐ Water purifier _____ _____

☐ Skillets: 1 qt., 2^1/$_2$ qt. _____ _____

☐ Saucepans: 1 qt., 2^1/$_2$ qt. _____ _____

☐ Ice cream maker _____ _____

☐ Ice cream scoop _____ _____

☐ Clay cooker _____ _____

☐ Fish poacher _____ _____

☐ Melon ball scoop _____ _____

☐ Tea kettle _____ _____

☐ Dutch oven _____ _____

☐ Roasting pan with rack _____ _____

☐ Thermometer/timer (for oven and meats) ____ _____

☐ Kitchen scale _____ _____

☐ Utensil set _____ _____

☐ Cookbook _____ _____

☐ Cookbook holder _____ _____

☐ Other _____ _____

Cutlery

	MANUFACTURER	MODEL
☐ Cutlery set	_____	_____
☐ Individual knives	_____	_____
☐ Sharpening tool	_____	_____
☐ Boning knife	_____	_____
☐ Carving knife and fork	_____	_____
☐ Knife block	_____	_____
☐ Cutting board	_____	_____
☐ Other	_____	_____

Electronics

	MANUFACTURER	MODEL
☐ Television	_____	_____
☐ Video system	_____	_____
☐ Stereo system (CD player, etc.)	_____	_____
☐ Telephone	_____	_____
☐ Radio/clock radio	_____	_____
☐ Camera equipment	_____	_____
☐ Portable music system	_____	_____
☐ Home computer	_____	_____
☐ Answering machine	_____	_____

Home Equipment

	MANUFACTURER	MODEL
☐ Iron	_____	_____
☐ Ironing board	_____	_____
☐ Vacuum	_____	_____
☐ Hand-held vacuum cleaner	_____	_____
☐ Toolbox	_____	_____
☐ Smoke alarm	_____	_____
☐ Carbon monoxide detector	_____	_____
☐ Security device	_____	_____
☐ Fire extinguisher	_____	_____
☐ Sewing machine	_____	_____
☐ Major appliances (refrigerator, dishwasher, washer, dryer, etc.)	_____	_____
☐ Other	_____	_____

Linens

	MANUFACTURER	STYLE	QTY.

Table Linens

☐ Formal tablecloth	_____	_____	___
☐ Formal napkins	_____	_____	___
☐ Casual tablecloth	_____	_____	___
☐ Casual napkins	_____	_____	___
☐ Place mats	_____	_____	___
☐ Extra napkins (for buffets, large gatherings)	_____	_____	___

Bed Linens

☐ Flat sheets	_____	_____	___
☐ Fitted sheets	_____	_____	___
☐ Pillowcases	_____	_____	___
☐ Pillow shams	_____	_____	___
☐ Blankets (winter and summer)	_____	_____	___
☐ Comforter or duvet cover	_____	_____	___
☐ Mattress cover	_____	_____	___
☐ Pillows	_____	_____	___
☐ Decorative pillows (neck rolls, European squares, etc.)	_____	_____	___

Bath Linens

☐ Bath towels	_____	_____	___
☐ Hand towels	_____	_____	___
☐ Face cloths	_____	_____	___
☐ Bath sheets	_____	_____	___
☐ Guest towels	_____	_____	___
☐ Beach towels	_____	_____	___

Bath Accessories

☐ Shower curtain	_____	_____	___
☐ Bath scale	_____	_____	___
☐ Showerhead massage	_____	_____	___
☐ Electric dental hygiene system	_____	_____	___
☐ Hair dryer	_____	_____	___
☐ Bath mat	_____	_____	___
☐ Bath rug	_____	_____	___
☐ Wastebasket	_____	_____	___
☐ Soap dish	_____	_____	___

☐ Toothbrush
holder   _____ ____ ___
☐ Other   _____ ____ ___

☐ Duffel   _____ _____ _____
☐ Sports bag   _____ _____
☐ Other   _____ _____

Decorative Accessories

	PATTERN	STYLE	MANUFACTURER
☐ Vases	_____	____	_____
☐ Candle-sticks	_____	____	_____
☐ Lamps	_____	____	_____
☐ Clocks	_____	____	_____
☐ Mirrors (various sizes)	_____	____	_____
☐ Area rugs	_____	____	_____
☐ Decorative bowls/ objects	_____	____	_____
☐ Art or craft pieces	_____	____	_____
☐ Other	_____	____	_____

Luggage

	MANUFACTURER	MODEL
☐ Garment/ hanging bag	_____	_____
☐ Suitcases	_____	_____
☐ Train case	_____	_____

Stationery

	COLOR	STYLE
☐ Letterhead	_____	_____
☐ Informals	_____	_____
☐ Address book	_____	_____
☐ Pen	_____	_____
☐ Other	_____	_____

General Style Manufacturer

	STYLE	MANUFACTURER
☐ Furniture (tables, chairs, bookcases, sofa, bed, mattress, box spring, etc.)	_____	_____
☐ Closet/storage system	_____	_____
☐ Exercise/sporting equipment	_____	_____
☐ Hobby	_____	_____
☐ Storage/ cedar chests	_____	_____
☐ Other	_____	_____

YOUR DINNERWARE

Dinnerware sets the tone for a beautiful table setting. The two of you will discover a wide variety of dinnerware colors, motifs, and textures. To help you choose, here's the dish on several types of dinnerware:

- **Fine china, porcelain** is quality dinnerware made from highly refined clays and minerals. It is completely nonporous and extremely durable.

- **Bone china** contains bone ash and is recognized by its translucency. If you hold it up to the light, you can see the silhouette of your hand through it. It is also high quality, nonporous, and extremely durable.

- **Stoneware** is made from coarser clays than porcelain, making it more informal in appearance. It is popular for casual designs and ovenware products.

- **Earthenware** is made from a mixture of clays, is semiporous, and is slightly less shock-resistant than other dinnerware materials. It can be vividly decorated, due to the low firing temperature required in its production.

- **Oven-to-tableware** includes porcelains and other glazes that do not crack or craze (develop fine lines in the glaze) when exposed to extreme heat.

How Much Will You Need?

Dinnerware is usually sold in five-piece place settings. A place setting for a fine china pattern would include a dinner plate, dessert/salad plate, bread-and-butter plate or rimmed bowl (great for pasta), and cup and saucer. (A casual dinnerware place setting substitutes a small bowl for the bread-and-butter plate.) You can register for as many place settings as you think you can use, based on how many people you usually serve when entertaining (aim for at least six to eight, though). In addition to place settings, also look at the extras available—vegetable dishes, platters, tea- or coffeepots, espresso cups, and service plates that sit under the dinner plate. They can be beautiful—not to mention functional—additions to your table setting.

Tips for Buying Dinnerware

- **Pick up cups.** Consider how they feel to hold, as well as how they look. Have your groom do this, too, as his grip is apt to be different from yours.

- **Notice plate shapes.** Is it a spacious coupe (rimless) or a deeper shouldered (rimmed) design? Decide which you prefer.

- **Look at different price ranges and notice the varying quality.** Whatever the price tag, make sure the weight of the plates and cups is well-balanced, that it has a smooth, blemishless surface, and that there's a refinement in the coloring of the design or metallic accents.

- **Check availability.** "Open stock" means you can usually buy individual pieces, not just as a place setting. Some stores will notify you if your pattern goes on sale. If the pattern is being discontinued, it may be available at a closeout sale. If necessary, you can contact the manufacturer and ask for some suggestions on how you can find missing pieces or how you can replace those that might someday break. Your gift registry should also be able to steer you to several companies that sell discontinued patterns by mail order.

DINNERWARE CHECKLIST

PATTERN NAME   Fine china _____   Everyday dinnerware _____

MANUFACTURER   Fine china _____   Everyday dinnerware _____

	FINE CHINA			EVERYDAY DINNERWARE		
	Quantity on hand	Quantity desired	Price	Quantity on hand	Quantity desired	Price
Dinner plates						
Salad plates						
Bread and butter plates						
Cups and saucers						
Fruit and cereal bowls						
Soup plates						
Cream soups						
Demitasse cups and saucers						
Vegetable serving dishes						
Platters						
Salad or serving bowl						
Gravy boat						
Butter dish						
Sugar bowl and creamer						
Teapot						
Coffeepot						
Tureen						
Salt and pepper shakers						

YOUR FLATWARE

You have several options when it comes to flatware. Popular and easy to care for is **stainless steel.** It can be sleek or ornate, contemporary or traditional. Many couples choose it for everyday use. **Sterling silver** has great beauty and intrinsic value that will be treasured for generations to come. Made from 925 parts pure silver and 75 parts mixed alloy for strength, each piece of this precious metal bears the imprint "sterling," as well as the maker's mark that attests to its value and quality. Sterling and more affordable **silver plate** (metal covered with silver; good silver plate has all the qualities of sterling silver) can be embellished by chasing (sculpting by hand), embossing (a die impression), or engraving (a light surface cutting).

Sterling as well as silver plate are available in a

bright mirror or satin finish. In time, and with regular use, they will develop a lustrous patina, or tiny scratches that give it a soft glow. Neither sterling nor good-quality silver plate will ever wear out; both will become more beautiful with time. If you have sterling or silver plate flatware, you can use it every day, with every meal. Rotate the items you use, so they develop a patina at the same rate. When you do polish it (perhaps twice a year), use a good-quality silver-cleaning polish, never a chemical dip, which can be too harsh and may remove the dark antiquing added to offset the detail on certain traditional designs.

Sterling and silver plate may go in the dishwasher (unless your manufacturer recommends hand washing). Make sure your silverware is loosely stacked (tight packing can encourage gauging), and knives should be dried by hand (the heat of the drying cycle can loosen the cement holding the knife blade to the knife handle). Also, take care not to place stainless steel in the same dishwasher compartment as sterling or silver plate. The combination of the metals could cause a reaction, marring the silver items.

Store your sterling or silver plate in a drawer or chest lined with protective, tarnish-preventing cloth. If you aren't using it often, store it in an airtight chest.

A typical six-piece place setting consists of a dinner knife, dinner fork, soup spoon, salad/dessert fork, teaspoon, and butter spreader. Serving pieces that are an excellent addition to your serving chest are gravy or sauce ladles; cold meat forks; serving spoons; items for lemons, butter, and condiments; trays; teas and coffee services; pitchers; and bowls. Just as with dinnerware, you can select serving and accessory pieces in patterns different from your place settings (e.g., simple versus ornate).

SILVER AND FLATWARE CHECKLIST

PATTERN NAME   Sterling/silver plate _____ Casual _____

MANUFACTURER   Sterling/silver plate _____ Casual _____

Item	STERLING/SILVER PLATE			CASUAL		
	Pattern	Manufacturer	Qty.	Pattern	Manufacturer	Qty.
Dinner knives						
Dinner forks						
Teaspoons						
Soup spoons						
Salad forks						
Butter spreaders						
Creamsoup spoons						
Demitasse spoons						
Iced beverage spoons						
Cocktail/oyster forks						

Item	STERLING/SILVER PLATE			CASUAL		
	Pattern	Manufacturer	Qty.	Pattern	Manufacturer	Qty.
Steak knives						
Serving forks						
Serving spoons						
Salad servers						
Soup ladle						
Gravy/sauce ladle						
Sugar tongs						
Sugar spoon						
Jelly server						
Butter server						
Pie or cake server						
Carving set						
Pasta server						
Teapot						
Coffeepot						
Sugar bowl and creamer						
Tray						
Large platter						
Smaller platter						
Vegetable serving dishes						
Gravy/sauce boat and tray						
Sauce bowl and tray						
Bread tray						
Butter dish						
Water pitcher						
Salt and pepper shakers						
Bowls for flowers, candy, fruit, nuts, etc.						
Compotes						
Candlesticks (high)						
Candlesticks (low)						
Coasters						
Ice bucket						
Wine cooler						
Trivets						

YOUR GLASSWARE

Glassware is either hand blown or machine made. When glass is **hand blown**, it's created one piece at a time by a skilled glassblower. The result is a very fine, delicate, uniquely shaped piece of glass—a work of art. **Machine-made** glass is either blown or molded mechanically, many pieces at a time, into uniform shapes. Technology has become so advanced that machine-made glass is now of superb quality. **Cut glass** is decorated by hand cutting on stone wheels, or it may also be achieved by machine. Typical cut glass decorations include leaf, flower, diamond, and geometric motifs. **Etched glass** usually has fine lines, lacy patterns, or geometric designs. **Full lead crystal** or crystal made with substitutes for lead is high-quality glassware. The lead or the lead substitutes give the glass its characteristic brilliance as well as softening the glass so designs can be cut into it. There are also **colored glasses** (produced by mixing various mineral salts with the other glass-producing materials), **milk glass** (which is an opaque white), and **cased glass** (which is coated with layers of colored glass to give it a two-tone effect).

Through the Looking Glass: How Much Glassware Will You Need?

There are two basic types of glassware: stemware (drinking glasses or other pieces that are on stems, such as wineglasses), and barware (drinking vessels without stems, such as glasses for everyday beverages or cocktails). You will probably start with a basic "all-purpose" stemware shape, such as a nine-ounce goblet for wine, water, and juice; champagne flutes; and several barware styles, such as short double old-fashioned glasses and taller highball glasses. Later, you can add wineglasses in different shapes for individual wines—red, white, sparking, and sweet wines, or sherry. Also add cordial glasses, brandy snifters, and accessories such as decanters.

Buying Tips

• Make sure the glasses feel **comfortable and balanced** when you hold them.

• **If you're buying hand-made versus machine-made glassware, you might notice very slight variations in size or an occasional bubble.** Think of these as beauty marks, not blemishes. They're a testament to the hand-crafted character of the glass, distinguishing it from the machine-made variety.

GLASSWARE CHECKLIST

Item	FINE CRYSTAL			EVERYDAY GLASSWARE		
	Pattern	Manufacturer	Qty.	Pattern	Manufacturer	Qty.
Water goblets						
Red wine glasses						
White wine glasses						
All-purpose stemware						
Champagne flutes						
Juice glasses						
Iced beverage glasses						
Double old-fashioned glasses						
Highball glasses						
Cocktail glasses						
Pilsners						
Sherry glasses						
Cordial glasses						
Brandy snifters						
Pitchers						
Decanters						
Dessert set						
Serving/salad bowls						
Individual plates and bowls						
Punch set						
Ice bucket						
Wine cooler						

YOUR COOKWARE

Here are some pointers for picking your pots and pans.

Aluminum

Aluminum is a popular cookware material. It is relatively lightweight compared to cast iron, but it just as quickly and evenly distributes heat through the sides and bottom of the pan. However, the heavier the gauge (thickness) of the pot or pan, the more durable and efficient it is. Aluminum is a good choice for stock pots, roasting pans, and other large, difficult-to-handle items. Aluminum pans work equally well with either a plain or a nonstick surface.

Stainless Steel

Stainless steel is extremely durable, doesn't stain, and is available with or without a nonstick coating. Stainless steel by itself is not a good conductor of heat. Therefore, it will be clad or sandwiched with copper or aluminum.

Cast Iron

Cast-iron utensils are excellent for browning, frying, stewing, and baking because they absorb heat slowly and distribute it evenly. Since cast iron is porous and rough, it must be seasoned periodically to prevent rusting and to keep food from sticking. Enameled cast iron has all the same advantages, but it doesn't require seasoning. Be careful not to overheat it, however, or the finish may chip or develop fine cracks. And for total ease of cleanup, some items, like skillets, are available with a nonstick coating.

Copper

Copper is the oldest cookware metal and the best conductor of heat. Copper serving utensils are also excellent for keeping food warm at the table. Copper items are always lined with silver, tin, stainless steel, or a nonstick finish because any direct contact with copper can cause foods to discolor. Polish the exteriors periodically with a commercial copper cleaner to maintain its appearance.

Porcelain Enamel

Also called enameled steel, porcelain enamel is metal covered with a durable glass. Porcelain enamel combines the heat-conducting qualities of metal with a surface that won't interact with food, stain, scratch, or peel. Higher-quality versions also have stainless steel rims. There is a wide variety of colors—white, cobalt blue, red, green—and motifs to choose from. You may even be able to coordinate your porcelain enamel cookware with your dinnerware.

Glass and Pyroceramics

One dish that goes from freezer to oven to table is ideal for busy cooks. Heat-tempered glass and pyroceramic utensils fit the bill and are easy to maintain due to their naturally nonporous surfaces or because of their nonstick coating. Be sure to look for a warranty against thermal breakage (due to extreme changes in temperature).

Microwave Cookware

Microwave cooking calls for microwave cookware (it won't damage the oven or prevent food from cooking properly). Look for cookware that's labeled safe for microwave use.

Nonstick Surfaces

Pots and pans with nonstick surfaces offer two big benefits: They're easy to clean, plus food slides right off them, so you don't need to grease the pan prior to cooking (which lowers the fat content of food). When cooking, always use wood or nylon utensils, as metals can scratch the surface. Nonstick surfaces are dishwasher safe, or they can be cleaned with detergent and a sponge or a nylon brush.

ON THE CUTTING EDGE: CHOOSING KNIVES

Good knives make dicing, chopping, slicing, and cutting practically effortless. Here is some knife knowledge:

• Knife blades are made from either high-carbon steel, stainless steel, or high-carbon stainless steel. **High-carbon stainless steel is usually the best choice,** since it is strong, does not rust, pit, or stain, and can be resharpened when it becomes dull. Serrated knives are offered only in stainless steel, which never needs resharpening.

• **Handles, too, come in various materials.**

Choose one that won't become slippery when wet or greasy and feels comfortable in your hand.

• **You'll probably need at least four good knives.** A **chef's knife** is a reasonably large, heavy knife for chopping whole foods. A **paring knife** is a miniature version of the chef's knife and is used for smaller cutting tasks. Use a long, thin **slicing knife** for cutting cooked meats and vegetables. A **serrated knife** has a scalloped edge and is used for cutting bread, tomatoes, or other foods with a tough skin and soft interior.

YOUR LINENS

"Linens" is a broad term, encompassing sheets, pillowcases, blankets, and towels, as well as table-cloths, napkins, and place mats. You can list all these items in your gift registry at department and bed and bath stores.

Bedding Basics: Don't Get Caught Snoozing

A generation or two ago, sheets were always white and needed ironing. Today, sheets come in a vast array of colors and patterns, and in a number of fabrics that eliminate the need for ironing. When buying sheets, consider **fabric.** The more threads per square inch that are woven into the fabric, the softer, stronger, and finer the sheet. Percale, a popular option, has a thread count of 180 or more. Also think about fit. Sheets today are generously sized. You should have no problem finding those that will fit your standard twin, full, queen, or king-size bed. Consider accessory and accent pieces in the same pattern as your sheets or in a complementary pattern. Look for coordinating or matching pillow-cases and shams, a matching comforter or duvet

cover, bed skirt, window treatments, accent pillows, and table skirts. Finishing touches: a mattress cover and a couple of blankets, of varying weight.

Towel Tips

• **Select a variety of sizes**—bath towels, bath sheets, hand towels, face cloths, and beach towels.

• **All towels are not created equal.** A velvety texture may feel soft, but it won't dry as well as terry.

• Don't forget about **guest towels.** They're the perfect choice when you're entertaining.

• **Personalize your towels** with a monogram or favorite motif.

• **Get coordinated.** For a stylish look, choose towels, rugs, and a shower curtain that complement each other.

Basic Linens List

A crisp stack of the smoothest sheets. Plump towels in natural hues. Soft blankets awaiting a cool night. Stocking your newlywed linen closet is a tactile pleasure. Register and enjoy!

Master Bedroom
  3 sets of sheets
  6 pillowcases
  6 pillow protectors
  4 or more pillows
  1 comforter or duvet cover
  4 blankets—2 winter weight, 2 summer weight
  1 mattress cover
  Accessory pillows (2 neck rolls, 2 European squares)
  1 bed skirt

Master Bathroom
  8 bath towels
  8 hand towels
  8 face cloths
  2 bath mats
  1 bath rug
  1 shower curtain
  2 beach towels

For Your Guests
  2 sets of sheets per bed

  2 pillowcases for each pillow
  1–2 blankets
  2–4 sets of towels
  6 fingertip towels

Table Linens: A Buyer's Guide

Your **linens can make a strong style statement.** Bold colors and interesting designs can change the mood of the table for each party and give a routine table setting a face-lift. Select table linens to go with your **dinnerware and your dining room decor.** You will probably need at least **one fine linen or lace tablecloth** for elegant dining, **a selection of casual ones for everyday use,** and a set of **place mats and coordinating napkins. Napkins** are a necessity and **should go with your tablecloths and place mats.** Also consider getting eight or a dozen colorful, unique, inexpensive, oversized cotton lap napkins for **when serving a casual buffet.** Team them with smaller napkins for hands and mouth. When entertaining, don't forget **cocktail napkins** for drinks and hors d'oeuvres.

YOUR MONOGRAM: AN INITIATION

A monogram can personalize just about anything—silver, linens, stationery, even stemware. The letters of the customary three-part monogram are the bride's initials—that of her first name, maiden name, and new last name (in that order). Other options include using your first-name initial, your husband's first-name initial, and your married-name initial either above or below the two—or smack in the center, between them. Keeping your name? Then consider a joint monogram—your first and last initials stacked over his. One word of caution: If your initials

spell a word—BAD, HAT, BAR, etc.—consider reworking the monogram, perhaps putting the last initial in the center. Some monogram styles include elaborate intertwined initials, block capital letters in a triangle, and tailored oval or diamond shapes.

Where to put your monogram? Consider the design of the piece and the space available. Silver flatware may call for a simplified monogram or a family crest reduced in size. A silver serving tray, however, probably has ample space. Plain linens display a monogram to its best advantage; unless the monogram is reserved for a border, patterned linens are best left unmonogrammed.

Last but not least, consider exactly what, if any, items you want monogrammed. Since many stores will not allow you to return monogrammed pieces, you might want to request on your registry that gifts *not* be monogrammed. You can always take care of it later, if you want.

GEE, THANKS! HOW TO WRITE A HEARTFELT THANK-YOU NOTE

It doesn't matter how many times you said thank you or gushed over the gift. You should still write a thank-you note. It doesn't have to be long, just sincere. Here are simple strategies for putting your heart and soul into it.

Getting Started

• **Order your thank-you notes early**— about the time you order your invitations. With notes at the ready, there's no excuse for putting off writing your thank-yous—which can pile up quicker than a bunch of single guys at the garter toss.

• **Be organized.** Have a master list of gifts you've received (see guest/announcement chart), who sent them (jot down addresses, too), and any brief thoughts you have about them (a compact food processor—great for our short-on-counter-space kitchen).

• **Write thank-you notes for gifts you receive before the wedding within two weeks of their receipt;** thank-you notes for gifts received after the wedding should be written within a month of their arrival.

Finding the Right Words

• **Describe the gift and how you'll use it.** If it's a place setting or crystal goblets, for example, mention how great they'll look on your table when you host your first Thanksgiving dinner this year. If it's a gift of money, give some indication of how you'll spend it—be it putting it toward a down payment on a house, home improvement projects, new furniture, whatever. Don't mention the amount.

• **Can't find something nice to say about, um, an *unusual* gift? Then just politely describe it.** Say how creative it is, how unique the design/material/shape is. If you think you might have a use for it—a goldfish-shaped punch bowl might be the perfect thing for a summer barbecue—say so.

• **Be gracious.** If you've never met the gift giver, mention what a pleasure it will be to do so in the near future.

• **You received two blenders?** Two identical crystal vases? The gift giver needn't know. Just politely thank him or her for the gift and the kind gesture. You can arrange to return a duplicate item without the gift giver knowing.

• **Divvy up the task.** Your groom can write thank-you notes for gifts received from his family and friends, while you can handle those received from your side.

• **Make sure you handwrite your notes,** no matter how atrocious your penmanship is. As any mass-mailing recipient knows, typewritten or computer-printed notes lack personal appeal.

Chapter 16:

GIFTS FOR GUESTS AND ATTENDANTS

Say thank you in style. Here are great gift ideas for attendants, family, and guests.

GIFTS FOR GUESTS: IN YOUR FAVOR

Wedding favors are both lucky souvenirs and tokens of appreciation for your guests. They can also say something personal and creative about you. Let these suggestions spark your imagination.

Traditional

- Beautifully boxed and monogrammed mints or chocolates
- Small picture frames (put guests' place cards in them at the reception)
- Votive candles and holders
- Sugar flowers from the wedding cake, presented in ribboned boxes
- Pieces of the groom's cake, placed in monogrammed white boxes

Ethnic

- Italian confetti—candy-coated almonds wrapped in a pretty piece of tulle or lace or in a linen pocket square
- Chinese fortune cookies (personalize the fortunes)
- Boxes of Scandinavian marzipan candies
- Miniature bottles of Japanese sake
- Irish linen handkerchiefs
- Small pieces of English bone china

Theme

- Southwestern: mini cacti
- Tropical: leis or shells
- Country: pottery mugs or dried flower arrangements
- Nautical: miniature toy boats filled with candy
- Hanukkah: wooden dreidels
- Christmas: tree ornaments engraved with the year
- New Year's: small, framed calendar
- Easter: hand-painted eggs (real or keepsake); gourmet jelly beans
- Halloween (or masquerade): ornate masks

Hand-made

- Miniature wreaths made with symbolic herbs (rosemary, for example, for remembrance)
- Sachets of satin or lace filled with potpourri or scented rose petals

• Small boxes hand-decorated with fabric, paint, paper, beads, etc., with the couple's name and wedding date inscribed inside the lid

• Fabric flowers tied with ribbons inscribed with your name and wedding date

• Framed decoupage flowers on hand-made paper

• Hand-decorated bird houses (a real love nest!)

Distinctive and Different

• Notes stating that you and your groom have made a donation to a charity in each guest's name

(or have a sign placed at an exit that lets guests know the name of the charity)

• Packets of seedlings or individual tree saplings for planting

• Lottery tickets

• Gift certificates

• Bagels and the Sunday paper (after a late Saturday-night wedding)

• Poetry printed on accordion-pleated paper and folded into fan shapes (great for a garden wedding)

• Handcrafted cookies, dressed with ribbon and tulle

• Miniature wedding cakes (a few inches tall)

GIFTS FOR ATTENDANTS: PRESENTS THAT REALLY SAY THANKS

They've shopped and schlepped. Listened and laughed. Calmed and comforted. Now say thanks.

Bridesmaids

• Silk scarf

• Makeup bag and brushes

• Crystal or porcelain vanity accessories

• Leather backpack

• Jewelry box

• Certificate for a body massage, facial, pedicure, or other spa treatment

• Photo album and memory snapshots of you and the bridesmaid, along with a note

• Silver-trimmed bookmarks

• A pretty journal or note cards

• Freshwater pearl necklace or bracelet

• Porcelain paperweight (a nice touch: monogram it, or have her initials hand painted on)

• Perfume bottles

• Hand-fabricated and personalized fabric hatbox to store keepsakes

Ushers

• Sports team memorabilia (cuff links, sweatshirt, hat)

• Bottle of vintage port or malted scotch

• Day of skiing (or golfing, or tennis, etc.)

• Portable CD player

• Binoculars

• Fine leather shaving case

• Great-looking vest for wedding day and beyond

• Monogrammed bathrobe

• Sterling silver money clips

• Pewter mint julep cups

• Gold-plated pen and pencil set

Bridesmaids or Ushers

• Two tickets to a concert, play, or sporting event

• Weekend bag

• Gift certificate to a favorite restaurant

- Engraved stationery
- Picture frame (add a photo of you with your bridesmaid—or of your groom with his attendant)
- Fountain pen
- Certificate to a movie theater, or for twelve (or more) video rentals
- Leather business-card case
- Engraved pilsner glass
- Sports watch

Children

- Charm bracelet
- Heart locket
- Crystal animal
- Stuffed animal
- Classic children's book
- Computer game software
- Autographed baseball
- Wedding-day accessory (petticoat, vest, bow tie)

Chapter 17:

JUST FOR THE TWO OF YOU

You've decided on the date, the place, the dress. The bridesmaids, the boutonnieres, the band. The food, the flowers, the favors. Now you need to address less celebrated (but just as important) issues of wedding planning. How do you get a marriage license? Should you think about having a trousseau? What's involved in getting your name legally changed? Here's help to get you started.

BRIDAL TROUSSEAU

"Trousseau" comes from the French word *"trousse,"* meaning "little bundle"—the clothes and linens a bride took with her to her new home. The idea expanded into a dowry, a larger collection of possessions that made the bride more attractive in the eyes of potential suitors.

In recent generations, the bride's trousseau has referred to the new clothes the bride bought before her wedding (as well as other possessions, such as linens, sheets, etc., she might bring to the marriage). Marriage was a rite of passage—a girl who lived with her parents became a young matron with the responsibilities of a home and community. For both her honeymoon and her new life, the bride needed an entire new wardrobe.

Although many brides today already have a wardrobe that reflects their lifestyle, there are still reasons why buying new clothes at this time makes sense:

- You're moving to a different climate.
- You're changing careers.
- You're traveling or entertaining more.
- You're traveling to a honeymoon destination for which you need suitable clothes.
- You want some special, sexy lingerie for your honeymoon and after.

If you fit any of these categories, then a shopping trip may be in your future. Just be sure to spend wisely.

HIS NAME OR YOURS?

While a full 87 percent of brides-to-be polled in a recent *BRIDE'S* Magazine survey say they will take their husband's name after the wedding, changing your name isn't a given anymore. Here are some options:

- **Keeping your name.** You may get some flak from his side of the family (if there's tension over your decision, sit down and talk with his Mother about it), but when you've built a professional, not to mention a personal, identity around a name, it's hard to give it up. Most people will understand and accept your decision, once they know you're not rejecting their name—or them.

• **Using both names.** You may decide to use your married name socially while keeping your maiden name professionally. Just be sure you sign all legal documents using your legal name—which, unless you formally change it, is your maiden name.

• **Hyphenating your maiden and married names.** If your two names aren't long or cumbersome, it could give you the best of both worlds. For example, if your husband's last name is Smith, you could now go by Sarah Jones-Smith. Or you could adopt the hyphenated name legally and use your husband's last name socially. Your husband may take on the hyphenated name as well, but he'll have to get the name changed in court if he wants it legally recognized.

• **He adopts your name.** Instead of your taking his name after the wedding, he takes *yours*.

• **Creating a new name.** Movie stars have been doing it for years, so why not newlywed couples? The two of you could decide to adopt a name that's a combination of your two last names (Baker and Taylor can become Baylor, for instance)—or pick out a new one altogether. Either way, if you want the name legally recognized, you'll have to go to court.

If you do decide to take his name (or legally change yours in any way), you'll have to fill out some paperwork. You will have to record the name change on all legal and official records, including:

• Social Security card
• Passport
• Tax forms
• Driver's license
• Will
• Checking and savings accounts
• Voter registration card
• Mortgage, deed, and lease
• Stock and bond certificates

• Employee ID
• Insurance policies
• 401K plan
• IRAs
• Utility and phone accounts (if the accounts are in your name)
• Post office address
• Credit cards
• Magazine subscriptions
• Professional associations and club memberships

Whether you decide to keep your name or not, let others know of your decision so they can address you properly. Here are some ways to spread the news to family, friends, and business associates:

• Use the name you've chosen on personal stationery, letterhead, and business cards and in all correspondence.

• Send at-home cards. These are printed cards listing your name and address, which can be enclosed with wedding invitations or announcements, or with thank-you notes.

• For business, you might want to send out cards stating something like "Sarah Jones has taken the surname of Smith and will now be known as Sarah Smith."

• If you're keeping your maiden name, or keeping it just professionally, say so in your newspaper wedding announcement.

• If you want to be known by your maiden name, introduce yourself as "Sarah Jones, Jim Smith's wife," at social gatherings.

• Ask your husband, family, and friends to introduce you using your maiden name.

• Respond to misaddressed invitations in your maiden name. "Sarah Jones and Jim Smith will gladly attend."

• Take the inevitable slip-ups in stride. You may politely correct the person or just let it slide at an informal gathering.

GIVE YOURSELF SOME CREDIT

Whether you're married or single, it's important to establish credit in your own name. Not knowing that Mrs. James Smith is the same person who paid off student loans and managed five charge cards under the name of Sarah Jones, the bank may deny you credit if you ever want to start your own business or buy a house in your name. Earning your own credit rating will help prevent that. How do you do it?

• Use your name in all your financial dealings. Instead of using Mrs. James Smith, for example, use Sarah Smith or Sarah Jones-Smith (whichever name you've adopted). Don't flip-flop back and forth between names. Be consistent.

• Maintain your own charge accounts.

• If you open a joint charge account, make sure you're each issued individual cards with your own names. Don't use an "authorized user" card for his account.

• Put some things in your name—not your husband's. It could be your phone, cable, or utilities service.

GETTING A MARRIAGE LICENSE: HOW TO APPLY YOURSELVES

You can't get married without it, so make this a top priority. Different states have different requirements. To wend your way through the bureaucratic maze, take note of the following:

• **Where to apply.** Call the town hall, town clerk's office, marriage license bureau, or health department in the city where you'll marry. In most cases, it's one of these offices that issues the license. If you live far away from where you'll be marrying, they can tell you how to proceed.

• **When to apply.** Check with the office that issues the licenses. Most are issued a few weeks before the wedding. There may be a waiting period—a few days between when you apply for the license and when it is issued and becomes valid. Some licenses may also expire within a certain period (if you don't get married within that time frame, the license is invalid).

• **Blood tests.** States have different requirements for blood tests (the office responsible for the marriage license can give you the specifics). If you

and your groom do need blood work done, you may go to a doctor or a health clinic and get the necessary tests. One caveat: In some states, blood test results are only valid for a certain period. Apply for your license after that period expires, and you may be asked to get new blood tests.

• **Docu-musts.** The license-issuing office can tell you exactly what you need, but be prepared to present your birth certificate (to verify age), proof of citizenship (if you weren't born in the United States), parental consent (if you're under the legal marrying age for the state), identification, and blood-test results (if your state requires them). If you're divorced, also bring your divorce decree. If you're widowed, bring along your spouse's death certificate. You may also be asked to bring a witness age eighteen or over who knows both of you.

• **Bring cash.** Ask what the license fee is, and then make sure you can pay it in cash (some offices will not accept checks).

MARRIAGE LICENSE CHECKLIST

Date we go for the license _____

Time _____

Office of City Clerk _____

     Building _____

     Address _____

     Phone _____ Fax _____ Fee $ _____

We need:

____ Identification (driver's license,   ____ Blood-test results

      birth certificate)   N/A Proof of divorce

____ Proof of age   N/A Death certificate

N/A Citizenship papers   ____ Witness (over age 18)

Waiting period _____ License is valid for _____ days

PRENUPTIAL AGREEMENTS: SHOULD YOU HAVE ONE?

No longer the exclusive domain of the rich and famous, prenuptial agreements are becoming more and more common. Prenuptial agreements are contracts drawn up before the wedding specifying who keeps what assets or inheritances should the marriage dissolve (in some cases, marital rights, duties, and responsibilities, as well as custody of any children, are also spelled out).

The very idea of prenuptial agreements is unsettling to a lot of people—they seem to feel there's a presumption that the marriage will fail. But these agreements can serve an important purpose beyond protecting your rights to personal property. Because many couples also spell out personal issues in the prenuptial agreement, such as whether or not they will have children and how their care will be divided up, they can help you clarify your goals for married life. But before you sign on the dotted line, *any* dotted line, make sure you carefully look over all documents and understand them fully. Also have your own personal attorney (not your groom's attorney) review them. Set up a mutually agreed upon timetable to reevaluate and revise the contract (say, every two years, every five years, or whatever you both think is sufficient).

Of course, whether or not you choose to have a prenuptial agreement is a highly individual decision. Many couples find them unnecessary, even unthinkable. Others wouldn't be caught at the altar without them. Some couples who have found them particularly useful are those with children from a previous marriage, a family trust fund, a large inheritance, lots of real estate, and heirlooms that they'd like to keep in the family should they divorce. If you think you might want to draw up a prenuptial agreement, consult your lawyer and financial planner or accountant.

COMMUNICATION 101

The wedding lasts a day, but the marriage—if it's a good one—will last a lifetime. Many counselors agree that one major cause of trouble in marriage is unfulfilled expectations and disparate goals. How much have you really talked about issues involving money, sex, and family? Even if you've discussed having children, have you discussed how you will raise and discipline them? Educate them? Save for them? How does religion fit into your lives? Will you attend services regularly? How will you handle holidays and family tensions if you're an interfaith couple?

The foundation of any good marriage is communication. And good communication involves more than talk—it involves *listening*. To communicate effectively, psychologists recommend using nonaccusatory language. For example, instead of saying "You spend way too much time with your family," say "I feel like you spend a lot of time with your family." Additionally, to get a better understanding of what is being said, paraphrase what you're hearing before responding.

Take some time out of wedding planning to really address issues that will affect your married life. Here are some questions to get you started.

Money

- Will we pool our incomes into one fund?
- Will we have a joint checking account or separate ones?
- Should we each have money of our own?
- Will one of us be the family financier, or will we share the responsibility?
- Do we have a budget? How much money should we try to save each month?
- Do my saving and spending habits bother you? Do yours bother me?

Career

- Would one of us be willing to move if the other was transferred or found a better job in another city?
- Will either one of us have many professional meetings or obligations outside of regular business hours?
- How many hours a day will we work?
- What sort of jobs do we see ourselves having in five years? Ten years?
- When do we see ourselves retiring?

Children

- Do we want children? If so, when? How many?
- If we have children, how will we divide child-rearing duties?
- Will one of us have more responsibility for day-to-day child raising?
- Will we both continue to work, or will one of us stay home with the children?
- If we found out one of us was infertile, would we seek infertility treatments or consider adoption?

Sex

• Have we talked openly and honestly about our sexual preferences and needs?

• Are we content with the frequency and quality of our sex?

• Are we happy with our form of birth control?

• If a sexual problem developed, would we seek professional help?

Leisure Time

• Will we spend all of our free time together? Do you feel it's important to take some time apart?

• Do we expect each other to share the same hobbies, interests? What if one of us doesn't enjoy the other's favorite leisure pursuit?

• Where will we take our vacations?

• If we have children, will we take them on vacation with us?

• How much money and time will we spend on leisure activities?

Friends

• Who will be responsible for scheduling social activities? Will we share the responsibility?

• How much time will we devote to our individual friendships?

• What if I don't like your friends—or you mine?

• Will we spend time with each other's friends whether we like them or not?

• Do you think I'm too influenced by my friends? Do I think you're too influenced?

Relatives

• How often will we see our families?

• How will we split up family holidays?

• Do you think I spend too much time with my family? Do I think you're too controlled by yours?

• Would we consider having a parent live with us someday?

Religion

• Will we attend religious services regularly? Together?

• Which religious traditions, if any, will we observe at home?

• Will we raise our children in a particular faith?

• Will we send them to religious school?

FAMILY PLANNING GUIDE

Once the wedding is over, you can be sure people will replace "When are you getting married?" with "When are you going to have kids?" If you want to put off having children or you've decided against parenthood altogether, you'll need some reliable birth control. To find the right contraceptive for you, study the following chart, then consult your physician. Cost will vary by the method, by whether or not you need a physical exam before it can be prescribed, and by how often you need to have it checked, refilled, or replaced. Note that both male and female sterilization methods are available for couples who are certain they want no children. The procedures are effective—and considered permanent, although in some cases they can be reversed. For more information, speak to your doctor or health-care provider.

Method and Effectiveness	Availability	How It Works
NORPLANT 99.96%	Prescribed by a physician.	Clinician inserts six matchstick-size capsules under the skin of the upper arm. Capsules continually release a hormone that suppresses ovulation and thickens cervical mucus, making it hard for sperm to penetrate. Provides effective contraception for five years (or as long as it's in place).
Depo-Provera 99.7%	Prescribed by a physician.	Provides protection from pregnancy for 12 weeks. Clinician administers a hormone shot to the arm or buttocks every three months to suppress ovulation and thicken cervical mucus so sperm cannot penetrate. The shot also prevents a fertilized egg from implanting in the uterus.
Intrauterine device (IUD) 97.4%–99.4%	Available only through a doctor. Annual checkups are necessary.	Clinician inserts a hormone-releasing or copper device in the uterus, keeping sperm from eggs and preventing a fertilized egg from implanting itself in the uterus. Copper IUDs may be left in place for up to 10 years; hormone-releasing IUDs for one year. You must check occasionally to make sure the device is still in place.
Combination pill/Minipill 97%–99.9%	Requires a prescription. Yearly checkup including Pap smear, breast exam, and blood pressure check recommended.	Combination pills suppress ovulation; minipills thicken cervical mucus, preventing implantation of a fertilized egg in the uterus. Most pills come in 21- or 28-day packs (the last seven of the 28 are placebos); one pill is taken orally each day.
Male condom 88%–98%	No prescription necessary; available in drugstores.	Thin sheath of latex, plastic, or animal tissue is rolled onto an erect penis before sex to keep sperm out of the vagina. Latex condoms should be used with water-based lubricants only. Leave a half inch of space at the tip (with air squeezed out) for sperm collection. Base of condom should be held in place during withdrawal.

Advantages	*Disadvantages*
Does not interrupt sex; can be used by women who can't take estrogen; safe for use during breast-feeding (beginning six weeks after delivery).	Irregular bleeding and menstrual cycles (e.g., heavy bleeding, spotting between periods, irregular intervals between periods, no menstrual bleeding at all); scarring above the implant site; slightly increased risk of heart attack or stroke, especially in women who smoke. May be hard to remove.
Does not interrupt sex; protects against cancer of the uterine lining and iron-deficiency anemia; can be used by breast-feeding women (six weeks after delivery) and those who can't take estrogen.	Irregular bleeding, weight gain, headaches, depression; may cause a delay in becoming pregnant after shots are discontinued.
Does not interrupt sex; does not affect hormone levels in the blood. Hormonal IUDs may reduce menstrual cramps and flow; copper ones may protect against ectopic pregnancy.	The IUD may be expelled; may cause discomfort, temporary increase in cramps and spotting, heavier or longer periods (with copper IUDs). Hormonal IUDs may increase the chance of ectopic pregnancy (a fertilized egg attaches outside the uterus), which can cause infertility. Increased chance of tubal infection, which may lead to sterility in women with multiple partners. Because of chance of infertility, may only be prescribed if you've had a child.
Does not interrupt sex; regulates your period and soothes PMS; protects against ovarian cysts, noncancerous breast tumors, ectopic pregnancy, gynecologic cancers.	Possible nausea, headaches, weight gain, spotting between periods, or temporary irregular bleeding. Rarely, the Pill is associated with heart attacks, strokes, blood clots, and liver and gall-bladder disease.
Easy to buy and use; can help reduce incidence of premature ejaculation. Lubricated condoms or nonlubricated ones used with a spermicide provide increased protection against pregnancy and the most effective protection against sexually transmitted diseases. No hormonal side effects.	Interrupts sex; may slip or break during sex; may decrease sexual pleasure. Some people may be allergic to spermicide or latex.

Method and Effectiveness	Availability	How It Works
Diaphragm/Cervical cap 82%–94%	Requires a prescription and fitting from a doctor.	Clinician fits you with a latex-rubber dome or cap that you coat with spermicide and insert into your vagina before sex, to cover the cervix. A diaphragm or cap keeps sperm from eggs; the spermicidal coating immobilizes sperm. Spermicide must be reapplied before each sex act. Both devices must be kept in place for six hours after intercourse.
Vaginal foams, gels, creams, suppositories, and female condoms 74%–97%	No prescription necessary; available at drugstores and/or clinics.	Vaginal foams, gels, creams, and suppositories are inserted into the vagina 15 minutes before intercourse. Spermicides in the products help immobilize sperm. The female condom is a polyurethane sheath with two flexible rings; one is inserted in the vagina, and one remains outside the body. The condom acts as a lining, keeping sperm out of the vagina.
Periodic Abstinence 80%–99%	Consult with your clinician. Involves using ovulation calendars and temperature charts as well as a basal thermometer. Free instruction at many health clinics and church centers.	You chart your menstrual cycle to predict your fertile period. Temperature and cervical mucus are also checked daily. Abstain from sex during unsafe times (five days before, the day of, and two days after ovulation).

Advantages	*Disadvantages*
Poses no major health concerns; can last several years; spermicide used with diaphragm or cap helps protect against certain sexually transmitted diseases (STDs), like chlamydia and gonorrhea.	Interrupts sex; some people may be allergic to latex or spermicide; should not be used during menstruation or if you have an infection; may become dislodged during sex. The diaphragm increases the risk of bladder infections and is not recommended for women with pelvic conditions. The cervical cap may be difficult for some women to use, and is not recommended for women with cervical conditions.
Easy to buy and insert; no known health risks to either partner. Female condom helps protect against STDs.	May interrupt sex; chemicals in some products may cause irritation or allergic reactions in some people. Female condom may slip or break during sex; it may decrease sexual pleasure. Some people may be allergic to spermicide or latex.
No medical or hormonal side effects; endorsed by most religions.	Don't use if you have irregular periods. Illness, stress, or lack of sleep may affect body temperature; vaginal infections and douching can change the consistency of cervical mucus, making fertile period difficult to identify. Both partners must be committed to this form of contraception.

Chapter 18:

WEDDING-DAY COUNTDOWN

If wedding planning were a baseball game, this would be the ninth inning. Here's a game plan for the home stretch.

WEDDING REHEARSAL

Do you hand your bouquet to your maid of honor after you walk down the aisle or before the exchange of rings? Do you kiss after the vows or at the end of the ceremony? Unless you're a wedding aficionado, you're not likely to know. Which is where your wedding rehearsal comes in. Generally, it's held from one to a few days before the ceremony. Your officiant is the master of ceremonies, so to speak, walking everyone through the wedding event and explaining each participant's role. He or she will tell you and your attendants when to stand, turn, sit, and speak. Don't worry if your wedding day comes and you can't remember a thing. You may not get married every week, but your officiant probably performs wedding ceremonies that often. He or she will guide you through it. More tips for a successful wedding rehearsal:

• Discuss ideas for personalizing your ceremony at premarriage meetings with your officiant. Don't wait until the rehearsal to get creative.

• Go over plans with parents and participants in advance, especially when there are variations. For example, if you'd like your mother to give you away, make sure she's comfortable with the idea beforehand.

• Bring along a faux bouquet or the ribbon bouquet from your bridal shower. Practice handing it to your honor attendant.

• Anyone who has a role in your wedding should attend the rehearsal (that includes child attendants, readers, candle lighters, etc.).

• Brief ushers on seating instructions and special duties such as spreading the aisle runner. They should also know where rest rooms and coat racks are located, and have directions to the reception site.

• Before the rehearsal is over, remind everyone about the times and places they should gather for the wedding.

• Have your clergyperson check the marriage license to make sure everything is in order.

WEDDING CEREMONY TIMETABLE

Wedding Morning
- Finish last-minute packing.
- Give wedding rings to your maid of honor and best man to hold at the altar.
- Make sure the outfits you both will wear when leaving the reception are ready and are brought to the reception site.
- Eat a light meal. You may be too busy or excited to eat much at your reception.

Two Hours to Go
- Start getting dressed. This is one day when you don't want to be hurried.
- Begin your makeup.

One Hour to Go
- Have formal portraits taken if they haven't been taken already.
- Attendants who've gotten ready elsewhere join you at your home to have pictures taken.
- Parents and siblings should finish dressing, too, so family photos can be taken.

Forty-five Minutes to Go
- Ushers should arrive at the ceremony site to begin seating guests (for instructions on who sits where, see page 214).

Thirty to Fifteen Minutes to Go
- The prelude music begins.
- Ushers continue seating guests.

Twenty Minutes to Go
- The groom and the best man arrive and await the bridal party in the vestibule (or hallway or a room away from guests).
- The officiant gives any last-minute instructions to the groom and ushers.

Ten Minutes to Go
- Bridal attendants arrive, followed by the bride's mother and the groom's parents.
- The wedding party and family wait in the vestibule (or other room away from guests); special guests are shown to their reserved seats.

Five Minutes to Go
- The groom's parents are seated (unless they are part of the processional). The groom's mother is escorted on the arm of an usher; her husband follows a few steps behind her. He takes a seat beside her, on the aisle.
- The bride and her father (or other escort) arrive. They remain in the limo or join the bridesmaids out of sight of guests.
- Late-arriving guests are shown to their seats.
- The bride's mother is seated by an usher or other important family member (but not your father if he is escorting you).

One Minute to Go
- Ushers fold back pew ribbons (if used) and then tie them to the last pew.
- Two ushers lay down the aisle runner (it protects the bride's gown from dirt and stays in place until guests have exited after the ceremony).
- Ushers assemble in the vestibule for the procession.

Ceremony Time
- The officiant takes his or her position at the front of the church.
- The groom, accompanied by the best man, stands ready (unless they are part of the processional).
- The processional music begins.
- Guests rise and turn to watch the procession in a Christian service and remain seated during a Jewish procession.

WHO SITS WHERE?

That depends on what sort of ceremony you're having. Here are some guidelines:

• If you're having a **Christian ceremony,** guests of the bride and her family should be seated on the left side of the church (as you face the altar); guests of the groom and his family on the right. If the church has a center pew, with aisles to the left and right, follow the same format—seating the bride's guests on the left, the groom's on the right. Both sets of parents sit on the center pew, with the bride's parents seated more toward the left, the groom's more toward the right.

• If you're having a **Jewish ceremony,** the bride's guests should be seated on the right, the groom's on the left. Both sets of parents stand under the chuppah.

• If **you and your family are inviting many more guests than your groom and his family are—or vice versa**—instruct ushers to fill up both sides of the church/synagogue. That way, things won't look lopsided.

• Ushers should seat your **parents** in the first pews, on their respective sides.

• **Grandparents and siblings** should be seated in the second pew.

• Additional pews can be reserved for **aunts and uncles**, **special friends**, **and the parents of any child attendants** (after the processional, these children may sit with their parents). Special pews should be marked with flowers, garlands, or ribbon. Pew cards can be sent with invitations or mailed out individually once you've received reply cards.

• **The rest of your guests** should be seated from front to back as they enter.

• Age has its advantages. **If several guests arrive together,** the oldest woman is seated first.

• Unless they need help walking, **male guests** are not escorted. Instead, they're simply shown to their seats.

• Once the bride's mother is seated and the processional has begun, ushers stop escorting and take their places. **Late-arriving guests** simply duck into a back pew.

Christian Ceremony

Christian Ceremony Positions:
1. *Bride*
2. *Groom*
3. *Honor attendant*
4. *Best man*
5. *Officiant*
6. *Flower girl*
7. *Ring bearer*
8. *Bridesmaids*
9. *Ushers*

Jewish Ceremony Positions:
1. *Bride*
2. *Groom*
3. *Honor attendant*
4. *Best man*
5. *Cantor*
6. *Rabbi*
7. *Flower girl*
8. *Ring bearer*
9. *Bride's parents*
10. *Groom's parents*
11. *Bridesmaids*
12. *Ushers*

Jewish Ceremony

STANDING ORDERS: WHO GOES WHERE?

The Processional

Christian

• Ushers begin the procession, walking in pairs (according to height) from the rear of the church. (In a Catholic wedding, however, the ushers may take their place at the altar from the front of the church.) If you have an odd number of ushers, have the shortest one walk down the aisle first.

• Bridesmaids proceed next, four to five pews behind the ushers. When your bridesmaids number four or fewer, have them walk down the aisle individually. If there are more, pair them by height. As with the ushers, if you have an odd number of bridesmaids, have the shortest one start the procession, heading down the aisle alone.

• Junior bridesmaids follow. If there are two, they should be paired together.

• The maid or matron of honor comes next. If you have chosen both a maid and matron of honor, they can walk together or individually. If

you choose the latter, have the honor attendant upon whom you've bestowed the most duties (i.e., fixing your train, holding your bouquet and the groom's ring, etc.) follow the other.

• Child attendants directly precede the bride. A ring bearer can walk with a flower girl, or they can walk separately.

• The bride and her father (or other escort) walk next. She is escorted on his left arm.

• Pages—if you're including any—carry the bride's train and end the procession.

Formal Jewish

• Customs vary by branches of Judaism, as well as by the rabbi's and by the family's wishes. In a formal Jewish procession, however, the rabbi and cantor (on the rabbi's right) start the procession.

• Next come the bride's grandparents, followed by the groom's grandparents (men are on the left, women on the right).

• The ushers follow in pairs (according to

Christian Ceremony

Jewish Ceremony

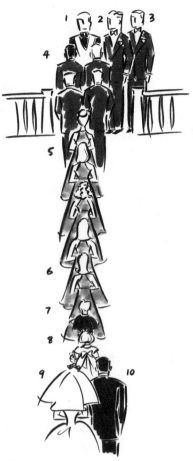

Christian Procession:

1. *Officiant*	6. *Honor attendant(s)*
2. *Groom*	7. *Ring bearer*
3. *Best man*	8. *Flower girl*
4. *Ushers*	9. *Bride*
5. *Bridesmaids*	10. *Father of the Bride*

Jewish Procession:

1. *Cantor*	9. *Groom's mother*
2. *Rabbi*	10. *Bridesmaids*
3. *Bride's grandparents*	11. *Honor attendant*
4. *Groom's grandparents*	12. *Ring bearer*
5. *Ushers*	13. *Flower girl*
6. *Best man*	14. *Bride's father*
7. *Groom's father*	15. *Bride*
8. *Groom*	16. *Bride's mother*

their height). Begin with the shorter ushers, followed by the taller ones.

• The best man comes next.

• The groom now enters with his parents. He stands on his father's right, his mother's left.

• The bridesmaids make their way down the aisle. If there are fewer than four, they walk singly, beginning with the shortest one. If there are four or more, they walk in twos. If there are

an odd number, have the shortest bridesmaid proceed down the aisle alone.

• The maid or matron of honor comes next. If there are two, the one with the most duties comes last.

• The ring bearer follows.

• The flower girl walks next.

• The bride now proceeds down the aisle, accompanied by her parents. She is escorted by her father on her right and her mother on her left.

Informal Jewish

- Ushers start the processional, walking in pairs (arranged by height) down the aisle.
- Bridesmaids follow—also in pairs, arranged by height.
- The best man comes next.
- The groom follows.
- The honor attendant(s) makes her way down the aisle.
- The flower girl walks next.
- The bride enters, escorted on her father's right arm.

Large, Formal Civil

- Let the site dictate. If there's a large center aisle, consider having everyone proceed in pairs or alone. If there's a narrow, small aisle—or none at all—scale down the processional, or simply enter through a door near where your officiant and groom are standing.

Small, Informal Civil

- Most brides marrying in small, civil ceremonies have one attendant. Have her precede the bride down the aisle.
- The bride's father or other escort walks with her into the room.
- The bride may forgo a procession altogether and stand with her groom before the officiant. Instead of being seated, guests can stand around the bride and groom.

Interfaith

- Depending on where you hold the ceremony and how much space you have, consider incorporating aspects of both kinds of processional into your ceremony. For example, perhaps both the bride's mother and father escort her down the aisle, but her grandmothers are seated beforehand.

The Ceremony

Christian

- The officiant usually stands facing the congregation.
- The bride stands facing him or her, on the left side of the congregation (after the procession, her father has slipped into the front pew—or the third pew if her parents are divorced; see chapter 3); her groom is on the right.
- The bride's honor attendant is on her left; the best man is on the groom's right.
- The attendants may stand in a diagonal line or straight row beside or behind the bride and groom (sometimes special chairs may be arranged for the attendants to sit on). Bridesmaids are on the left, ushers on the right. Flower girls stand just in front of the bridesmaids, the ring bearer in front of the ushers (or young children can slip into pews with their parents). Attendants may also stand in a semicircle around the bride and groom, but facing the congregation.

Jewish

- The rabbi and cantor stand facing the congregation; the cantor is on the rabbi's left.
- The bride and groom, wedding party, and both sets of parents stand under the chuppah for the entire wedding ceremony. In some cases, the poles of the chuppah may be held aloft, usually by ushers, during the ceremony.
- The bride stands on the right, facing the rabbi and cantor; the groom is on the left.
- The maid or matron of honor stands one step behind the bride, at a diagonal angle. The best man does likewise, behind the groom.
- The bride's parents stand one step behind the maid or matron of honor, diagonally. The groom's parents stand likewise, behind the best man.
- Bridesmaids and ushers situate themselves in a diagonal line next to the parents (ushers next to the groom's parents, bridesmaids next to the bride's parents).

• The ring bearer stands to the right of the ushers, flower girl to the left of the bridesmaids. Or they can sit with their parents in a front pew.

Civil

• Consider the amount of space you have and whether or not you'd like to acknowledge any religious customs (if you're Jewish, that might mean having your parents stand up with you, as well as your bridal party).

Interfaith

• Decide with your groom what traditions from each of your religions you'd like to honor; also consider any space constraints.

The Recessional

Christian

• The bride and groom (the bride taking his right arm) turn and walk up the aisle together, leading the recession.

• The flower girl, walking on the ring bearer's right, follows.

• The maid or matron of honor takes the right arm of the best man and walks up the aisle.

• The attendants follow in a similar manner, each on the right arm of an usher.

• If you have more bridesmaids than ushers, have one usher escort two attendants; if there are more ushers than bridesmaids, have the extras walk together or alone.

• Once the recessional of the bridal party ends, the ushers can return to the front of the church and escort the mothers of the bride and groom and other honored guests, such as grandmothers.

• Immediately after the recessional, the bride, the groom, the best man, and the maid or matron of honor may be asked to meet the clergyperson in his or her chambers to sign the marriage certificate.

Christian Recession:
1. Bride
2. Groom
3. Flower girl
4. Ring bearer
5. Honor attendant
6. Best man
7. Bridesmaids
8. Ushers

Jewish Recession:
1. Bride
2. Groom
3. Bride's parents
4. Groom's parents
5. Flower girl
6. Ring bearer
7. Honor attendant
8. Best man
9. Bridesmaids
10. Ushers
11. Cantor
12. Rabbi

Jewish

- The bride and groom lead the recession.
- The bride's parents follow, with her mother being escorted on the left arm of her father.
- The groom's parents follow, in similar suit.
- Child attendants come next, with the flower girl walking on the left side of the ring bearer.
- The maid or matron of honor is escorted down the aisle next, on the left arm of the best man.
- Bridesmaids and ushers follow similarly.
- The cantor and rabbi end the procession, with the cantor on the rabbi's left.
- The recession is customarily followed by the yichud. The bride and groom spend about fifteen minutes alone together in commemoration of ancient times when a new groom brought his bride to his tent to consummate their marriage and break their fast. Today, the yichud is a time for quiet reflection before the wedding reception begins.

Civil

- Again, consider space and plan accordingly. In many small, informal civil ceremonies, the recessional is usually eliminated, and the couple simply turns and greets their guests.

Interfaith

- Discuss with your groom and your officiant(s) how you'd like to borrow from different recessional styles.

ON THE RECEIVING END: FORMING A RECEIVING LINE

Your guests have just witnessed one of the biggest events of your life—take a moment to welcome them to your wedding and receive their congratulations. If your wedding is very large, the receiving line may be your only opportunity to speak with every guest. Here is what you should know.

When

The receiving line forms directly after the ceremony but before the reception. If you're Jewish and observing the yichud, your receiving line should form after you've emerged from your time alone together.

Where

Move to an entrance of your ceremony site (the vestibule of church/synagogue) and form your line. Or, weather permitting, form the line outside. If your photographer has scheduled pictures directly after the ceremony and/or there is no room for a receiving line at your ceremony site, form the line at the place where you'll hold your reception.

Who

The wedding's hosts, typically the bride's parents, begin the line. Your mother is first, your father on her left. Next to your father is the groom's mother, then his father on her left side. Next comes the bride, the groom, the maid or matron of honor, and the rest of the bridesmaids. Or consider having fathers and attendants not stand in the line and instead have them mingle with the guests. Besides helping to get guests chatting and mixing, this will cut down on the time guests spend in the receiving line.

Receiving Line Order:
1. *Mother of the bride*
2. *Father of the bride (optional)*
3. *Mother of the groom*
4. *Father of the groom (optional)*
5. *Bride*
6. *Groom*
7. *Bride's honor attendant (optional)*
8. *Bridesmaids (optional)*

Receiving Line Order

When Parents Are Deceased or Divorced

An honored guest can stand in for a deceased parent. If your father has passed away, for example, consider having your grandfather stand next to your mother in the receiving line. If either set of parents is divorced, have the fathers mix among the guests rather than stand in line. If parents are divorced and a father is hosting or cohosting the reception, allow him to stand in line—just don't place him next to his ex-wife.

What to Say

Thank guests for being a part of your wedding day. If they don't know your groom or other members of the wedding party, introduce them (your groom should do the same with guests you don't know). You might include a brief comment about the person (i.e., "Janet is my best friend from high school") so the person becomes more memorable to your groom and others who don't know her. Here is some more receiving line protocol:

• The two of you should go over the guest list with your parents so all names will be fresh in your minds.

• If you don't know a guest, introduce yourself.

• Leave gloves off. If you're worried about sweaty palms, lightly apply antiperspirant or powder to them prior to forming the receiving line.

• Keep guests entertained. Have music playing. If you're at your reception site, ask that food and drink be served to guests waiting in line. Perhaps even set up a photo display of you and your groom as children.

RECEPTION TIMETABLE

Wondering when you might have your first dance? Cut the cake? Throw the garter? Here is a timetable for a four-hour reception. Yours may be shorter or longer, so while the order of events will remain about the same, the time between them will vary. Fill in the estimated times for your reception, then appoint a close friend, relative, or your bridal consultant to oversee the schedule and make sure the caterers, musicians, and photographer are on track.

The Reception's Start

_____ You and all members of the wedding party arrive at the reception site.

The First Hour

_____ Form a receiving line if one wasn't assembled at the ceremony site. Photos of you, your groom, and the wedding party may also be taken. The band or DJ starts the music. The band leader could announce the wedding party. Drinks are poured. Hors d'oeuvres are served. Guests mingle and begin to pick up their table cards, if any. You and your groom mix among the guests. The photographer begins capturing the action on film, the videographer on tape.

After One Hour

_____ Dinner is announced. The wedding party takes their places at the head table; guests take their seats at their assigned tables. If there is a blessing to be said over the food, it is done now (by your clergyperson or some other honored guest). The first course is served, first to the wedding party, or guests are invited to the buffet table. Champagne is served and the best man proposes the first toast, perhaps succeeded by the honor attendant; other toasts may follow. Guests begin their meal.

Head Table:
1. Bride
2. Groom
3. Bride's honor attendant
4. Best man
5. Bridesmaids
6. Ushers

Head Table

After One And One-Half Hours

_____ The first course is cleared from the head table, then guests' tables. You and your groom dance your first dance (this may be done earlier, before you've had your first course). Father-daughter and mother-son dances can follow. Your musicians or DJ keep playing music. The main course is served (your musicians may continue with the music, stop, or play quiet dinner music).

After Two Hours

_____ Tables are cleared. Your bandleader or DJ signals the start of the cake-cutting ceremony. The cake is cut. Dancing resumes. Dessert is served.

The Last Half Hour

_____ The bride throws her bouquet to the single women; the groom removes the bride's garter (or a substitute garter) and throws it to the single men. If they're not staying until the very end, the bride and groom slip out of the reception to change into their going-away clothes. After they return, they say good-bye to their parents, are showered with rose petals or confetti, and duck into the getaway car. Shortly thereafter, the parents signal the musicians to stop playing, the bar to close. They then bid farewell to the guests.

Parent's Table

Parents Table:
1. *Mother of the bride*
2. *Father of the bride*
3. *Father of the groom*
4. *Wedding officiant*
5. *Mother of the groom*
6. *Wedding officiant's spouse, or assistant, or another honored female guest*

YOUR RECEPTION: AN ANATOMY

The Guest Book

A guest book is a keepsake that records the names of your wedding guests. Available in stationery stores, a guest book should have space for guests to write sentimental messages as well. You can place your guest book on a table near the entrance to your reception site or at the end of the receiving line. A friend or usher can circulate the book later in the reception to make sure everyone signs it.

The First Dance

The traditional first dance is your first as husband and wife. But there's no reason why your guests shouldn't begin dancing as soon as the receiving line is over and the music starts playing. After you've caught your breath from greeting guests, there is a pause in the music. An announcement is made, the floor clears, and the bride and groom circle the floor alone, dancing their first dance. (You could also wait and have the first dance after the first course has been served and cleared.) The bride is next claimed by her father for "the father-daughter dance." They dance this alone on the dance floor. The groom next takes his mother to the floor for the "mother-son dance.". They also dance this alone on the dance floor. The father-of-the-groom then dances with the bride and the mother-of-the-bride dances with the groom to the same dance. The bride and groom then dance with the best man and maid/matron of honor respectively. The bride will probably dance with each usher and the groom with each bridesmaid before the dancing ends. It's also customary for each man in the wedding party to dance with each bridesmaid and both mothers.

The Toasts

Toasting can begin anytime after the receiving line has ended and everyone has a glass of champagne or other toasting beverage in hand. Toasts can be given just before the meal, after the meal, or several times throughout the reception. The best man always begins the toasts by saluting the bride and groom. The groom usually responds by thanking the best man and toasting the bride, his new in-laws, and his parents. The bride may then add her own toast, honoring the groom and his family and thanking her parents and the maid of honor. Attendants and other guests may add short toasts. After the toasts are completed, the best man reads aloud any congratulatory telegrams. How do you make a heartfelt, yawn-proof toast? Refer to your relationship with the person being toasted and add a wish for their future good fortune. Be succinct, be sincere, and be loving. For example, you could say: "To my parents, for helping me put together this wonderful day and for showing me the beauty of true love. May we have many more happy family gatherings."

Cutting the Cake

The wedding cake should be beautifully displayed on a cloth-covered table with decorations and flowers. The bride and bridesmaids can also place their bouquets there. Position the table where guests can admire the arrangement, but far enough out of the way that it won't get toppled. The wedding cake can be cut approximately an hour after the receiving line disbands at a tea or cocktail reception, or before dessert at a dinner reception. There are several ways to alert guests that the ritual is about to take place: The band might signal with a drumroll or fanfare, your wedding consultant or banquet manager might gather guests around, or you and your groom might beckon guests over. With his hand over her hand, the bride and groom cut the first piece of cake from the bottom layer. Customarily the bride and groom feed a piece of the first slice to each other, then perhaps serve pieces to each of their parents. The rest of the cake (excluding the top layer, of course, which is kept for your first anniversary) is then cut by someone on the catering staff for the rest of your guests. If there is a groom's cake, it is sliced by the catering staff and boxed for guests to take home. Sometimes the groom's cake is served at the wedding as well, or at the rehearsal dinner.

Throwing the Bouquet and Garter

The bandleader usually asks all single women to come forward for the traditional bouquet toss (your florist can make up a throwaway bouquet for the occasion; if a prayer book decorated with flowers is your bouquet, set aside the book and throw the flowers). Most brides turn and toss the bouquet over a shoulder, but if you want better aim, face the group as you throw. Tradition says that the woman who catches the bouquet will be the next bride. With the bouquet caught, the bandleader will signal the garter toss. The groom removes the bride's garter from her leg or is handed a substitute, and then throws it to the single men. Whoever catches it is said to be the next to marry. In some parts of the country, it's customary for the bachelor who caught the garter to place it on the leg of the woman who caught the bouquet.

Chapter 19:

YOUR HONEYMOON

Back in the days of old, newlyweds spent a full month basking in each other's glow, drinking a fermented honey drink (honey is a symbol of life, vitality, and fertility) until the moon waned. Hence the term honeymoon. A lot's changed since then. Nowadays, honeymoons are long or short. Newlyweds travel across continents or just county lines. Sometimes they even honeymoon before or well after the wedding, when work and family schedules are more allowing. Whatever sort of honeymoon you ultimately decide to take, remember that preparation is crucial. No amount of sexy lingerie or tropical drinks can make up for poor planning.

PAINLESS PLANNING

If ever you need a vacation, it's after the whirlwind of planning a wedding. To make sure your honeymoon goes off as flawlessly as your wedding, you need to get organized. Here is when to do what:

• **One Year to Six Months Before:** For some honeymoons, it's never too early to start planning. Top accommodations in the best resort areas should be booked up to a year in advance. Time is even more of the essence if you'll be honeymooning during any major holiday. Soon after your engagement, start working on your honeymoon wish list together. Do you want lazy days on the beach, swinging nights in the disco? Research your dream destination in guidebooks and the travel sections of magazines and newspapers. Contact the tourist offices of the places you're considering (if you'll be traveling internationally, call a consulate located in the United States; many have toll-free numbers) to request brochures and guides.

• **Six Months Before:** Ask friends, relatives, or colleagues to recommend a good travel agent; firm up your budget and the length of time you can be away. If you don't have a major credit card, apply for one now (or see if you can get a rider on your parents' card). Many hotels and car rental agencies require that you have one. But go easy on your plastic, and pay outstanding bills before leaving (a credit card isn't much good if you've already reached your limit).

• **Five Months Before:** If you're traveling to a foreign destination, you'll need passports or some proof of citizenship—usually notarized copies of your birth certificate (for information on getting a passport, call the Federal Information Center at 800-688-9889). While there's no need for special inoculations for domestic and most foreign travel, double-check with the tourist boards and consulates of the countries you plan to visit.

• **Two Months Before:** Book your honeymoon—and that includes hotel, airline tickets, rental car, etc. (If you'll be traveling during a peak season or holiday period, you may need to do so sooner.) Be very specific. If you'd like a room with an ocean view that's away from the disco, say so. Check your closets. Will you need new ski pants? New shoes? New bathing suits? Do last summer's shorts still fit and look stylish? While you're at it, take stock of your luggage situation.

Will your old bags do the job, or is it time to invest in a new set? If you're traveling to a place with a different electrical current, will you need a transformer for your blow-dryer plus the right kind of adapter plug? Check the batteries in your camera; buy a phrase book to familiarize yourself with key foreign expressions.

• **One Month Before:** Refill important prescriptions (including any for birth control). Start collecting travel-size toiletries. Shop for sunscreen.

• **Two Weeks Before:** Do you have airline tickets, seat assignments, hotel and car rental confirmations? If not, call your travel agent (or airline or hotel) and alert them. Arrange transportation from the reception to the wedding-night hotel, and from the hotel to the airport.

• **One Week Before:** Buy traveler's checks.

Purchase enough foreign currency (at a bank or currency broker) to pay for taxis, tips, and that first round of margaritas (you can exchange more money once you've arrived). Research ATM locations at your destination. Make photocopies of passports, traveler's checks, and airline tickets; leave them with friends or relatives. Begin packing.

• **One Day Before:** Finish packing. You should have one suitcase sitting by the door, ready to go into the car or limo, and one carry-on bag (leave it open; toss last-minute items like makeup, medication, and keys into it before you leave). Leave copies of your itinerary with family or friends. Confirm your outbound flight and transportation to the airport. Have a great trip!

DECIDING ON A DESTINATION

1. Start fantasizing. After all, that's what a honeymoon is all about. Imagine being serenaded in a Venetian gondola or relaxing with a fruity drink under a swaying palm. Let your mind play out the perfect honeymoon. Travel books, brochures, and even the Internet can help you (depending on what service you use, you can get things like weather reports, restaurant reviews, information on first-rate hotels and inns, color pictures of romantic beaches, etc.). Write to airline tour departments (or call their ticket offices)

for information on timetables, fares, package tours, etc.

2. Compromise. What happens if you see yourself enjoying high tea, shopping for fine linens, and swooning over an English accent while he sees himself rolling in the surf and playing golf? Meet halfway. Ever think about British-accented Bermuda?

3. Shop for deals. See a travel agent and start discussing destination possibilities. She'll try to match your fantasy with your (fiscal) reality.

BUDGETING FOR PARADISE

Does an out-of-this-world honeymoon have to carry an out-of-this-world price tag? Not necessarily. Here's how to keep down costs:

1. If you have frequent flier miles saved up, use them. For a fee, you may be able to buy

more miles, which may entitle you to a companion ticket or an upgrade in class.

2. See if any of your credit cards offer discounts or free upgrades when used to book transportation and accommodations.

3. Register for your honeymoon with a travel agency (but be sure you're planning a honeymoon you can afford, in case gifts don't cover it entirely).

4. Consider joining a discount travel club. You pay a club membership fee (which varies by club), but you could wind up saving a bundle on your honeymoon travel.

5. Honeymoon off season, when prices are lowest. But before you book, check the weather. Do you want to risk running into a hurricane just to save a few bucks?

6. Once you're on your way, **stay out of the resort gift or sundries shop.** Bring shampoo, sunscreen, film, books, and other pricey gift-shop staples from home.

7. Do as the locals do. Take local transportation whenever possible.

8. Venture beyond hotel doors for great eats and local color at prices you can swallow. And think twice about ordering room service. It's no friend of the budget conscious.

9. Read the fine print. Before you leave a tip, check to see whether it's already included in your bill.

10. Talk isn't cheap when you're phoning from your room. Keep calls—even local ones—to a minimum. Better yet, find a pay phone.

11. Compare exchange rates at banks before changing your money at the hotel. But watch out for hefty commissions—banks and exchange counters often charge them, but hotels don't.

12. Steer clear of the minibar. Like room service, it will take a big bite out of your budget. Some hotels, upon request, will empty your minibar so you can use the fridge for your own eats.

13. Buy a youth-oriented travel guide before you go—it will point you in the direction of low-priced hotels, eateries, etc.

14. This trip is for *you*. You don't have to come back loaded with presents for every friend or relative.

HONEYMOON LIFESAVERS: DON'T LEAVE HOME WITHOUT 'EM

1. Get a plan of action. Decide with your groom who'll carry the camera, who'll hold the maps, who'll confirm all air flights, who'll call about the ground transportation. And it's probably a good idea to split up the money, too—just in case. Now's as good a time as any to start thinking like a team.

2. At least ten days before you leave, your travel agent (or package tour operator) should have sent you all your essential traveling documents—your airline tickets, itinerary, hotel confirmations, transfer coupons, etc. If you don't have them, call.

3. Pack some can't-do-without items in his carry-on luggage—and he can do the same with yours. This way, if your checked luggage is lost or if one or the other of you misplaces your carry-on bag, you can each get by. For a while anyway.

4. Put ALL essentials—a bathing suit, toothbrush, change of clothes, medications, and your birth control—in your carry-on bag. Even if your checked luggage is delayed, you can still start enjoying yourselves immediately.

5. Tag your luggage—inside and out—with your name and business address.

6. Check—and then double-check—that

you have important documents, such as your passport, traveler's checks, hotel confirmations, and travel agent's number, before you leave home. Do the same every time you check out of a hotel.

SHOULD YOU BOOK A PACKAGE?

The choice is yours, but before you sign up for a package honeymoon know what you're getting. Here is how to check them out:

• **Do some research.** Inquire with your travel agent or the tour operator about exactly what it is your package offers. Are all meals included—or just dinner and a continental breakfast? Is the hotel near the beach action—or nestled smack dab in the middle of the island, where you'll only get an ocean view with the help of binoculars? Tour books that mention the hotel or even your point of destination can help you decide if the deal is too good to pass up.

• **Figure the prices.** A package is a good idea if it saves you money. See what the package offers—and then what each item would cost you were you to pay for it individually.

• **Is it practical?** If you plan on eating all your meals away from the hotel, for example, a package that includes a meal plan is really no bargain.

• **Don't necessarily go for the honeymoon package.** Okay—so you might have to forgo that bottle of free champagne, but if you think you'd get more use out of a tennis or golf or water-lovers package, then book that instead.

• **Check the fine print.** Are there any restrictions that would make you think twice about the package (meals are included, but only if you order off a certain menu)?

HONEYMOON TRAVEL CHECKLIST

Travel agent / address _____

Phone _____ Fax _____ Confirmation No. _____

24-hour hotline number _____

TRANSPORTATION

Air, rail, or ship line _____

Ticketing address _____

	Departure	Return
Date	_____	_____
Ticket number	_____	_____
Airport/station	_____	_____

	Departure	Return
Flight/train number	_____	_____
Class	_____	_____
Departure time	_____	_____
Arrival time	_____	_____

Confirmation date _____ Transportation cost _____

Car rental agent _____

Address _____

Phone _____ Fax _____

Make and model of car reserved _____

Pickup and drop-off site _____

Dates car is rented _____ From _____ to _____

Terms of charges _____

Estimated car rental cost _____

YOUR ROOM

Hotel/resort _____

Address _____

Phone _____ Fax _____

Confirmation No. _____

Manager, assistant manager, or reservations manager _____

Check-in date _____ Time _____ Check-out date _____ Time _____

Description of room _____

Daily rate _____ Total room cost (with tax) _____

MEAL PLAN

No meal plan _____ Continental (breakfast only) _____

Modified American (breakfast and dinner) _____

American (breakfast, lunch, and dinner) _____

Other _____

MONEY

Cash $ _____

Traveler's checks $ _____

Foreign currency (if any) _____

Credit cards _____

Current balance(s) _____ Current limit(s) _____

Location of ATM machines _____

Total pocket money $ _____

Total cost of honeymoon $ _____

TO CARRY WITH YOU

_____ Driver's license

_____ Passports or visas (if needed)

_____ Proof of age and citizenship (if you're not carrying a passport, bring your birth certificate or

voter registration card)

_____ Birth control, medications

_____ Money, any valuables (but keep valuables to a minimum)

_____ Address book (to write your friends and family postcards, and in case you need to contact

them because of an emergency; note any time differences between where they live and your

honeymoon spot)

_____ Your doctors' names, addresses, and phone numbers

_____ Copies of prescriptions for medications you're currently taking

_____ List of all credit card numbers

_____ List of all traveler's check numbers

_____ Checking account numbers

_____ ATM card

_____ Gift-idea/size list

_____ List of luggage contents

_____ List of recommended restaurants, sites, etc.

HONEYMOON CATASTROPHES: HOW TO SAVE THE DAY

As dreamy as your honeymoon should be, sometimes nightmares occur. You lose your tickets. You get food poisoning. The hotel never booked your room. Here is what to do when disaster strikes:

• **You lose your tickets.** Contact someone in the know—your travel agent, the airline, or your tour/cruise operator. He or she will tell you how to proceed—whether it's by filing a lost-ticket claim (so your money can be refunded if no one uses your tickets within a certain time frame) or showing proof of purchase (e.g., a credit card receipt), etc.

• **You miss the boat/plane/train.** An airline will rebook you on another flight (even another airline's flight). If you had restricted tickets, there may be a fee. You should also be able to hop the next train—possibly with a penalty fee. If a late flight caused you to miss your boat, the cruise company will get you to the next port of call at no expense to you (provided you booked your flight in combination with a cruise package). If you booked your air on your own, you can still catch up with the ship, via a launch, or meet it in its next port of call—but you're likely to have to cough up the dough.

• **Your luggage doesn't show.** Hold on to your claim check and notify the airline immediately. Don't leave the airport without filing a loss report. Different airlines have different procedures for reimbursing you (to get a more accurate assessment of what your luggage items are worth, keep a detailed list of what you pack—and their approximate cost). Taking pictures of your valuables and holding on to their receipts will also help you if you have to make a claim with your insurance company (most homeowners' policies cover personal property lost anywhere). If the airline finds your luggage during your stay, many will deliver it directly to your hotel.

• **There's no room at the inn.** Have your confirmation letter at the ready and ask to speak with a senior hotel staff person. In most cases, hotels will find ways to accommodate you. That may mean getting a hotel upgrade or being transferred to an equivalent hotel property free of charge.

• **Your room is rotten.** Call the front desk and ask to speak to a manager. Explain why you find the room unsatisfactory. Chances are good you'll be switched to a different room.

• **You get sick.** Contact the front desk and tell them you need a doctor. Many hotels have physicians on call or at least can get you in touch with local doctors. And go prepared. Bring prescription medicines (in their prescription bottles) from home. Take along aspirin and an antidiarrheal medication. Depending upon your destination, pack plenty of sunscreen, insect repellent, and an anti-itch cream. Check with your travel agent and your doctor about food and drink precautions you should take in foreign countries. When in doubt, drink bottled water, and avoid milk, unpeeled fruits and vegetables, ice made from local water, and food that is not thoroughly cooked.

• **You lose your passport or visa.** Report the loss immediately to the nearest U.S. consulate. They'll take it from there. Keep a record of your passport number and its date and place of issuance in a safe place, such as a zipped compartment in a carry-on bag. Also keep a copy with friends or family back home (and while you're making copies, make one of all traveler's check numbers as well).

• **You run out of money.** If you have an ATM card, you can probably find a machine and withdraw some cash. If you have a credit card, you can use that—and likely extend your limit if need be. As a last resort, call home and have some money wired to you.

• **You're too tired to make love.** You're in good company. Given the whirlwind of the wedding and the stress of traveling, hot wedding-night sex is more fiction than reality for many couples. Don't make sex a big issue the first day or two.

HONEYMOON TIPPING

Wondering how much to give—and to whom? Read on. These guidelines are general—your hotel concierge or travel agent can give you more specifics. And remember, a tip shows appreciation for good service. If you feel your treatment's been substandard—or sensational—tip a little or a lot.

• **Taxi driver:** Generally, it's 15 to 20 percent of the meter fare. Some countries, however, have different tipping customs. Inquire with the concierge at your hotel about what's the norm.

• **Airport sky cap/train redcap:** A dollar per bag.

• **Bellboy:** A dollar per bag; add a little more if the bellhop performs extras for you—opening windows, turning on the air conditioner, etc.

• **Chambermaid:** One to two dollars a night. (Instead of tipping her daily, leave her tip in an envelope in your room at the end of your stay.)

• **Cabin steward (on a cruise ship):** Five to six dollars per couple, per day. Use the tipping envelopes slipped under your cabin door at the end of your cruise; leave the steward's tip in your room.

• **Cabin steward (on a train):** About five dollars per person, per night.

• **Doorman:** A dollar for hailing a taxi.

• **Maître d' or head waiter:** Five dollars per week for extra special, very courteous service.

• **Waiter:** Fifteen to 20 percent of the bill (unless gratuities are already included in the bill). This also goes for the room service waiter.

• **Waiter (on a cruise ship):** Five to six dollars per couple, per day. Tip at the end of your cruise, when tipping envelopes are generally slipped under your cabin door; bring the envelope with you to your last dinner.

• **Busboy (on a cruise ship):** About three dollars per couple, per day. Again, use a tipping envelope and bring it with you to your last dinner.

• **Instructors (golf, tennis, water skiing, etc.):** Fifteen to 20 percent of the bill, unless he or she is an owner of the business.

• **Tour guide:** About five dollars per couple, for a half-day sight-seeing trip.

PACK LIKE A PRO

It's your honeymoon—you want to feel light, unfettered, carefree. About the last thing you need is to be buckling under the weight of nearly all your worldly possessions. Pack right.

1. Know the weather. Ask your travel agent, consult a guidebook, cruise the Internet, or flip on the Weather Channel to see what's coming down and heating up where. You'll pack a whole lot smarter if you know what to expect, climatically speaking.

2. Make a list. There's a lot on your mind right now. Remembering to pack a bathing suit, your sunscreen, even your birth control may be far from it. Make a list—and consult it as you pack—to make sure you don't forget essentials.

3. Limit yourself. Try to fit everything into one carry-on bag. You won't have to wait in line to check your luggage or risk the airline's losing it.

4. Think versatility. You want to make the most of what you pack. The leggings you wore around town on Thursday can serve you well at the gym on Friday. Your basic black sheath dress can look casual with a cardigan sweater, siren hot with strappy sandals. And while you're thinking versatility, also think easy care. Jersey, knits, and cotton-Lycra blends are the best friends of packers. Linens and pure cotton are not.

5. Minimize wrinkles. Place shoes, heel to toe, against the hinge side of the bag. Place large items (jackets, sweaters, jeans) on the bottom of the bag, followed by noncrushables like T-shirts, knit shorts, bathing suits, etc. (roll them tightly, then place them snugly against each other). Place easily wrinkled clothes on top, and put plastic dry-cleaner bags between layers to cushion against creases.

6. Maximize your space. Stuff socks and underwear into shoes. Roll a T-shirt or nightgown into the spaces and crevices around the edge of your suitcase. Bring only travel-size toiletries (share whatever you can with your groom). Call the hotel and ask if they have blow-dryers and irons available for your use so you can leave yours at home.

7. Leave your valuables at home. A honeymoon is no place for the family gems or your pricey portable CD player. Keep them locked in a safe-deposit box at home.

8. Pack your carry-on bag carefully. You could be living out of it for a few days if your luggage is lost. Make sure your carry-on bag contains all your medications, birth control, jewelry, camera and film, eyewear, a bathing suit, and a change of clothes (at least some fresh underwear).

9. Put all essentials in your purse. Tickets, passports, confirmation letters, traveler's checks, your travel agent's number, and other honeymoon vitals belong on your person.

10. Leave space for souvenirs. A foldable tote bag will come in handy.

HONEYMOON WARDROBES

For a Week in the Sun

Her
1 blazer
1 cardigan sweater
2 pairs of casual pants (make one a pair of jeans, in case you do any horseback riding)
1 sundress
2 pairs of shorts
5 tops/T-shirts
2 evening looks (a sarong is sexy; a black jersey tank dress is packable, stylish, versatile)
7 sets of underwear
7 pairs of socks
1 slip (if needed)
1 nightgown
1 travel robe
1 pair of slippers
2 bathing suits
1 beach cover-up
1 pair of sneakers
1 pair of casual sandals
1 pair of dress sandals
1 evening bag
1 sun hat

Him
1 blazer
1 sweater
2 pairs of casual pants (one being jeans)
1 tie (just in case)
2 pairs of dress slacks
2 pairs of shorts
5 shirts/T-shirts
5 button-down shirts
7 pairs of dress and sport socks
7 sets of underwear
1 pair of sneakers

1 pair of dress shoes
1 pair of sandals
1 pair of pajamas
1 travel robe
2 bathing suits
1 hat for the sun

For Two Weeks Abroad

Her
1 all-weather coat
1 collapsible umbrella
2 skirts/casual dresses
2 pairs of casual pants
1 pair of dress pants
1 blazer
6 washable tops/T-shirts
1 sweater
2 evening outfits
1 evening bag
3 pairs of panty hose
1 slip
7 sets of underwear (bring hand-wash detergent)
1 pair of sneakers or walking shoes
1 pair of dress shoes

1 pair of slippers
1 nightgown
1 travel robe

Him
1 all-weather coat
1 collapsible umbrella
2 pairs of casual pants
2 pairs of dress pants
6 casual shirts
3 dress shirts
1 blazer
1 sweater
7 sets of underwear (bring hand-wash detergent)
7 pairs of sports socks
3 pairs of dress socks
1 pair of sneakers or walking shoes
1 pair of dress shoes
1 pair of pajamas
1 travel robe

If summer add: one bathing suit, cover-up, sandals, one or two pairs of shorts
If winter add: boots, lined gloves, wool scarf and hat, two wool sweaters

HONEYMOON BEAUTY

Go from blushing bride to hot, sensual honeymooner. Here are beauty essentials to keep you looking relaxed and ravishing.

Take It with You:

1. Lip balm with sunscreen
2. Skin freshener
3. Bottled water
4. Pared-down skin care—cleanser, moisturizer, and sunscreen (with the dermatologist-recommended SPF of 15 or higher)
5. Makeup essentials—lipstick, foundation, pressed powder (to save space, opt for a two-in-one product), eye liner and shadow, blush and mascara, and purse-size cologne. You won't need much else—you'll still be glowing from the wedding!
6. Sunglasses
7. Compact curling iron
8. Hair accessories—a rhinestone clip, headband, etc.
9. Breath mints

Chapter 20:

YOUR HOME

Marriage merges you—in body, soul, and address. If you'll be looking for a new place to share together, you'll have to do a little investigating.

FINDING A NEW HOME

Check the real estate and classified sections of newspapers in the towns where you want to live (if you're out of the area, order a subscription to the paper or check the library). See what kinds of homes and apartments are available in your price range. If a phone number is provided, call it to see what other information you can acquire about the property; also see when you can come and inspect it. Registering with a real estate broker is another good idea (however, in some states you will have to pay him or her a fee, usually a percentage of the purchase price or the rent). Home-buying and apartment-renting books at your local library or bookstore can provide invaluable insights. But before you go much further, ask yourselves these questions.

Needs

- In what area do you want to live?
- How will you commute to work? (Make sure any home or apartment you consider is in a convenient location.)
- How many bedrooms will you need? Do you want space for a child, home office, guests?
- Do you want a furnished or unfurnished place to start?
- If you want an apartment, do you want one with a doorman, alarm system, or other security measures?
- Are other features important to you—access to an elevator, pool, or exercise room?

Budget

- How much can you afford in rent, mortgage, and/or maintenance payments?
- Are the costs of gas, water, electricity, taxes, garbage pickup, parking, etc., included in the monthly payment?

FURNISHING YOUR HOME

When faced with empty rooms and an enormous selection in furniture and floor and wall coverings, decorating may seem like an overwhelming task. Here are some tips on getting started:

• **Determine your taste.** Don't assume he won't have an opinion—or can be talked out of it. Talk about what you both like and dislike. Together, window-shop and flip through decorating magazines to get ideas about the colors and styles that please you both.

• **Draw up a floor plan.** Be sure the furniture you choose will fit into each room. Using graph paper, figure out a scale (for example, one quarter inch on paper equals one foot) and sketch the room, indicating the location of windows, radiators, doors, and other built-in features. Next, draw furniture shapes to scale on another piece of paper, cut them out, and arrange them to suit your needs and traffic patterns. And whenever you shop for furniture, always go with the exact measurements of the room, corner, or nook where you want to place the item.

• **Work out a budget.** Calculate your monthly discretionary income—money available after all essentials (rent, utilities, loan payments, food, and transportation) are paid. Each month, deposit a portion of these available funds in a separate account. Let money accumulate until you're ready to buy. If you decide to buy on credit, be sure that the monthly payments will not strain your budget.

• **Work with what you have.** You both probably already own some furniture. Tie everything together with your choice of window treatments, paint color, and decorative accessories. Reupholster or get slipcovers for an old sofa or chairs for a fresh new look.

• **Determine what to buy first.** Here are some basics:

Living Room
• Sofa
• Love seat
• Chairs
• Coffee table
• End tables
• Lighting
• Entertainment unit

Dining Room
• Table with chairs
• Hutch or china cabinet
• Sideboard
• Lighting

Bedroom
• Bed
• Armoire
• Dresser with mirror
• Lamps
• Bedside tables
• Chair with ottoman

For more decorating inspiration (as well as information on how to select quality pieces you can afford), consult decorating magazines and interior design books.

Blending Two Styles

He's silly for stripes, you're nuts about plaid? You love anything in Queen Anne, he's mad for modular? Relax—compromise is the soul of marriage. Here is how to meld your styles and still have a home with taste:

1. Make tradeoffs. If you love bold colors while he likes traditional furniture, reupholster his traditional pieces in vibrant fabric.

2. Use accessories to blend together your styles. You can give a room with traditional furnishings a contemporary style by painting it in a hip color, papering it in a stylish pattern, etc. Window treatments, accessory pillows, area rugs, and decorative objects can work the same magic.

3. Divide up the rooms and decorate according to your own individual tastes—but remember, you both need to feel comfortable.

DECORATING PLAN

LIVING ROOM

Square footage _____

Wall color _____ paint ☐   paper ☐

Floor covering color _____ carpet ☐   area rugs ☐   price _____

Drapery color _____ dimensions _____ fabric _____ price _____

Period or type of furniture _____ finish _____

Sofa_____ style_____ brand_____ color_____ price _____

Chair_____ style_____ brand_____ color_____ price _____

Chair_____ style_____ brand_____ color_____ price _____

Chair_____ style_____ brand_____ color_____ price _____

Tables_____ coffee _____ end _____ occasional _____

Television_____ brand _____ price _____

Stereo components _____ brand(s) _____ price(s) _____

Desk_____ price _____ Desk chair _____ price _____

Lamps_____ floor _____ table _____ wall _____ ceiling _____

Storage units (chest, etc.) _____

Paintings, prints, wall hangings, other accessories _____

_____

_____

DINING ROOM OR AREA

Square footage _____

Wall color _____ paint ☐   paper ☐

Floor covering color _____ carpet ☐   area rugs ☐   flooring ☐   price _____

Drapery color _____ dimensions _____ fabric _____ price _____

Table size _____ style _____ finish _____ brand _____ price _____

Chairs, number _____ style _____ finish _____ brand _____ price _____

Sideboard or chest _____ style _____ finish _____ brand _____ price _____

Serving cart _____ style _____ finish _____ brand _____ price _____

Lamps_____ floor _____ table_____ wall _____ ceiling _____

Paintings and other accessories _____

_____

_____

BEDROOM

Square footage _____

Wall color _____ paint ☐   paper ☐

Floor covering color _____ area rugs ☐ carpet ☐ price _____

Drapery color _____ dimensions _____ fabric _____ price _____

Bed size _____headboard style _____ brand _____ price _____

Mattress/box spring _____ brand _____ price _____

Dresser/chests_____ style _____ finish _____ brand _____ price _____

Mirror _____ style _____ finish _____ brand _____ price _____

Chair_____ style _____ finish _____ brand _____ price _____

Vanity table or desk _____ style _____ finish _____ brand _____ price _____

Night table _____ style _____ finish _____ brand _____ price _____

Lamps_____ floor _____ table_____ wall _____ ceiling _____

Paintings and other accessories _____

_____

_____

YOUR BUDGET

One thing you're bound to have all your married life: bills. Good budgeting will help you take control over them. Look into computer software programs that do the figuring for you, or follow these tips:

1. Set goals. Discuss how you both see yourselves living in the next year, five years, ten years. Write down your goals and estimate how much money you will need to achieve them.

2. Size up weekly income. Write down what each of you makes after taxes, Social Security, 401K contributions, and other deductions from your paycheck. Include any other income, such as bonuses or stock dividends.

3. Calculate fixed expenses. Fixed expenses are the ones that remain unchanged on a monthly, quarterly, or annual basis. They usually include rent or mortgage, insurance, loan payments, and the amount of money you want to allocate to savings.

4. Estimate flexible expenses. These are items that change from month to month—food, telephone, clothing, entertainment, transportation. The only way to accurately determine these expenses is to keep a record of *everything* you spend for about three months.

5. Draw up a weekly budget. Use the following worksheet to record your estimated income and expenses. If expenses exceed your income or if there is not enough left for saving toward your goal, cut back on flexible expenses, the easiest part of your budget to control. If that's not enough, consider whether it's possible to cut back on fixed expenses (maybe move into a less expensive apartment, find extra work, etc.). If what you make is more than what you spend, save a set amount of each paycheck. Call a financial planner to inquire about investments.

6. Review your budget. Go over it at least every six months. Your lives change—so should your budget.

WEEKLY BUDGET CHART

INCOME

Add: Her weekly income	$ _____
His weekly income	$ _____
Total	$ _____

PERIODIC FLEXIBLE EXPENSES
(estimate annually)

Her clothing	$ _____
His clothing	$ _____
Vacations	$ _____
Other	$ _____
Total	$ _____

Convert to weekly estimate

Total for estimated periodic flexible expenses $_____ ÷ 52 = $ _____

FLEXIBLE WEEKLY LIVING EXPENSES

Food/beverage $ _____

Transportation $ _____

Household (upkeep, etc.) $ _____

Laundry (dry cleaning, etc.) $ _____

Entertainment $ _____

Gifts/donations $ _____

His personal items $ _____

Her personal items $ _____

Total $ _____

FIXED MONTHLY HOUSING EXPENSES

Rent/mortgage $ _____

Water $ _____

Heat $ _____

Electricity $ _____

Telephone $ _____

Total $ _____

Convert to weekly estimate

Total for fixed monthly housing expenses $_____ ÷ 52 = $ _____

PERIODIC FIXED EXPENSES

(figure each annually)

Loan payments $ _____

Insurance premiums $ _____

Medical checkups $ _____

Other (tuition) $ _____

Total $ _____

Convert to weekly estimate

Total for periodic fixed expenses $_____ ÷ 52 = $ _____

PLANNED SAVINGS/EMERGENCIES

(estimate per week)

Total $ _____

ADD TOTAL WEEKLY EXPENSES $ _____

COMPARE TO TOTAL WEEKLY INCOME $ _____